Albertus Magnus

Covering one of the most fascinating yet misunderstood periods in history, the MEDIEVAL LIVES series presents medieval people, concepts and events, drawing on political and social history, philosophy, material culture (art, architecture and archaeology) and the history of science. These books are global and wide-ranging in scope, encompassing both Western and non-Western subjects, and span the fifth to the fifteenth centuries, tracing significant developments from the collapse of the Roman Empire onwards.

SERIES EDITOR: Deirdre Jackson

Albertus Magnus and the World of Nature *Irven M. Resnick and Kenneth F. Kitchell Jr*

Christine de Pizan: Life, Work, Legacy *Charlotte Cooper-Davis*

Margery Kempe: A Mixed Life *Anthony Bale*

Albertus Magnus

and the World of Nature

IRVEN M. RESNICK AND
KENNETH F. KITCHELL JR

REAKTION BOOKS

Published by Reaktion Books Ltd
Unit 32, Waterside
44–48 Wharf Road
London N1 7UX, UK
www.reaktionbooks.co.uk

First published 2022
Copyright © Irven M. Resnick and Kenneth F. Kitchell Jr 2022

Printed and bound in India by Replika Press Pvt. Ltd

A catalogue record for this book is available from the British Library

ISBN 978 1 78914 513 7

CONTENTS

ABBREVIATIONS

Note: Unless otherwise indicated, all translations are our own.

Alb.	Albertus Magnus
De anima	*De anima* (ed. Colon., vol. VII/1, pp. 1–284)
DA	*De animalibus* (reference by book and number; Stadler, 1916–20)
De bono	*De bono* (ed. Colon., vol. XXVIII, pp. 1–329)
ed. Borgnet	*Opera omnia, ex editione lugdunensi, religiose castigata, et pro auctoritatibus ad fidem vulgatae versionis accuratiorumque patrologiae textuum revocata, auctaque B. Alberti vita ac Bibliographia suorum operum a PP. Quetif et Echard exaratis etiam revisa et locupletata cura et labore A. Borgnet*, 38 vols (Paris, 1890–99)
ed. Colon.	*Sancti Doctoris Ecclesiae Alberti Magni ordinis fratrum praedicatorum episcopi opera omnia, ad fidem codicum manuscriptorum edenda apparatu critico notis prolegomenis indicibus instruenda curavit Institutum Alberti Magni Coloniense* (Monasterii Westfalorum, 1951–?)
CPE	*On the Causes of the Properties of the Elements*, trans. Irven M. Resnick (Milwaukee, WI, 2010)
De gen. et corr.	*De generatione et corruptione* (ed. Colon., vol. V/2, pp. 109–219)
De homine	*De homine*, ed. Colon., vol. XXVII/2
DM	*The Book of Minerals*, trans. Dorothy Wyckoff (Oxford, 1967)
De mot. an.	*De motibus animalium* (ed. Borgnet, vol. IX)
De mul. forti	*De muliere forti* (ed. Borgnet, vol. XVIII, pp. 1–242)
De nat. loc.	*De natura loci* (ed. Colon., vol. V/2, pp. 1–282)
DNL	Jean Paul Tilmann, *An Appraisal of the Geographical Works of Albertus Magnus and His Contributions to Geographical Thought* (Ann Arbor, MI, 1971)
De nutr.	*De nutrimento et nutribili* (ed. Colon., vol. VII/2a, pp. 1–18)
De res.	*On Resurrection*, trans. Irven M. Resnick and Franklin T. Harkins; Fathers of the Church, Mediaeval Continuation 20 (Washington, DC, 2020)

De veg.	*De vegetabilibus* (Jessen, 1867)
Meteora	*Meteora* (ed. Colon., vol. vi/1)
Phys.	*Physica* (ed. Colon., vol. iv/1–2)
QDA²	*Albert the Great's Questions concerning [Aristotle's] 'On Animals'*, trans. Irven M. Resnick and Kenneth F. Kitchell Jr; Fathers of the Church, Mediaeval Continuation 9, (Washington, DC, 2008)
Sent. [*i–iv*]	*Super* [*i–iv*] *librum Sententiarum* (ed. Borgnet, vols xxv–xxx)
Summa	*Summa theologiae: Summa de mirabili scientia Dei* (ed. Borgnet, vols xxxi–xxxiii)
sz	*Albertus Magnus 'On Animals': A Medieval 'Summa Zoologica'*, trans. Kenneth F. Kitchell Jr and Irven M. Resnick, revd edn, 2 vols (Columbus, OH, 2018)

Alex. Hales — Alexander of Hales
Summa theol. — *Summa theologica sive summa universae theologiae*, 4 vols (Quaracchi, 1924–48)

Ar. — Aristotle (line references are to the appropriate Loeb editions whenever possible; note, however, that these are frequently inaccurate and that correlation to the actual Greek text will often be approximate)
HA — *Historia animalium*

Avic. — Avicenna
Can. — *Liber canonis medicine. Cum castigationibus Andree Bellunensis* (Venice, 1527; repr. Brussels, 1971)

Barth. — Bartholomaeus Anglicus
De prop. — *De proprietatibus rerum* (Frankfurt, 1601; repr. Frankfurt am Main, 1964)

Caesarius of Heisterbach
Dial. — *Dialogus miraculorum*, ed. Joseph Strange, 2 vols (Cologne, 1851)

Isidore of Seville
Etym. — *Isidori Hispalensis episcopi Etymologiarum sive originum libri xx*, ed. W. M. Lindsay, 2 vols (Oxford, 1911)

Michael Scot
Lib. phis. — *Liber phisionomiae* (Venice, 1486)

Pliny

HN   *Historia naturalis*

Thomas of Cantimpré

ThDNR   *Liber de natura rerum*, ed. H. Boese (Berlin, 1973)

ThDA   *Bonum universale de apibus*, ed. George Colvenerius (Douai, 1627), cited by book and chapter

VfOP   Gérard de Frachet, *Vitae fratrum ordinis praedicatorum; necnon Cronica ordinis ab anno* MCCIII *usque ad* MCCLIV, *pars 3, cap. 14*, ed. Benedict Maria Reichert, vol. I (Leuven, 1896)

Vincent of Beauvais

Spec. nat.   *Speculum naturale*, vol. I of *Speculum quadruplex, sive, Speculum maius: naturale, doctrinale, morale, historiale* (Douai, 1524; repr. Graz, 1964)

ONE

The Life and Works of Albertus Magnus

I n his masterful *Divine Comedy*, the Italian poet Dante Alighieri (d. 1321) places Pope Nicholas III (d. 1280) upside down in the eighth circle of hell with the soles of his feet ablaze. He imposed that cruel punishment upon the pope who had once been the protector of the Franciscan Order by placing him among the simoniacs, that is, those accused of buying and selling church offices for profit. On 15 November 1280, and only a few months after Nicholas's death, Albertus Magnus, one of the shining lights of the Dominican Order, also died. Dante, who was himself educated by Dominicans at Santa Maria Novella in Florence, placed Albertus far from Nicholas, in Paradise among the wise spirits of Heaven and the Sun and beside Thomas Aquinas, his celebrated student and brother Dominican. In his prose *Banquet* (*Convivio* book three, Chapter Five), Dante refers to him as Albert the Great (*Alberto della magna*), and the poet acknowledges his own substantial debt to Albertus' teaching on astronomy, geography and natural philosophy, and in particular to Albertus' treatises *On the Nature of Places* (*De natura locorum*) and *On the Causes of the Properties of the Elements* (*Liber de causis proprietatum elementorum*). The fate of the two Dominicans, Albertus and Thomas, differed dramatically from that of Pope Nicholas III.[1]

Dante's judgement is shared by Albertus' near contemporaries, who placed him on a level equal to that of the ancient

philosophers. Even his rather jealous rival, the Franciscan friar
Roger Bacon (d. 1292), referred to Albertus as 'the most noted
of Christian scholars',[2] and praised him as one of the 'wise men'
(*sapientes*). Siger of Brabant, a younger contemporary, referred
to him as one of the most eminent men in philosophy, while
Albertus' student Ulrich of Strasbourg (d. 1277) described him
as 'so godlike in every branch of knowledge that he can properly be called the wonder and marvel of our age'.[3] According
to Henry of Herford's fourteenth-century *Chronicle*, just as God
established the sun and the moon as two great lights to illumine

Giovanni di Paolo, miniature of Dante and Beatrice in the sphere of the sun being greeted by Aquinas and Albertus Magnus, while ten other great intellectual authorities (the Doctors of the Church) are seated below, including Peter Lombard, Siger of Brabant, Bede, Ambrose, Isidore and Boethius. From Dante Alighieri, *Divina commedia* (c. 1444–50).

the world, so Thomas Aquinas and Albertus were the two great lights of the Dominican Order. Since during Henry's lifetime (c. 1300–1370) Thomas had been canonized as a saint and Albertus had not, Henry compared Thomas, the renowned theologian, to the greater light of the sun, and Albertus, the distinguished natural philosopher, to the lesser light of the moon; but because natural philosophy logically precedes theology among the sciences, Henry also praised Albertus as 'the brightest sun from among all of the philosophers of the whole of Christendom'.[4] Similarly, towards the end of the fifteenth century, the Cologne Dominican Rudolph of Nijmegen remarked that Albertus illuminated the entire world by his understanding of all things capable of being known, while the epitaph at Albertus' tomb in the Dominican church of Cologne describes him as 'a prince among philosophers, greater than Plato, and hardly inferior to King Solomon in wisdom'.[5]

When Albertus died on 15 November 1280, he was likely an octogenarian, although the year of his birth is uncertain. Based on later medieval testimony, most modern biographers reckon that Albertus was born about 1200. But Albertus' younger Dominican contemporaries Bernard Gui (d. 1331) and Tolomeo of Lucca (1236–1327), who composed brief biographies or *vitae* for both Albertus and Thomas Aquinas, remark that at his death Albertus was 'more than eighty', while in the fifteenth century, the Dominicans Luis of Valladolid and Rudolph of Nijmegen both insisted that Albertus was 87 when he died, indicating that he may have been born before 1200. Just as no firm date can be established for the year of Albertus' birth, there is no clear consensus for many of the details of his early life.

A variety of sources supply material for Albertus' biography. In addition to Albertus' few statements of a personal nature scattered throughout his writings, there are archival materials (episcopal acts, correspondence relating to his activities on behalf of the Dominican Order, municipal documents, and so on). Although a brief early biographical account is found circa 1260 in the *Lives of the Brothers of the Order of Preachers* (*Vitae fratrum ordinis praedicatorum*), compiled by Gérard de Frachet, the primary medieval sources for Albertus' life first appear in the late fourteenth and fifteenth centuries as part of an effort to promote Albertus' canonization. These include Henry of Herford's *Chronicle* (*Chronicon, c.* 1355) or *Book of Memorable Events* (*Liber de rebus memorabilioribus*), Luis of Valladolid's *Account of Albertus Magnus* (*Tabula Alberti Magni,* 1414), the anonymous mid-fifteenth-century *Cologne Legends* (*Legenda Coloniensis*), Peter of Prussia's *Life of Blessed Albert, the Great Doctor* (*Vita B. Alberti Doctoris Magni, c.* 1485), and Rudolph of Nijmegen's *Legends of Albertus Magnus* (*Legenda Alberti Magni, c.* 1488). Although some of the later sources are aware of con-tradictions in Albertus' early biographical history and attempt to reconcile them, the result is less than satisfactory. Simon Tugwell admirably summarizes these contradictions for the modern reader in his 'Life and Works of Albert the Great',[6] but contradictions they remain. Indeed, exhibiting a notable gift for understatement, James Weisheipl remarks that 'the first 40 years of Albert's life are relatively obscure.'[7] Nevertheless, we shall attempt to present a brief yet plausible summary of Albertus' life and early career.

As Albertus' birth year is uncertain, so too are his place of birth and his family name. Albertus contributes to the historian's frustration by referring to himself at one time as Friar Albertus of Lauingen and at another as Albertus of Cologne. A seal Albertus received upon becoming a theology master in Paris in 1245 identified him as *Albertus Lauigensis*, however, so it seems likely that either his family name was Lauingen or that he was born in Lauingen, a small town in Swabia situated on the Danube, approximately 500 kilometres (300 mi.) southeast of Cologne and 130 kilometres (80 mi.) northwest of Munich in the diocese of Augsburg.

Although some modern historians maintain that Lauingen is Albertus' family name, most medieval chroniclers suppose that Lauingen is Albertus' birthplace. Lauingen itself promoted the

Statue of Albertus in front of the Lauingen town hall (detail).

medieval tradition by constructing a chapel in Albertus' name
during the fourteenth century. A monument to Albertus Magnus
that stands before Lauingen town hall was erected in the late
nineteenth century, and a designated 'Albertus Path' conducts
tourists through the old town.

Albertus' parents' names and the number of his siblings are
unknown, but we know the name of a brother, Henry. Most

historians have rejected Rudolph of Nijmegen's assertion that Albertus belonged to the noble family of the counts of Bollestat (or Bollstadt), whose now-ruined castle lies only about 30 kilometres (19 mi.) from Lauingen. It seems more likely that Albertus was descended from a family of lesser knights, or *ministeriales*, that had served the Holy Roman Emperor Frederick I (d. 1190), that is, Frederick Barbarossa (Red Beard), who was also duke of Swabia. Indeed, Emperor Frederick I Barbarossa had constructed Lauingen's defensive walls, and its medieval burghers placed the emperor's image on the town seal to identify Lauingen as an imperial town. Lauingen continues to enjoy widest acceptance as Albertus' birthplace.

Even though Albertus' was not a high noble family, they must have been prosperous since, in a rare observation about his youth, Albertus describes hunting with falcons and dogs, practices associated with the upper classes:

> Now I myself have had experience . . . [with] falcons
> when I was a lad. Whenever I led my dogs with me into
> the field (they are called 'bird dogs' [*canes avium*] because
> they know how to find birds), falcons would follow me to
> the field, flying above me in the air, and they would strike
> the birds which the dogs had put to flight. These birds
> came back to earth trembling and allowed themselves
> to be picked up in our hands. At the end of the hunt we
> gave one to each falcon and then they left us. (*DA*, 8.110;
> *SZ*, vol. I, p. 716)

Albertus reveals too that:

> I once had a horse that suffered from rheum, and mucus
> [*coryza*] flowed to the nostrils drop by drop. I fumigated the
> horse often after having spread dried cow dung over coals

and after having covered its head, so that, though he had
seemed on the verge of death, he escaped. (QDA², p. 58)

Since Dominicans were forbidden to ride on horseback like great
lords, his description of this cure for equine rheum likely recalls
an event from his youth as well.

Although these references to his life before entering the
Dominican Order do not specify a location around Lauingen in
Upper Swabia, Albertus does offer abundant testimony later to
his experiences in Swabia. In his *On the Causes of the Properties
of the Elements*, he mentions an extinct or inactive volcano in
Swabia and elsewhere remarks on the large number of black
ravens nesting in Augsburg (in East Swabia, approximately
55 kilometres (35 mi.) from Lauingen), where they found an
abundant source of food 'because of the multitude of cobblers
preparing animal hides there'. He also questions Swabian fowlers on the habits of goshawks. Rather more ambiguously, Albertus
mentions observations of eagles' nests by 'fowlers *of our land*,
which is upper Germany' and remarks too that 'we ourselves saw,
in parts of upper Germany, a mouse which held a candle and
provided light for those who were dining, doing so at the behest
of its master.' If these references to 'upper Germany' are references to Upper Swabia, then Albertus seems to identify Upper
Swabia, in which Lauingen is located just to the west of the
Danube River, as 'our land'.[8]

Although Albertus' signet ring's seal suggests his origin in
Lauingen, he was known by various names or titles during his
lifetime. Henry of Herford identifies Albertus more generically
as 'Albertus the German' (*Albertus Theutonicus*), and his student
Thomas of Cantimpré refers to him simply as 'Master Albertus
the Theologian' (*magister Albertus Theologus*).[9] Others identify
him as 'Albertus the Great' (*Albertus Magnus*) or as the 'Universal
Doctor' (*Doctor universalis*), a title he shared with only one

other medieval author, the French theologian Alan of Lille
(d. *c.* 1202).

Albertus was sent to Padua as a young man, where, under
the care of an uncle, he received some education in the arts. In
his treatise *On the Nature of Place*, which he completed circa
1251–4, he mentions that in Padua the study of letters had
flourished for a long time (*De nat. loc.*, 3.2), anticipating
Shakespeare's 'fair Padua, nursery of arts'. Did Albertus study at
the University of Padua? It depends on the date of his arrival
there. From his own works, we know that Albertus spent time
as a young man in Venice and that in 1222 Albertus 'witnessed
an earthquake in Lombardy when the sun was in the sign of
Capricorn', most likely referring to the one that devastated northern Italy at Christmas 1222. The University of Padua was also
established in 1222, and if Albertus arrived in Padua after wit-
nessing the earthquake, he may have studied at the university.
If he arrived prior to the earthquake, then perhaps he studied at
a precursor to the university.[10]

During the summer of 1223, Jordan of Saxony (d. 1237)
visited Padua. Jordan had become the master general of the
Order of Preachers, more commonly known as the Dominican
Order, after the death of its founder, St Dominic. According
to the *Lives of the Brothers of the Order of Preachers*, Jordan of
Saxony visited Padua, 'where there was a great centre for learning', to recruit students for this relatively new mendicant movement (*vfop*, 3.14, p. 110). Although initially he found little
enthusiasm for this novel religious experiment, Jordan remarks
that ten prospective unnamed students did seek admission to
the Order, adding that two were the sons of German lords,[11]
whereas the *Lives of the Brothers of the Order of Preachers* mentions
only that in Padua Jordan received 'a German nobleman in the
flower of youth with gracious manners' (*vfop* 3.14, p. 110).
Some medieval sources identify Albertus as one of these German

students at Padua, leading the normally cautious Weisheipl to
remark that 'it is certain that Albertus joined the Dominican
Order when he was a student in Padua, receiving the habit from
Jordan of Saxony around Easter of 1223.'[12] But if Albertus was
not from a German noble family, Jordan's testimony does not
refer to Albertus at all and does not reliably date Albertus' entry
to the Dominican Order. Indeed, other medieval sources suggest
that Albertus first entered the Order not in Padua but in Cologne,
creating a 'double tradition', which, Simon Tugwell claims, 'is
something of an embarrassment to Albertus biographers'.[13]

These discordant medieval traditions make it difficult to
establish where or when Albertus joined the Dominican Order.
Although some sources suggest that Albertus was a sixteen-year-
old youth when he entered the order, this seems impossible if
he was first drawn to the Dominicans in 1223 and was born in
1200 or earlier. Did Jordan of Saxony recruit him for the order
in Padua in 1223? Simon Tugwell concludes that it is quite
probable that Albertus *did* meet Jordan of Saxony in Padua, but
that Jordan sent him almost immediately to Cologne, where he
later entered the Dominican Order. Tugwell also revives an older
tradition that Albertus first heard Jordan preaching in 1229,
when he was studying at the already-established University of
Padua, and that he first arrived at Cologne in 1229 or early
1230.[14] These varying accounts mean that Albertus could have
entered the Dominican Order sometime between just after his
sixteenth birthday and not later than his 37th!

One would also like to know *why* Albertus joined this rather
new religious experiment, which had only received approval
from Pope Innocent III in December 1216. The Dominican
Order's emphasis on higher education as a necessary foundation
for its members' activity as preachers and inquisitors combat-
ting heresy may have appealed to Albertus. Albertus himself
alludes to these roles in his *Commentary to the Gospel of Luke*

(16.21), where he employs a popular pun that identifies the Dominicans as *Domini Canes*, or 'Watchdogs of the Lord'. Since Albertus was plausibly the son a wealthy family of ministerial rank, other career opportunities certainly would have presented themselves, including military service, and given his impressive intellect, service in the imperial administration was a real possibility. Since many of the most prestigious ecclesiastical foundations in Germany were still closed to those of ministerial rank at the beginning of the thirteenth century, the new Dominican Order also may have offered to men like Albertus (and his brother Henry) a better opportunity for advancement in the Church.[15] This new religious order promoted the ideal of apostolic poverty, however, and demanded that its members embrace not only the individual poverty of Benedictine monasticism but even corporate poverty, asking its members to provide for their daily needs by begging (hence a 'mendicant' order, from the Latin *mendicare*, 'to beg'). Such requirements likely would not have appealed to Albertus' parents, who may have expected him to pursue a career that would elevate his family's wealth, rank and political influence.

Parental opposition to the mendicant orders is a common motif in medieval hagiography. According to legend, when St Francis of Assisi, the founder of the Franciscan Order (Order of Friars Minor), resolved to profess a vow of apostolic poverty, giving up his inheritance and his father's merchant business, his father was so angry that the young Francis hid himself in a cave for a month. When his father was unable to force him to abandon his intention, he publicly disowned his son. Similarly, when Thomas Aquinas dashed his family's hopes that he would become a Benedictine monk and, ultimately, follow his uncle to become abbot of the wealthy Italian abbey of Monte Casino, his family imprisoned him in a family castle for almost a year until Thomas 'escaped' through a window and was received into the Dominican Order. The *Lives of the Brothers of the Order of Preachers* includes a similar legend for the unnamed German nobleman that Jordan of Saxony recruited in Padua. The youth's 'teacher and companions, foreseeing [his] entry [to the Order], just like ministers of the devil, confined a certain beautiful woman with him in the room in order to turn his mind away from a holy intention by the desire of the flesh'. Not only did their stratagem fail, but the text adds that Christ drew the young nobleman so strongly that later he even persuaded his teacher to join the Order. Meanwhile, the young man's rich and powerful father and his retinue travelled to Lombardy, intending either to recover his son or to kill Jordan of Saxony. The father was so impressed by Jordan's holiness that he commended himself and his entire retinue in service to God across the sea (that is, on Crusade). This young nobleman could not have been Albertus, however, since the text clearly states that the father sought to recover him because 'he had no other son.' Albertus' brother Henry of Lauingen followed Albertus into the Dominican Order.[16]

It will become part of the lore of these mendicant orders, then, that their most distinguished members had to overcome serious obstacles before they could enter. In Albertus' case, we have no record of such family opposition.

Medieval sources also credit Albertus' conversion to the direct intervention of the Virgin Mary. It is reported that she appeared to the young Albertus in a vision and instructed him to flee from the world to the Dominican Order. According to medieval legend, she promised that by his devoted study he would acquire the understanding and wisdom to illuminate the entire Church. She is even said to have miraculously provided him with his prodigious philosophical learning, although on the condition that before his death he should be completely stripped of it and restored to a childlike innocence.

Friedrich Walther, *Sermon of St Albertus Magnus*, c. 1430–95, oil on
wood. The banner inscription reads: 'Furcht got wan die stund seyns
urteils ist zukunfftig apock / xiiii' (Fear God . . . for the hour of his
judgement is come; Revelation 14:7).

For his contemporaries, the intellectual confusion and memory lapses Albertus displayed before his death confirmed that the terms of his agreement with the Virgin Mary were fulfilled. According to Rudolph of Nijmegen, when Albertus' memory failed him as he addressed a large audience in Cologne Cathedral, he understood this to be a sign of his imminent demise and begged to receive last rites. When this was reported to his friend Siegfried II of Westerburg, archbishop of Cologne (r. 1274–97), the archbishop hastened to Albertus' cell. He knocked on the door and inquired, 'Father Albertus, are you there?' Albertus did not open the door to him but replied, 'Albertus is not here, but he was.' He died soon after, on 15 November 1280.

Life in Thirteenth-Century Cologne

Although Albertus was likely born in Lauingen and received his early education in Padua, it was in Cologne that he spent much of his life, creating a lasting bond with the German city. Not only is it likely that Albertus completed his novitiate (a probationary period for those seeking admission to the Order) and his early theological training in the Dominican house in Cologne, but he would return there several times for extended periods of residence. He spent at least the last ten years of his life at the Dominican priory of the Holy Cross in Cologne. Whenever Albertus speaks of his 'family', he refers to his Dominican brethren and speaks hardly a word of his birth family.

Thirteenth-century Cologne was a major port on the west bank of the Rhine and a centre of industry, producing textiles, cloth and metal goods. It was one of Europe's largest cities, with more than 40,000 inhabitants, compared to contemporary London's estimated population of 25,000–28,000.[17] Cologne's merchants transported wine, finished metal goods (principally weaponry) and luxury Italian goods to England, and returned to Cologne with English wool and raw metals. Although its economy was quite vibrant and prosperous, its political interests often put it in conflict with the Hohenstaufen dynasty, which had risen to prominence as dukes of Swabia and went on to become German kings, emperors of the Holy Roman Empire and kings of Sicily.

Civil war beset the German realm in the early thirteenth century after the death of Emperor Henry vi (d. 1197) and during the reign of Henry's brother, Philip of Swabia. Peace was temporarily restored only following the election of Henry's son and Philip's nephew, Frederick ii (d. 1250), as king of the Germans in 1212 and shortly thereafter as Holy Roman Emperor. Frederick is remembered as *immutator mundi* – 'one who changed the world'. But change often evokes opposition, and this was especially so during Frederick's reign. Caesarius, a monk at the nearby abbey of Heisterbach, records a Cologne monk's apocalyptic revelation foretelling the schism in the Holy Roman Empire following Henry's death and Frederick ii's disputed election. During this period of civil unrest, the monk proclaimed that

> a cruel beast [Antichrist] will be revealed to the ten lost tribes [of the Jews] . . . After the darkening of the sun, the cruel beast will raise up certain Jews as if from the dead by black magic, but they will not be Jews, but false messengers, saying that they have risen from the dead, and promising vain hope to the real Jews, encouraging the Jews in their faithlessness and error and deceiving many.[18]

Political strife readily evoked apocalyptic fears of the coming of Antichrist. According to medieval Christians, it is he whom

the Jews await as their long-anticipated messiah who will free
them from their political captivity in Christendom, restore
the Davidic kingdom and rebuild the Temple in Jerusalem in
preparation for the resurrection of the dead. The Jews' hopes are
in vain, Caesarius insists, but fear of the advent of Antichrist
is real. Frederick's political enemies, including Pope Gregory IX
(d. 1241), later identified the emperor as, if not the Antichrist
himself, then his forerunner. Cologne's mendicant orders,
including the Dominicans, sided with the papacy when Pope
Gregory IX excommunicated Emperor Frederick II in 1227 for
his failure to embark on a planned crusade to the Holy Land.
Despite this first excommunication – a second followed in 1239
– Frederick departed for the Holy Land in June 1228 and, as a
result of negotiations with Sultan al-Kāmil of Egypt, obtained
the cities of Jerusalem, Nazareth and Bethlehem. On 18 March
1229 Frederick crowned himself king of Jerusalem at the Church
of the Holy Sepulchre.

View of Cologne in Master of the Small Passion, *Martyrium der heiligen Ursula vor der Stadt Köln* (Martyrdom of St Ursula before the city of Cologne), 1411, oil on canvas.

Cologne's present cathedral dedicated to St Peter was built on the site of older Christian churches that date from the fourth century. It was likely during the construction of Cologne's high Gothic cathedral, begun in 1248 on the site of fourth-century Christian churches, that Albertus himself encountered evidence of Cologne's ancient past. In his *Book on the Causes of the Properties of the Elements*, which he composed in Cologne between 1251 and 1254, he says: 'we have also seen in Cologne that deep pits are made and at their bottom paving stones of marvelous design and beauty were found, and it is agreed that ancient peoples produced them there and that the ground was built up over them after the buildings fell to ruin' (CPE, pp. 51–2). The cathedral promoted its Roman origins, too, with the claim that it possessed among its sacred objects St Peter's staff and part of the chains with which he had been bound during his imprisonment first in Jerusalem (Acts 5:17–25) and later in Rome. Emperor Frederick Barbarossa's chancellor, Rainald of Dassel, visited Milan, where he obtained relics alleged to be the bodies of the Three Kings or Magi who, according to Matthew's Gospel (Matthew 2:1–2), brought gifts of gold, frankincense and myrrh to the infant Jesus. According to legend, these relics had first been discovered by St Helena, mother of the Emperor Constantine I (the Great; d. 337), who had brought the relics to Constantinople, and from there, they later travelled to Milan. On 24 July 1164 Rainald solemnly translated the relics to Cologne Cathedral, having separated three fingers from the bodies to be sent to the cathedral of Hildesheim.

By the end of the twelfth century, a collection of written legends about the Magi was housed in Cologne Cathedral, and this collection would provide the basis for John of Hildesheim's early fourteenth-century *History of the Three Kings* (*Historia Trium Regum*), which established a connection between the Three Kings and the fabled priest-king of the East, Prester John, whose legend was already well known by the later twelfth century. Albertus mentions his own visit to Cologne's Shrine of the Three Kings and describes an onyx stone cameo on the shrine that depicts two heads in profile (DM, pp. 130–31). Based on Albertus' description, Dorothy Wyckoff tentatively identifies the gem as the 'Ptolemy' cameo that disappeared sometime after Albertus' description. It currently resides in the Kunsthistorisches Museum in Vienna and dates from 278–269 BCE.

Under Rainald's successor, Archbishop Philip of Cologne, the relics were enshrined in a gold reliquary, which later made the cathedral a centre of European pilgrimage to rival Rome, Compostela and Canterbury. The height of the Gothic cathedral's spires at 157 metres (516 ft) made it the tallest structure

Ptolemaic Cameo with the portraits of Ptolemy II and Arsinoe II,
3rd century BC, ten-layered onyx.

in the world, until in 1884 the Washington Monument's height
of 169 metres (555 ft 5 in.) surpassed it.

In addition to the cathedral, thirteenth-century Cologne
boasted sixteen parish churches, eleven collegiate churches,
three Benedictine monasteries, six religious houses for women
(two Benedictine, three Augustinian and one Cistercian), a
church of the Teutonic knights and sixteen chapels.

During Albertus' lifetime, new religious orders established
themselves in Cologne. In 1221 two of the recently formed
mendicant orders – the Dominicans and the Franciscans –
arrived in Cologne. The Franciscans, or Order of Friars Minor
(*Ordo fratrum minorum*), obtained property for an oratory in
St Severin's parish in Cologne, but later moved their house
to St Columba parish, where they consecrated a church in 1260.
The adjacent street is still known as *Minoritenstrasse*. The
Franciscan community in Cologne, like the city itself, had

strong ties to England: the eminent Oxford-trained Franciscan philosopher and theologian Scotsman John Duns Scotus (the 'Subtle Doctor', *Doctor subtilis*) spent the last two years of his life teaching in Cologne, which aspired to surpass Paris as a centre for study. After his death in 1308, he was buried in Cologne's *Minoritenkirche*.

In 1221 or 1222 the Dominicans also founded a priory and small chapel dedicated to the Holy Cross in Cologne on the *Stolkgasse*. Its first prior, Henry of Cologne, had been recruited to the order while a student at the University of Paris by St Dominic himself. Gradually, the chapel, a short distance from Cologne Cathedral, was enlarged to become a great church. Albertus Magnus laid the foundation stone for its expanded choir in 1271 and left a sizeable bequest to complete its construction following his death. Albertus also endowed the enlarged

Shrine of the Three Kings, Cologne Cathedral, *c.* 1185–1200.

Cologne Cathedral, 2017.

church with holy relics, which included a splinter from the True Cross – hence the chapel's dedication to the Holy Cross – as well as a thorn from Jesus's crown of thorns. Albertus brought these sacred objects to Cologne from Paris, where St Louis, King Louis IX of France (d. 1270), had presented them to him. With these relics, the Dominican chapel could compete with the Cologne church of St George the Martyr, which, according

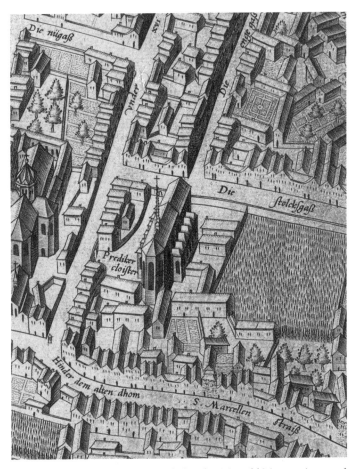

Detail of the Dominican priory and church in Arnold Mercator's map of
Cologne, *Colonia agrippina*, 1571, engraving.

to the Cistercian Caesarius of Heisterbach (*Dial.*, 8.25), also
possessed a bejewelled gold cross that contained a piece of the
True Cross.

By the middle of the thirteenth century, the Hospitallers, or
Order of Knights of the Hospital of St John of Jerusalem, had
established a church in Cologne dedicated to St John and St
Cordula. Albertus had close ties to this community. According
to the anonymous fifteenth-century *Cologne Legends* (*Legenda*

Coloniensis), in 1263 Albertus bestowed indulgences upon the Hospitallers' church; in 1267 he confirmed under his seal donations made to this community by Theodoric of Heinsberg. While tradition states that St Cordula died in Cologne in the fifth century, it was Albertus Magnus who uncovered Cordula's bones in Cologne in a spot to which a vision had directed his fellow Dominican, Isbranda. Albertus then translated the bones to the chapel of the Hospitallers on St Valentine's Day, 14 February 1278.

Medieval Jewish Cologne

In addition to the many Christian institutions of thirteenth-century Cologne, Albertus could hardly have avoided contact with its sizeable Jewish community. That community was already well established in the late Roman Empire, when the edicts of Emperor Constantine I imposed onerous duties upon the Jews of Cologne. By the eleventh century, the Cologne synagogue had become a place of regular assembly for Jewish scholars from across the Rhineland, and members of Rhenish Jewish communities met three times each year during the triannual Cologne market fair. The Cologne Jewish quarter was in the very heart of the city next to the cathedral, and the city hall, or *Rathaus*, was in the middle of the Jewish quarter. Archaeological evidence indicates that by 1115 the Jewish community had rebuilt its synagogue, almost twenty years after Rhineland Jewish communities had been nearly destroyed by Christian Crusaders preparing to depart for Jerusalem on the First Crusade. Shortly thereafter, it had bought land for a community hall (*domus universitatis*) and constructed a *mikveh*, or ritual bath, that utilized flowing groundwater from the Rhine. Current excavations of the medieval Jewish quarter in Cologne have uncovered important evidence of the Jewish community, which will be on view in the long-awaited Jewish Museum in the Archaeological Quarter of Cologne.

Between 1135 and 1159, for the first time, we find a Cologne Jew named 'Bishop of the Jews' (*episcopus Judaeorum*), who, although not a bishop in the Christian sense, nonetheless served as religious and legal administrator and as a liaison between the Jewish community and Christian authorities. By about 1250 the Jewish community had expanded to at least five hundred members. One of its many scholars, R. Asher b. Yehiel (d. 1327), emerged as Cologne's most important Talmudist during the second half of the thirteenth century. The Jewish community's financial importance is evident from the hundreds of property transactions in St Lawrence parish recorded in Latin and Hebrew in the Cologne *Judenschreinsbuch* for the thirteenth and early fourteenth centuries, some of which involve sales between Jews and Christian religious houses. Thanks to the *Judenschreinsbuch*,

Conrad of Hochstaden holding plans for the cathedral's construction, floor mosaic, Cologne Cathedral.

we can identify the *episcopus Judaeorum* at the time of Albertus' death as a certain Moses, who transferred a house in 1280 to his son Suskint and his son's wife, Brune.

The growing importance of Cologne's thirteenth-century rabbinical court was supported by privileges or protection charters issued or reissued in 1252 to the community by Archbishop Conrad of Hochstaden (d. 1261), who is memorialized in Cologne in starkly different ways. Inside Cologne Cathedral, where he is buried, Conrad is depicted in a mosaic holding the architectural plan for the new cathedral, whose foundations he established in 1248. But on the outside of the city hall, constructed at the beginning of the fifteenth century, Conrad is depicted in a column statue that stands upon an obscene sculpted base revealing a male exposing his bottom and engaging in autofellation. The image may recall the troubled relationship that Conrad had with the city of Cologne or, at least, a certain later disdain for ecclesiastical authority.

As one of three German archbishops among the seven imperial electors, Conrad of Hochstaden crowned Richard, Earl of Cornwall, as king of the Germans in the city of Aachen in 1257. In Cologne, Conrad pledged not only to protect the Cologne Jewish community from violence, but to support the community's juridical autonomy. Both Conrad's authoritarian policies and his jurisdiction over Cologne's Jews alienated much of the Cologne citizenry, however, since the archbishop and not the city benefited from taxes imposed upon the Cologne Jewry. Hostilities broke out between the archbishop and the city, and from 1249 through to the next decade, Albertus Magnus served as a mediator to bring a measure of peace to the city. In the Great Arbitration of 1258, Albertus sought to resolve numerous points of conflict between the city of Cologne and Conrad, and recognized the archbishop's sovereignty over the Jews as serfs of the archbishop's chamber: 'nothing regarding his

Conrad of Hochstaden, Cologne City Hall, c. 1410.

Jews concerns the citizens of Cologne . . . for he holds the Jews
themselves in fief from the empire' (*quod nichil ad Cives
Colonienses pertinet de suis Judeis . . . tenet enim ipsos Judaeos in
feodo ab imperio*). Although Albertus upheld Conrad's rights over
the Jews, within a year of the Great Arbitration, the city won
concessions to impose a municipal tax upon the Jews, resulting

Customary rights of Cologne's medieval Jews,
stone tablet, Cologne Cathedral.

in recognition of the jurisdiction of both the archbishop and of the city of Cologne over the Jewish community. Tensions created by such dual jurisdiction continued long after Conrad's death.

Conflict arising from dual jurisdiction over the Cologne Jewish community erupted again following Albertus' death when Archbishop Siegfried II of Westerburg was defeated by a coalition that aligned the duke of Brabant and the citizens of Cologne against the archbishop at the Battle of Worringen in 1288. Siegfried was captured in the battle and subsequently moved his archiepiscopal seat from Cologne to nearby Bonn, where he continued to assert his rights over Cologne's Jews at the same time the citizens of Cologne asserted their independence as a self-governing city.

Although there is little evidence of Albertus' *direct* involvement with the Jews of Cologne, since Jews and Christians regularly interacted there, it is reasonable to assume that Albertus had more than a passing acquaintance with Cologne's Jewish representatives. Indeed, Albertus authenticated and confirmed with his seal Pope Gregory x's papal bull *Sicut Judaeis* of 1272 and submitted it to the newly elected King Rudolf I. This bull, which can be traced back to Pope Gregory I (d. 604), codified the legal protections to which Jews were entitled in Latin Christendom. It also condemned the accusation that Jews regularly murdered Christian children and used their hearts and blood as a sacrifice, and ordered that any Jews imprisoned under such accusations be freed.

Although the Jewish population of Cologne grew to 750 by 1340, a violent persecution on 23–24 August 1349, following unsupported rumours that Jews were poisoning town wells, forced Cologne Jews to seek refuge elsewhere. On 2 January 1360 Archbishop William of Cologne reissued the *Edict in Favor of the Jews* (*Edictum in favorem Judaeorum*), which reiterated customary imperial protections and privileges accorded to Jews in German lands.[19] The community was revived after 1372, but only about two hundred Jews resettled in Cologne, and the community's importance declined. In August 1423 the Cologne city council failed to renew the charter of protection for the Jewish community, and by 1 October 1424 all Jews were forced to leave the city.

Albertus' First Period in Cologne

Although it is likely that Albertus was first sent to Cologne to study theology (rather than to Bologna or Paris to study philosophy, as some sources suggest), the date of his arrival in Cologne and the exact chronology of his period of study there are difficult to ascertain. Tugwell suggests that because of Albertus' maturity and previous study, his training there followed an accelerated path. Henry of Herford attests that in Cologne Albertus twice 'read' or lectured on Peter Lombard's *Four Books of Sentences* (*Sententiarum libri* iv), an essential and standard instructional textbook in theology. Therefore, even before Albertus was named a lector, whose role was to give theological lectures to the members of the community, in Hildesheim in 1233, he may have served as a sort of 'apprentice' lector in Cologne. Although the earliest constitutions of the Dominican Order required four years of theological studies before one could receive an appointment as lector, it is not certain that this requirement had been introduced in Cologne before Albertus' arrival. Depending upon the date one assigns to his arrival in Cologne, therefore, Albertus may have become an 'apprentice' lector there as early as 1229.

As a lector, Albertus offered theological instruction to the Dominican community. Essential to the theological curriculum were the Bible and the *Scholastic History* (*Historia scholastica*) of Petrus Comestor (Peter the Eater, d. 1178), which, drawing on the writings of the Church Fathers, presented a 'harmonized' biblical narrative from creation to the Acts of the Apostles. At the centre of instruction, however, lay the *Sentences* of Peter Lombard (d. 1160), bishop of Paris. Dominicans also received training in canon law and sacramental theology. Only after completing these studies was the friar permitted to preach. After Albertus completed this training, he was sent as a lector to other Dominican houses. For nearly a decade, Albertus wandered across Germany to teach at Dominican priories, whose students would have received from him the same basic training he had received in Cologne.

It is also during this period that Albertus began to write compositions of his own. His first work, *On the Nature of the Good* (*De natura boni*), treats the virtues and various ethical

Albertus lecturing to students, miniature from Albertus Magnus, *De animalibus* (14th century).

questions, citing ten of Aristotle's works, including six of his books on nature (the *libri naturales*) in their older versions, which still were proscribed in Paris. Albertus also began writing texts for theological instruction: *On the Sacraments* (*De sacramentis*), *On the Incarnation* (*De incarnatione*) and *On Resurrection* (*De resurrectione*). Later, these three would be incorporated into Albertus' six-part *Parisian Summa* (*Summa Parisiensis*), which purportedly arose out of his formal public disputations at the University of Paris. The *Parisian Summa* contains all six treatises: (1) *On the Sacraments* (*De sacramentis*), (2) *On the Incarnation* (*De incarnatione*), (3) *On Resurrection* (*De resurrectione*), (4) *On the Four Coequal Principles* (*De IV coaequavis*), (5) *On the Human* (*De homine*) and (6) *On the Good* (*De bono*). *On the Four Coequal Principles*, which explores the relation between matter, time and celestial bodies, and *On the Human* sometimes circulated independently or as parts of a larger treatise on the work of creation bearing the title *Summa de creaturis*. It is likely that Albertus began all six treatises during the 1230s while serving as a lector in Germany and before he was sent to Paris to study. Nonetheless, Albertus often revised his earlier works in Paris, where he incepted as master in 1245. Inception is a step that indicates not only that a candidate has received his master's degree, but that he has completed certain formal academic acts. Following inception, a new university master enters a two-year period of regency and will be known as a regent master. With this new status, Albertus was ready for the next phase of his career, one that would shape the rest of his days.

TWO

From Cologne to Paris

Albertus departed Cologne to become a lector in Hildesheim around 1233. As a lector, Albertus provided instruction to Dominican communities on the Bible and theology. Theological instruction turned especially to Peter Lombard's *Sentences*, which had become *the* standard instructional textbook. Peter, who would be known as the 'Master of the Sentences' (*Magister Sententiarum*), sought to create a systematic theology that reconciled discordant opinions found among the Church Fathers, and the *Sentences*' four books treat the mystery of the Trinity, Creation, the Incarnation and the Sacraments. In his role as lector, then, Albertus introduced his students not only to the interpretation of biblical texts but, equally important, to Lombard's theological model.

From Hildesheim, Henry of Herford claims that Albertus went to teach at Freiburg, then to Regensburg for two years, then to Strasbourg, and finally to Paris. Whether Albertus left Hildesheim for Freiburg-im-Breisgau or Freiberg in Saxony is unclear. Freiburg-im-Breisgau is in southwest Germany, whereas Freiberg in Lower Saxony is located to the northeast. Dominican houses existed in both locations in 1235–6, and arguments can be made for either place. From Hildesheim to Freiberg in Saxony is a distance of 303 kilometres (188 mi.), while it is about 550 kilometres (340 mi.) to Freiburg-im-Breisgau. It might have made sense, then, to send Albertus to the nearer city. Albertus himself notes, moreover, that he was in Saxony in 1240 when he saw a comet passing near the north pole of the ecliptic. In addition, he remarks elsewhere that 'at one time I became a wanderer, making long journeys to mining districts, so that I could learn by observation the nature of metals,' and on his travels he visited copper mines in Saxony at Goslar (*Goselaria*) and observed silver ore at Freiberg (*Vuriebeg*).[1] If he saw this comet while a lector in Freiberg in Saxony, then Albertus would have arrived in Hildesheim in 1233 and sometime later departed for Freiberg, where he remained at least until 1240. He likely was in Regensburg from 1240 to 1242, in Strasbourg for either 1242 or 1243, and from there travelled to Paris in either 1243 or 1244.[2] Tugwell offers an alternative chronology, however, in which Albertus was a lector in Freiberg from 1236 to 1237, in Regensburg from 1237 to 1239 and in Strasbourg from 1239 to 1240. Tugwell adds that Albertus only visited Saxony in 1240, for reasons unknown, and that he arrived in Paris as early as 1240.[3] Both chronologies are plausible, with the latter placing Albertus in Paris several years earlier than the former.[4]

Since both timelines are possible, we can only assert with confidence that Albertus arrived in Paris between 1240 and 1243, where he pursued his studies and lectured on Peter Lombard's *Sentences*, with the goal of becoming a master in theology. The Dominican priory of St James in Paris, incorporated into the University of Paris soon after 1220, was the only international study house (*studium generale*) the Dominicans had at that time and could enrol only about 110 Dominican externs (that is, foreign students) annually. Dominican provinces were therefore permitted to send to Paris no more than three students each year. Only in 1246 did the Dominicans move to create four new international study houses in the provinces of Provence, Lombardy, England and Germany. Until then, Paris remained a highly selective academic environment for those who held the most promise. Albertus' selection for study at the Dominican house in Paris was quite a distinction.

Already in the 1220s, Caesarius of Heisterbach had identified Paris as 'the fount of all knowledge and the well of the Holy Scriptures'.[5] In the geographical study he completed between 1251 and 1254, Albertus rightly describes Paris as 'the city of the philosophers'. In his 1255 bull *Quasi lignum vitae*, Pope Alexander IV recognizes the corporation of university scholars in Paris 'as the tree of life in God's Paradise and the lamp of glory in God's house'. According to Albertus' student Thomas of Cantimpré, once the scheduled university lectures and debates had concluded for the day, Albertus devoted himself to the Psalms and lay prostrate in prayer both day and night. Such was Albertus' dedication, Thomas added, that when a demon assumed the appearance of another Dominican brother and sought to divert him from his studies, Albertus immediately signed himself with the cross and forced him to depart. It is no surprise, Thomas concludes, that Albertus' knowledge surpassed that of other men.[6]

In Paris, Albertus would have encountered other inquiring minds of his own generation. At the Dominican priory of St James, he found an international community of students and teachers sharing his intense interest in the natural world. Albertus claims the stone *topasion*, which Wyckoff identifies in this context as *hephaestites*, is an effective remedy for haemorrhoids and for attacks of lunacy. When placed in boiling water, it makes the water stop bubbling and cool 'so that soon the hand can be put in, to take it out; and a member of our Order', said Albertus, 'actually did this in Paris'. Albertus also remarks on images or fossilized impressions ('sigils') he found among the rocks of Paris, and he adds that when he was in Paris 'in the number and company of scholars', another student, the son of the king of Castile (likely Philip of Castile, the son of King Ferdinand III of Castile and León, who studied in Paris

and was the younger brother to King Alfonso x, 'the Wise', who
reigned as king of Castile from 1252), presented him with an
oyster shell that had been found in the belly of a fish. On its
concave side were images of three serpents, and on its convex
side ten more were incised. Albertus concludes that just as
nature produced these images on the oyster shell, so too nature
produces fossilized impressions on the surfaces of stones. He
cherished the shell, adding that 'I kept this shell for a long time
and showed it to many people, and later I sent it as a gift to
someone in Germany.'[7]

After his arrival in Paris, Albertus likely offered a series of
required lectures on Peter Lombard's *Sentences*. It was there,
however, that Albertus also encountered theological controversy. The Fourth Lateran Council (1215) required assent to
the proposition that 'all will rise with their own individual
bodies, that is, the bodies which they now wear.'[8] Caesarius of
Heisterbach complains of theologians in Paris who gave greater
authority to the poet Ovid than to St Augustine and denied the
resurrection of the body while affirming that heaven and hell
only signify an interior state reflecting one's knowledge or igno-
rance of God (*Dial.*, 5.22). Heated debates at the University of
Paris continued into the 1240s and led William of Auvergne,
bishop of Paris, and Odo of Châteauroux, the university chancellor, to condemn ten theological errors on 13 January 1241
and again in 1244. They especially condemned the teaching
that those resurrected as blessed will not see the divine essence.[9]
Among those scholars at Paris who may have been targeted by
the condemnation was Guerric of Saint-Quentin. Albertus
addresses many of the condemned errors in his *On Resurrection*,
which indicates that Albertus often wrote with an eye turned
towards real debates that divided scholars of his generation.

This controversy addressed by the 1241 condemnation of
ten theological errors was not the only one to trouble the

University of Paris. Towards the beginning of the thirteenth century, a theology master in Paris, Amalric or Amaury of Bène (d. 1206), was charged with pantheism, based partially on his interpretation of Aristotle and partially on his interpretation of the ninth-century philosopher-theologian John Scotus Eriugena's treatise *On the Division of Nature* (*De divisione naturae*, or *Periphyseon*). In 1204 the Parisian faculty of theology placed Amalric on trial, and he was summoned to the papal court. After Pope Innocent III censured his theories, he recanted before his fellow scholars at Paris. The Council of Paris even convicted him posthumously of heresy in 1210 and ordered that his body be exhumed and reburied in unconsecrated ground. Ten of his followers, known as Amalricians, were also convicted of heresy and publicly executed in 1210. Canon 2 of the Fourth Lateran Council (1215) reaffirmed Amalric's condemnation, adding that his doctrine is not so much heretical as insane.

The Council of Paris also condemned for heresy and pantheism David of Dinant, who earlier had translated works of Aristotle at the papal court. In David's *Quaternuli*, which was rediscovered in the early 1930s, David explains that he had travelled to Constantinople to read Aristotle's works on natural philosophy. His interest in Aristotle's zoological and biological treatises characterizes him as a natural philosopher with a strong interest in medical doctrine, however, rather than a metaphysician. Nonetheless, in 1210 a council of bishops in Paris ordered the *Quaternuli* burned and forbade the public or private reading of Aristotle's treatises on natural philosophy, the *libri naturales*. A 1215 papal regulation of studies in Paris reaffirmed these condemnations and prohibited the study of Aristotle's works on metaphysics and natural philosophy, either in their original or summary forms. However, students were expected to study Aristotle's *Nicomachean Ethics*, as well as the Aristotelian works on logic that formed the *Organon*.

The *Organon* (*Instrument*) includes both the *logica vetus*, or 'old' logic, which consisted largely of Aristotelian works that had been translated by Boethius in the sixth century – namely the *Categories*, *On Interpretation*, Porphyry's *Isagoge* or introduction to Aristotle's *Categories* – and the *logica nova*. The 'new' logic appeared during the twelfth century, principally as a result of the translation work of James of Venice (d. after 1147), who had travelled to Constantinople in search of Greek source texts. The *logica nova* introduced a Latin audience to previously unavailable works of Aristotle: the *Prior Analytics*, *Posterior Analytics*, *Topics* and *On Sophistical Refutations* (*Sophismata*). James of Venice also translated Aristotle's *Physics*, a work of natural philosophy, and Aristotle's *On the Soul* and *Metaphysics*. From about 1220 to 1230, with support from the imperial court of Frederick II and from the papal court, Michael Scot produced Latin translations from Arabic sources of Aristotle's *Physics* and *On Animals* (*De animalibus*, completed c. 1220),[10] and translated commentaries on various Aristotelian works by the Iberian Islamic philosopher Ibn Rushd (d. 1198, known to the Latin world as Averroes), Avicenna's *On Animals* (which Michael Scot dedicated to the Emperor Frederick) and Nur ad-Din al-Bitrūǧī's *On the Movements of the Heavens*. Although Lynn Thorndike, a pre-eminent historian of medieval science, remarks that 'Michael Scot may be regarded as the leading intellectual in western Europe during the first third of the thirteenth century,'[11] Albertus Magnus, who was dependent upon Michael Scot's translation of Aristotle's *On Animals*, nonetheless complained that Michael was 'ignorant' of the truth of nature and did not properly understand the works of Aristotle.[12]

Despite Albertus' criticism, the work of these twelfth- and thirteenth-century translators transformed the intellectual world of Europe. The *Organon* was uncontroversial, but Aristotle's natural philosophy or science represented a special challenge to Christian theologians, for in that body of work they found that Aristotle, the 'Master of Those Who Know', presented arguments demonstrating the eternity of the universe and challenging the immortality of the individual soul. Given this challenge, ecclesiastical authority responded with suspicion to Aristotle's natural philosophy. At first, it sought to prohibit scholars in Paris from reading such texts, as seen above in the papal regulation of 1215. Shortly thereafter, confronted with the failure of this policy in the face of growing interest in Aristotle's work, ecclesiastical authorities sought to 'Christianize' Aristotle by promoting interpretations of his philosophy that could be harmonized with Christian doctrine. In a final stage, ecclesiastical authority once again sought a 'purge' when in 1270 the bishop of Paris, Étienne Tempier, condemned a list of thirteen propositions that were defended on the basis of Aristotle's authority. Among these thirteen 'errors' were the propositions that the world is eternal, that there was never a first man and that the soul is corrupted with the body. Again in 1277 Tempier condemned a list of 219 theological and philosophical errors attributed to radical Averroism or heterodox Aristotelianism.

Looking back upon these early prohibitions, Caesarius of Heisterbach remarks that 'it was enjoined in Paris that no one should read the books on natural science [libros naturales] for the next three years. The books of Master David [of Dinant] . . . were subject to everlasting condemnation and burnt' (Dial., 5.22). In 1225 Pope Honorius III added condemnations of Scotus Eriugena's doctrines and ordered a public burning of his writings. On 7 July 1228 Pope Gregory IX demanded that Paris theologians reaffirm philosophy's subordinate rank to theology as ancilla theologiae (the handmaiden of theology) and warned them against 'adulterating the word of God with the fictions of philosophers'.[13]

In April 1229 a faculty strike known as the 'Great Dispersion', protesting the killing of a number of students during a drunken riot at Carnival by soldiers of Queen Regent Blanche of Castile, began. Gregory IX's 1231 bull *Parens scientiarum* brought the strike to an end and the return of scholars to Paris by establishing the legal privileges of university scholars under ecclesiastical and not royal jurisdiction. The bull also recognized the scholars' prerogative to renew their strike, as would occur several times during the second half of the thirteenth century, should their rights be infringed in the future.

The Great Dispersion also generated anger towards the university scholars who belonged to mendicant orders because although most secular masters – that is, scholar-ecclesiastics who were not members of religious orders – ceased instruction, the mendicant scholars did not participate in the strike. Their role as strikebreakers soured relations, as did the refusal of Dominican scholars to take the oath to abide by university statutes. Anger against them culminated in William of Saint-Amour's *On the Dangers of the Last Times* (*De periculis novissimorum temporum*), which William published in 1256. The work is an antimendicant polemic identifying Dominicans in particular as harbingers of the Antichrist. William, who had been chosen dean of the university theology masters around 1250, was a French philosopher and theologian who led the seculars' opposition against the mendicant scholars. He arranged to have the Dominican masters at the university suspended during the winter of 1254 and in July obtained from Pope Innocent IV a decree that would limit each mendicant religious order to one university master's chair. But when Innocent IV died in December of that year, he was succeeded by Pope Alexander IV, who was a staunch ally of the mendicants generally and of the Franciscans in particular. During his reign, *On the Dangers of the Last Times* was formally condemned on 5 October 1256 by a papal commission at Anagni. The pope ordered the destruction of all copies, although some survived. William was exiled, but under Pope Clement IV was permitted to retire to Saint-Amour until his death in 1272. We will return to this episode again since Albertus played a significant role in formulating a Dominican response.

To return to *Parens scientiarum*, this papal bull recognized the university scholars' right to direct student and university life, including the right to establish regulations governing academic dress, lecture schedules and the price of student lodgings. It established the length of the summer vacation (one month) and prohibited students – sometimes a rowdy bunch – from carrying weapons in the city. It also deprived those who called themselves students from enjoying the legal protections afforded scholars if they failed to attend lectures. It reaffirmed that the Aristotelian works on natural science were forbidden – although technically only for scholars in the arts faculty – until purged of error. It appears that Gregory IX appointed a commission under the leadership of the Parisian scholar William of Auxerre to examine Aristotle's prohibited books that were available in Latin translation, but since William died in November 1231, it is not clear that the commission ever convened. The larger concern, clearly stated in a university statute from 1272, was that members of the arts faculty would apply Aristotle's natural philosophy to theological doctrines, that is, the Trinity or Incarnation, arrive at heretical conclusions and trespass upon the domain of the theologians. Finally, *Parens scientiarum* warned students and theology masters especially not to appear as philosophers but to strive for knowledge of God, using only the 'sacred language' – that is, Latin, one of the three sacred languages, after Hebrew and Greek – and eschewing the vernacular.

Although Albertus Magnus arrived in Paris three decades after David of Dinant's condemnation, at the request of Pope Gregory IX, he undertook to rehabilitate Aristotle for a Christian audience. Albertus' *Summa of Theology* (*Summa theologiae*) attacks David of Dinant's 'pantheistic' claim that equates Aristotle's

prime matter and God, as well as David's materialistic doctrine
of the soul based on Aristotle's *On the Soul*.[14] In a later identi-
fication of heretical theses, in the *Compilation on the [Brothers
of the] New Spirit* (*Compilatio de novo spiritu*, written after 1262),
Albertus identifies David of Dinant with the 'error' of Alexander
of Aphrodisias, a late second- and early third-century CE philosopher and commentator on Aristotle. Albertus declares that

> to say that every creature is God is the heresy of Alexander
> [of Aphrodisias] who said that prime matter and God and
> *nous* – that is, the intellect – are identical in substance,
> which later was followed by a certain David of Dinant,
> who fled France in our time for this heresy.[15]

At the University of Paris during this time, lectures by bachelors
(that is, churchmen who had obtained a bachelor's degree)
explaining Peter Lombard's *Sentences* were a basic element of
theological instruction in systematic theology. There were other
bachelors who explained the biblical text (the *baccalaureus
biblicus*), and there was disagreement between secular scholars
and the Dominicans over which should come before the other
in one's educational preparation. Nonetheless, the study of both
the Bible and *Sentences* formed essential parts of the theological
curriculum. One could not advance to become a master, moreover, without serving as a bachelor. In addition to lectures,
however, theological education witnessed a major innovation
in Paris: the introduction during the regular academic year of
the quodlibetal disputation. In its most formal structure, the
quodlibetal disputation was an exercise held twice each year and
convened by a master at which anyone in the audience could
ask a question on any topic whatsoever (*de quolibet*). At the first
of these sessions, the master's assistants would provide responses
to questions posed, with arguments *pro et contra*. Then, typically

on a second day, the master would provide his own systematic response in an often lively session.

By the time of Albertus' arrival in Paris, the quodlibetal disputation had become a popular exercise, and it spread from Paris to other universities. It seems that the earliest recorded quodlibets belong to the Dominican Guerric of Saint-Quentin, who held one of the two Dominican chairs at the university in theology. The other was occupied by Godfrey of Bleneau (r. 1235–42). Albertus was probably promoted to master of theology in June 1245 and to regent master (*magister regens*) in September 1245, likely as the successor to Guerric. Albertus was the first German Dominican to hold the chair in theology in Paris, and he remained there until 1248 in distinguished company, alongside the bishop of Paris William of Auvergne, the Dominican Robert Kilwardby and the Franciscans Odo Rigaud, Roger Bacon and John of Fidanza (St Bonventure).

Albertus and the Condemnation of the Talmud

While Albertus was regent master in theology, he was drawn into another significant Parisian controversy concerning the Jews' Talmud. This controversy erupted circa 1236 when a recent Jewish convert to Christianity, Nicholas Donin, complained to Pope Gregory IX that the Talmud contains numerous blasphemies against Christianity. Donin, who had earlier been excommunicated by rabbinic authorities and repudiated as an apostate and heretic, may have collaborated with one or more Christian scholars to prepare a list of 35 articles against the Talmud, presented to Pope Gregory IX. On 9 June 1239 the pope sent documents related to Donin's complaint to William of Auvergne, bishop of Paris, that were hand-delivered by 'our beloved son, Nicholas, a former Jew', and instructed the bishop to share these texts with the kings of France, England, Aragon,

Navarre, Castile and León, and Portugal. Royal support was essential, since Jews were subject to royal rather than ecclesiastical jurisdiction. On the same day, the pope wrote to the archbishops of France and lamented that the Talmud's offensive doctrines 'are a source of shame to those who repeat them and a horror to those who hear them'. He ordered the French ecclesiastics to 'have all the books belonging to the Jews in your province seized' with the assistance of secular authorities 'on the first Sabbath of next Lent' (3 March 1240), when the Jews were in their synagogues, and to be held for safekeeping by the Dominicans and Franciscans. On 20 June 1239 Pope Gregory IX sent a similar instruction to the king of Portugal. In another letter on the same date addressed to Bishop William of Auvergne, to the prior of the Dominicans and to the minister general of the Franciscans in Paris, Gregory ordered that 'those [books] which you find to contain errors of this kind you shall have burned together in a bonfire.' Just as the appearance of Aristotle's books on natural philosophy were a perceived threat to Christian doctrines and resulted in papal efforts to restrict their use in Paris, so now a deeper awareness of the content of the Talmud prompted papal instructions to confiscate the Talmud and to investigate it for blasphemy and error.[16]

Donin's 35 articles, having cast a harsh light on the Talmud's alleged blasphemies against God, Jesus, the Virgin Mary and the Church, prompted the pope to act. Not only did he order the confiscation of these books, but he put them on trial at a public disputation in Paris in late June 1240, at which the 'errors' of the Talmud were investigated by ecclesiastical authorities. Gregory's exhortations to secular authorities succeeded only in France, however. King Louis IX confiscated rabbinic texts and called Jewish scholars to Paris, initiating a series of medieval show trials. Four rabbis were called upon to defend the Talmud against Nicholas Donin: Rabbi Judah ben David of Melun, Rabbi Samuel ben Solomon of Falaise, Rabbi Yehiel ben Joseph of Paris and Rabbi Moses ben Jacob of Coucy. The outcome seemed foreordained, and some twenty cartloads of the Jews' books were burned in Paris at the Place de la Grève, likely in June 1241.

Pope Gregory IX's letters from June 1239 award a significant role to the Dominicans and Franciscans for the confiscation, investigation and destruction of the Talmud. Thomas of Cantimpré (1201–1272), a Dominican friar who later studied under Albertus Magnus in Cologne, was sent to the Dominican priory of St James in Paris in 1237 to study the arts at the university and was present in Paris for some of the events described above. Thomas likely had contact in Paris with the convert Nicholas Donin, who, some scholars have suggested, had also entered the Dominican Order. Thomas reports, too, on the efforts of fellow Dominican Henry of Cologne (Henry of Marsberg, d. 1254) to confiscate the Talmud in Paris, and it has been suggested that Henry was the collaborator who worked with Nicholas Donin to produce the 35 articles. Although the Dominicans appear to have supported enthusiastically the papal assault on the Talmud, the Jews found some, especially from among the secular clergy, to defend their traditional right to possess their sacred texts. Thomas attests that among them was an influential archbishop, likely the archbishop of Sens Walter of Cornut (d. 1241), who allegedly accepted bribes from Jews and persuaded King Louis IX to return the confiscated books of the Talmud temporarily. The Jews, says Thomas, ordered that the day on which the books were returned be celebrated annually. Their joy was premature, however, as the archbishop died on that very same day the following year, and the king reversed his decision as a result. Thomas insists that he witnessed these events himself.

Not long after the burning of the Talmud in Paris, Gregory IX died (22 August 1241). Only in June 1243 did the cardinals elect the new pope, Innocent IV. In a letter of May 1244 to King

Louis IX, Innocent reaffirmed Gregory's charges against the Talmud. He expressed approval for the public burning of the Talmud in Paris, which the clergy had previously 'partially read and examined',[17] and exhorted the king to continue a policy that would confiscate, examine and destroy the Jews' blasphemous texts. In a subsequent letter to King Louis IX dated 12 August 1247, however, Innocent moderated his position. The pope indicated that he had received a Jewish delegation which insisted that the Talmud is essential to Jewish religious life and practice, and that as such it should enjoy the same protections as the Jews, who were a tolerated minority in Christian Europe. Already in 1245, Innocent IV had ordered Odo of Châteauroux, a former chancellor of the University of Paris who had been named cardinal bishop of Tusculum and apostolic legate to France (and who accompanied King Louis IX on crusade to the Holy Land, Egypt and North Africa from 1248 to 1254), to reopen the investigation of the Talmud. The pope rather vaguely instructed Odo that after examining the Jewish books he should return those that could be tolerated to the Jews. It seems that just as in 1231 Gregory IX had been willing to tolerate Aristotle's books on natural philosophy once they had been examined and purged of error, so now Innocent IV suggested that the Jews be allowed to keep the Talmud once errors had been removed from it. This anticipated a new stage in the conflict, in which the Church sought not to destroy the Talmud but to censor it.

Odo challenged the Jews' contention that the Talmud is essential to their religious life and defended the policy of Gregory IX that led to its destruction. Nonetheless, he ordered the Jews to 'deliver up to me the Talmud and all their other books', although he later complained that 'they have only delivered to me five extremely vile volumes' for inspection. In compliance with the pope's directive, Odo reluctantly convened a new commission to examine the Talmud. This commission completed an investigation and on 15 May 1248 issued a report signed by 41 scholars and clerics. Albertus Magnus was among the eleven professors of theology to sign the commission's report. Indeed, this seems to have been the first document to which Albertus was a signatory, identifying himself as 'Albertus Theutonicus' (Albertus the German). Like most of the other members of the commission, Albertus Magnus knew no Hebrew or Aramaic, but his academic prestige as a regent master of theology recommended his appointment. Odo of Châteauroux confirmed the commission's report that because the Jewish books 'contain innumerable errors, insults, and offensive things . . . the aforesaid books cannot be tolerated in the sight of God'. Odo added that they must not be returned to the Jews and declared that they were condemned 'by judicial sentence'.[18] It is not clear whether the Talmud was burned following the decision of the commission, as it had been in Paris in 1241. The Talmud does appear to have been burned in 1250 in southern France, however, perhaps again in 1255 according to a decree of the Council of Béziers, in 1319 at Toulouse, and in 1320 in Paris and Pamiers.[19]

In this 1248 inquisitorial proceeding against the Talmud, very few of the actors could read the Talmud's tractates in the original Hebrew and Aramaic. They relied, then, on translations of Talmudic texts. Donin provides translations of select passages in his 35 articles against the Talmud, whose Latin prologue describes Donin as 'very learned in Hebrew even according to the testimony of the Jews'. Donin likely translated Talmudic passages into the French vernacular and then relied on a collaborator, perhaps the Dominican Henry of Cologne, to translate the vernacular into Latin. A second translator of Talmudic materials was Theobald of Sézanne. Theobald composed a polemical assault on the Talmud, the *Errors of the Jews* (*Errores Iudaeorum*), and he, like Donin, was a Jewish convert to Christianity. Theobald had become a Dominican, moreover, and was subprior of the Dominican priory of St James in Paris when he participated in the commission's condemnation of the Talmud on 15 May 1248. In order to satisfy Innocent IV's demand to reopen the investigation of the Talmud, Odo of Châteauroux sought to provide more evidence for its condemnation, and therefore around 1245 commissioned a Latin translation of Talmudic materials that far exceeded in size the 35 articles presented earlier by Donin. This Latin Talmud, known as the *Extractiones de Talmud*, contains 1,922 passages from the Babylonian Talmud and may have been produced by a team of translators at the Dominican priory in Paris for examination by the commission in 1248.[20]

Albertus Magnus played a role alongside other professors and clerics, then, in the Talmud condemnation of 1248, and his work for the commission gave him access to the *Extractiones*. Alexander Fidora has suggested that Albertus later carried a copy of the *Extractiones*, or at least portions of it, with him from Paris to Cologne.[21] Although the criticism of the Talmud in Paris focused especially on the Talmudic passages thought to disparage Jesus, the Virgin Mary and the Church, Albertus invokes the Talmud – either directly or indirectly – in his own works to challenge its biblical interpretations or theological claims. In his commentary to the fourth book of Peter Lombard's *Sentences*, which Albertus completed in 1249 (that is, the year after the 1248 commission condemned the Talmud), Albertus identifies as a Talmudic 'heresy' the claim that the Book of Job denies the doctrine of resurrection. Albertus attributes this heresy to a 'Rabbi Nasse' who, he claims, composed the Talmud.[22] He may have had in mind Rabbi Judah ha-Nasi, who is credited with the codification around 200 CE of the Oral Law, or Mishnah, one component of the Talmud. Albertus adds that 'Rabbi Nasse' is also the author of a second heresy because he viewed Job not as a real person but rather as a fictional device to veil

the real author of the biblical book, namely Moses, thereby
implying that Moses too denied resurrection. For Albertus, such
a claim represents a serious heretical deviation from biblical
orthodoxy.

In his commentary on the *Ecclesiastical Hierarchy* of Pseudo-
Dionysius the Areopagite, Albertus again criticizes the Talmud
for its teaching on resurrection. Albertus had lectured on the
neo-Platonic pseudo-Dionysian theological writings while still
regent master in Paris and began his written commentary to the
Ecclesiastical Hierarchy in 1248. There, Albertus does not suppose
that Jews reject our resurrection *per se* but instead complains
that they understand resurrection only in a 'carnal' sense and
that this is, in fact, the Talmudic 'heresy'. As evidence of their
'carnal' interpretation, Albertus remarks that the authorities of
the Talmud say that following the resurrection the righteous will
dine on geese and Leviathan in a messianic banquet.[23] Albertus
dismisses the notion that the resurrected body needs to consume
food, however, as an error shared by Jews and Muslims. Instead,
he proclaims that resurrected bodies will be like angels and will
enjoy only spiritual nourishment. In his early treatise *On Resurrection*, which he began before arriving in Paris, Albertus acknowledges that although resurrected bodies possess the *power* to
consume food, they will not do so out of need, and any food they
do consume will be converted into the 'subtle, airy matter' of the
glorified body.[24]

In his *Commentary on Matthew*, completed between 1257
and 1264, Albertus also attributes to Talmudic sages, including
a Rab Vasse, the claim that God gave to the Jews a 'double law':
the first written on stone tablets and the second in the hearts
of the wise. The claim that Jews recognize another law found
outside the Bible that God delivered to them orally – later to
form the Talmud – was a frequent charge directed against the
Jews during the Paris Talmud controversy. Among the 35 articles

composed for Pope Gregory IX, Donin charges that Jews confer more authority upon the law of the Talmud than upon the Bible, while Theobald of Sézanne's *Errors of the Jews* (c. 1244/5) charges that contemporary Jews prefer the Talmud even to the books of Moses. About two decades later, an anonymous German Dominican inquisitor who compiled a text known as the *Passau anonymous* adds that among the Jews' many errors are the assertions that God's covenant with Israel is based not on the law of Moses but upon the law of the Talmud,[25] that it is more necessary to follow the law of the Talmud than the law of Moses, and that it is more important to study the Talmud than the Bible. Because they chose the Talmud over the Bible, this inquisitor adds, God rejected the Jews and chose the Gentile Christians as his elect. The *Passau anonymous* also addresses the Jews' deficient understanding of our resurrection and identifies various Talmudic 'heresies' as signs of the imminent advent of Antichrist.[26] An early 1270s redaction of the *Passau anonymous* incorporated, too, Albertus Magnus' academic judgement against numerous heretical propositions found in his *Compilation on the [Brothers of the] New Spirit*.

Finally, in his commentary on Aristotle's *On Animals*, Albertus introduces the Latin plural noun *Talmudisti* to identify Jews who err in their understanding of the habits of certain marine animals. Curiously, *Talmudisti* is a term that, Alexander Fidora has indicated, is unattested in other thirteenth-century and fourteenth-century texts.[27] Fidora hypothesizes that Albertus introduced this term and applied it not to the rabbinic authorities cited in the Talmud but rather to contemporary Talmud commentators or Tosafists he may have encountered in Regensburg both before and after he became bishop there. Although his references to the Talmud remain limited, Albertus returns to it with far greater frequency than his more famous student, Thomas Aquinas.

Albertus' criticism of the Talmud extends even to natural philosophy. In a discussion of the feeding habits of lobsters and the octopus, Albertus remarks, 'The Talmudic scholars of the Jews have spoken incorrectly when they said that the *galahe* is carnivorous within its own species.'[28] As we have indicated in a note to our English translation, the text had become jumbled in the process of translation. In the original Greek, Aristotle refutes the contention that the octopus eats its own body. For Albertus' text, however, 'eats itself' has become *intra se*, which Albertus glosses as 'in its own species'. Later in this same passage, Albertus merely adds that 'almost all fish feed on the young of the *galahe*' during their breeding seasons. The identity of the *galahe* is uncertain. Clearly, Aristotle had never mentioned *Talmudisti* in the text upon which Albertus commented, since the Talmud began to emerge as a written collection more than 1,000 years after Aristotle's death. Michael Scot's Latin translation, which Albertus employed, mentions the erroneous view of certain Jews, but Albertus' mention of *Talmudisti* is his own unique contribution.

Albertus appears to identify another Talmudic 'error' in *On Animals* when he discusses the nature of the *thamur* or *samyr*, a type of vermin; he says, that '[King] Solomon used to split marble at will.' In this passage, Albertus seems to allude to a Talmudic legend that the *shamir*, a small worm, has a marvellous power that can split stones to any desired shape and that Solomon used this worm to fashion the stones used in the construction of the Solomonic Temple in Jerusalem. Thomas of Cantimpré identifies this worm in his *Book on the Nature of Things* (ThDNR, 9.44) as 'Solomon's worm' (*vermis Solomonis*). But it is Albertus alone who adds that 'this is a fable and I think it is one of the errors of the Jews', whereas his contemporary and fellow Dominican Vincent of Beauvais transmits the story of the wondrous power of 'Solomon's worm' without reservation.[29]

Albertus often uses the term 'fable' (*fabula*) or 'myth' to denote rabbinic or Talmudic extrascriptural legends and often expresses disdain for them. In his early work *On the Human* (*De homine*), completed about 1242, Albertus rejects as a 'fable' the Jews' claim that Lilith was created before Eve and that because she was unwilling to submit to Adam she had intercourse instead with a demon to give birth to demons known as progeny of Asmodaeus, a demon mentioned at Tobit 3:8 who killed the husbands of Sara.[30] Although the *Extractiones* identifies Lilith as a 'demoness with whom Adam lay',[31] Albertus supplies information not found there. He could have learned the legend of Lilith from earlier Christian sources or perhaps from encounters with contemporary Jews in Paris, since the Hebrew account of the public disputation in Paris in 1240 identifies Lilith as the 'mother' of demons and goblins.[32] Thomas Aquinas may have derived his information concerning Lilith from his teacher Albertus, since Thomas repeats the claim that it is a 'fable' found in the Talmud that Adam once had another wife from whom the demons were born.[33] Elsewhere, Thomas warns Christians to reject the 'fables' proffered by those who misunderstand the law. Thomas understands Paul's injunction at 1 Timothy 4:7 – 'have nothing to do with worldly fables fit only for old women' – to refer to fables that were transmitted orally in the Talmud, which include the tale of Lilith. Albertus also rejects as a Jewish fable or myth the claim that Adam was originally a hermaphrodite and possessed both sexes. Those who adopt this view, says Albertus, wrongly follow 'the heresy of the Jews', since were Adam originally a hermaphrodite, he would have been unable to fulfil the first commandment to 'be fruitful and multiply'.[34]

For Albertus, the growing attraction of such *fabulae* is a sign of the end times. In a work titled *On a Woman of Valor* (*De muliere forti*) that is likely an authentic Albertian treatise, the author cites 2 Timothy 4:2–5 as an admonition to his fellow Dominicans:

Folio from the beginning of book 26, 'On the Nature of Vermin', in Albertus Magnus, *De animalibus* (14th century).

Preach the word: be instant in season, out of season:
reprove, entreat, rebuke in all patience and doctrine.
For there shall be a time, when they will not endure
sound doctrine . . . And they will indeed turn away
from hearing the truth but will be turned to fables.[35]

He identifies his own age as the time when many will 'be turned
to fables' – not only Jews who turn to the Talmud, but Christians
who heed false preachers.

The influence of Jewish sources upon Albertus was not confined to passages excerpted from the Talmud in the *Extractiones*.
According to Görge K. Hasselhoff, between 1244 and 1246,
Albertus also was the first scholastic author to cite a Latin trans-
lation of Maimonides's *Guide of the Perplexed*, bearing the title
Dux neutrorum, which was translated in Paris and possibly at the
priory of St James.[36] Albertus knew a Latin translation of this
work for the first book of his commentary on Peter Lombard's
Sentences, which he wrote in Paris in 1243. Maimonides, or
Rabbi Moses ben Maimon (d. 1204), who was born in Cordoba
but died in Fustat near Cairo, is not the only Jewish author
Albertus cites. In addition to Maimonides, whom Albertus identifies as Rabbi Moses the Egyptian (*Moses Aegyptius*), Albertus
was acquainted with the work of Isaac ben Solomon Israeli
(a Jewish physician-philosopher, d. c. 955); with Avicebron
(Solomon ibn Gabirol, d. c. 1057), the author of the influential
Fons vitae; with a David Judaeus, whom Albertus thought was the
redactor of the *Book of Causes* (*Liber de causis*); with Avendauth
(Abraham Ibn Daud) for his transmission of Arabic logic; and
with the Persian Jewish astronomer Māshā'allāh (d. 815), some
of whose works had been translated into Latin in the twelfth
century by John of Seville and Gerard of Cremona.[37]

Albertus and Thomas Aquinas

When Albertus was regent master in Paris, students flocked to his lectures. Among them were Ulrich of Strasbourg, Blessed Ambrose Sansedoni of Siena, and the twenty-year-old Thomas Aquinas (1225–1274), who arrived in Paris towards the end of 1245 or early 1246. Thomas's medieval biographer, William of Tocco, reports that Thomas rejoiced exceedingly at having so quickly found in Albertus that which he had come to Paris to seek. After attaching himself to Albertus as his teacher, Thomas 'began to be more than ever silent, more than ever assiduous in study and devout in prayer'.[38] Thomas impressed Albertus with his quick mind and his dedication to study, and Albertus famously stated that although the taciturn Thomas may be called the 'dumb ox', one day his bellow would resound throughout the whole world. It is certain that Thomas heard Albertus' lectures in Paris on the works of Pseudo-Dionysius, which Thomas then copied down in a manuscript written in his own hand (Naples, Bibl. Naz. I B 54).

Although Albertus' reputation was at its height in the early fourteenth century, Thomas's reputation soon eclipsed his master's. Just as Thomas's early canonization in 1323 enhanced his fame, the 608 years that passed before Albertus' canonization in 1931 had the opposite effect. Albertus' canonization was delayed largely because his name was associated with suspect or spurious works treating necromancy, sorcery and magic, attributed to him in the later Middle Ages. We will return to this subject in our final chapter.

Albertus Magnus instructing St Thomas Aquinas. The banner reads: 'Vos bovem mutum istum esse dicitis, sed talem adhuc dabit in doctrina mugitum, ut totus mirabitur mundus' (You say that he [Thomas Aquinas] is a dumb ox, but one day he will produce such a bellow in learning that the entire world will be amazed).

THREE

From Paris to Cologne

In 1248 the Dominican Order returned Albertus to Cologne to open an international school, or *studium generale*, for members of the Order. Thomas Aquinas accompanied Albertus on this journey, on foot, from Paris to Cologne. Thomas, Ulrich of Strasbourg, Thomas of Cantimpré and Giles of Lessines are Albertus' better-known pupils from this second sojourn in Cologne. In Cologne, Albertus began his very influential commentaries upon Pseudo-Dionysius the Areopagite's treatises *On the Celestial Hierarchy, On the Ecclesiastical Hierarchy, On the Divine Names* and *On Mystical Theology*.

Among Albertus and his contemporaries, it was generally accepted that these texts had been written by Dionysius the Areopagite, a New Testament figure baptized in Acts 17:34 when Paul was preaching the resurrection on the Areopagus, a hill in Athens jutting out off from the Acropolis. The first historical reference to these Greek mystical texts dates, however, from the early sixth century. These works quote verbatim the Neo-Platonist philosopher Proclus (d. 485 CE) and thus could not have been written much before 500. Some modern scholars have tried to identify the author as the Patriarch Severus of Antioch (d. 538).

The medieval assumption that the author was a companion to the apostle Paul endowed these works with great authority when they entered Latin Christendom after Byzantine emperor

Michael II presented the Greek texts to the Holy Roman Emperor Louis the Pious (d. 840). Louis's son, King Charles the Bald, commissioned John Scotus Eriugena in the early 860s to prepare a Latin translation. The cloud of confusion that surrounded their author's identity only increased, however, when the abbot of Saint-Denis near Paris, Hilduin (d. c. 860), who was also the archchaplain to Louis the Pious, mistakenly identified the author with another Dionysius, namely St Denis/ Dionysius, the third-century martyr-bishop and patron saint of France, who was thought to be buried at the abbey. For centuries, French national pride complicated every effort to identify Pseudo-Dionysius. During the twelfth century, the irascible scholar Peter Abelard (d. 1142), who had praised Dionysius the Areopagite as a 'great philosopher',[1] was nearly murdered by his fellow monks at the abbey of Saint-Denis when he argued that the patron saint of France, St Denis/Dionysius, and Dionysius the Areopagite were not one and the same.

During the thirteenth century, the influence of these Pseudo-Dionysian works increased. St Bonaventure called their author the prince of mystics. Robert Grosseteste (d. 1253), bishop of Lincoln, produced a new Latin translation and commentary, most likely during the 1240s. After leaving Paris, Albertus Magnus continued his lectures on the Pseudo-Dionysian literary corpus in Cologne and wrote his own commentaries to these works, utilizing the Latin translations of John Scotus Eriugena and of the twelfth-century translator and commentator John the Saracen, who taught at Poitiers. According to the *Cologne Legends*, Albertus began his exposition of *On the Ecclesiastical Hierarchy* after he had completed his commentary to Pseudo-Dionysius's *On the Celestial Hierarchy* but began to despair that he could never complete the task. However, one day after matins, as if in a dream, the apostle Paul spoke to him and gave him the confidence he needed to explicate these books.[2]

Albertus' Aristotle Project

Albertus' creation of commentaries on the Pseudo-Dionysian texts is a significant accomplishment from his second Cologne period. But the work that Albertus began during this same time and for which he is best known is his 'Aristotle project'. With this project, which occupied Albertus' attention for roughly twenty years (from about 1250 to 1270), Albertus paraphrased and commented on the entirety of Aristotle's philosophical and scientific work available to him in Latin.

This project began when Albertus returned to Cologne from Paris during the summer of 1248 to establish a *studium generale* in Cologne at the priory of the Holy Cross (*Heilige Kreuz*). Modelled after the one at the Dominican house of St James in Paris, the new Cologne *studium generale* was one of four to expand educational opportunities for talented friars in the Dominican provinces of Provence, Lombardy, Germany and England. A *studium generale* was intended for the most advanced students who had already completed basic instruction in the arts (reading, grammar, logic and so on). These centres trained the very best students to become the Order's lectors or teachers and, in even fewer instances, groomed them to become theology masters.

Even while still regent master in theology in Paris, Albertus had been an outspoken defender of the need for the Dominican friars to study not only theology but philosophy and, in particular, natural philosophy. Perhaps as a result of his influence, by 1262, the Dominican province of Provence added *studia naturarum*, or schools for the study of natural philosophy, that rotated among the priories in the province. Natural philosophy includes disciplines that today we designate as natural sciences: biology, zoology, physics, chemistry, geology, botany and many more. Albertus' defence of the study of philosophy responded directly to criticism from secular masters such as William of Saint-Amour, who had accused the mendicants of being false apostles who had perverted Christian theology with arguments drawn from logic and philosophy. In his *On the Dangers of the Last Times*, discussed above, William takes aim especially at the Dominican 'Watchdogs of the Lord' by comparing them to dogs and false apostles who 'bark and bite irrationally against the truth'.[3]

By instructing Albertus to establish the new *studium generale* in Cologne and naming him as its first head, Humbert of Romans expressed implicit approval for Albertus' vision for the friars' educational preparation and curriculum. At the Cologne *studium*, Albertus departed radically from a standard theology curriculum to introduce a course on Aristotle's *Nicomachean Ethics*, which had only recently been made available in a complete Latin translation from the Greek by Bishop Robert Grosseteste of Lincoln around 1246–7. Before Grosseteste's translation, only books one through three had been available to Latin readers. Although Aristotle's *Ethics* is a safer topic for Christian theology, since it addresses issues pertaining to the moral life, the decision to lecture in Cologne on the entirety of Aristotle's *Ethics* was a bold statement in defence of philosophy and of Aristotle, who would come to be known as 'the Philosopher' or the 'Master of Those Who Know'. This was not the first time Albertus had relied on Aristotle's writings: in his first work from circa 1233–4, *On the Nature of the Good* (*De natura boni*), which treats the virtues and ethical questions, Albertus had already cited ten of Aristotle's works, including six of his books on nature (the *libri naturales*), which had been proscribed in Paris in 1210. A 1215 papal regulation had reaffirmed these condemnations in Paris and prohibited the study of Aristotle's works on metaphysics and natural philosophy, although students were expected to study the *Nicomachean Ethics*. But Albertus took a risk when he lectured in Cologne not merely on books one through three but on all ten books of the *Nicomachean Ethics*. Thomas Aquinas copied down Albertus' lectures before leaving Cologne for Paris in the autumn of 1252 to become bachelor in the *Sentences* to the Dominican master Elias Brunet de Bergerac, who had succeeded Albertus in the chair in theology.

Albertus was not content to introduce only Aristotle's *Nicomachean Ethics* to the students at the Cologne *studium*. In 1231 Pope Gregory IX had reaffirmed that the Aristotelian works on natural science were forbidden to Parisian scholars – although technically only for scholars in the arts faculty – until purged of error. But how could they be purged of error if scholars did not investigate them? Albertus clearly established this as a principal goal: to investigate and rehabilitate Aristotle for a Christian audience. As a result, at the very same time that he lectured on Aristotle's *Nicomachean Ethics*, he began a lengthy commentary on Aristotle's *Physics*, remarking that he had been pressed over several years by some of his Dominican brothers to compose for them a commentary 'in which they would have the whole of natural science and from which they could competently understand the books of Aristotle'.[4] Albertus did not stop with the *Physics*, but instead continued his labour until he had treated *all* of Aristotle's philosophical writings, including some that were erroneously attributed to Aristotle, like the *Book on Causes* and *On the Causes of the Properties of the Elements*. In this project, Albertus does much more than comment, however. He explores problems Aristotle's texts raised for Christian theology, engages in frequent lengthy digressions in order to pursue his own solutions and supplements the Aristotelian corpus available to him by creating entire books (like Albertus' own *On the Nature of Place, De natura loci*) that he imagined Aristotle must have written but that were absent from his Latin sources. Albertus' intuition was proved right in at least one instance: in Italy around 1256–7, Albertus stumbled upon an anonymous Latin translation of Aristotle's previously unknown *On the Movement of Animals* (*De motu animalium*), not long after Albertus had written his own treatise with the name *On the Movements of Animals* (*De motibus animalium*) to fill a lacuna in Aristotle's natural philosophy. Albertus would later write a separate paraphrase circa 1263 with the title *On the Principles of Progressive Motion* (*De principiis motus processivi*) after he encountered in Italy William of Moerbeke's new translations of *On the Movement of Animals* (*De motu animalium*) and *On the Progression of Animals* (*De progressu animalium*). Based on Albertus' work, modern scholarship has attempted to reconstruct the anonymous medieval Latin translation of *On the Movement of Animals* (*De motu animalium*).[5]

Albertus continued his 'Aristotle project' well into the 1260s. Between 1251 and 1254 he completed not only his own

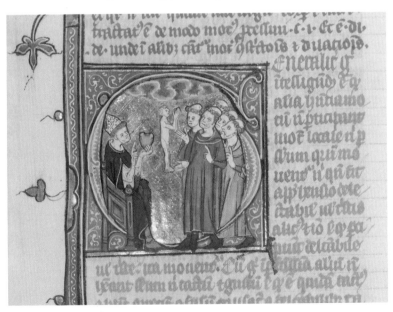

Miniature from the beginning of *On the Principles of Progressive Motion* (*De principiis motus processivi*), in Albertus Magnus, *De animalibus* (14th century).

On the Nature of Place (*De natura loci*) and commentary on Pseudo-Aristotle's *On the Causes of the Properties of the Elements* (*Liber de causis proprietatum elementorum*), but commentaries on Aristotle's *On Generation and Corruption* (*De generatione et corruptione*) and *On Heaven and the World* (*De caelo et mundo*). After he was elected prior provincial for the Dominican province of Germany in 1254, which released him from the burden of lecturing in Cologne, the 'Aristotle project' accelerated. Between 1254 and 1257 he commented on Aristotle's *Meteorology* (*Meteora*), *On Categories* (*De praedicamentis*), *On the Soul* (*De anima*), the *Prior* and *Posterior Analytics*, the *Parva naturalia* (a collection of shorter, empirically orientated works treating phenomena common to both body and soul), and produced his own *On Minerals* (*De mineralibus*).

In 1257 Albertus resigned as prior provincial and returned to Cologne to teach. But he continued his work on Aristotle's natural philosophy and once more introduced an important Aristotelian natural-philosophical text to the theological curriculum when he lectured in 1258 on Aristotle's *On Animals* (*De animalibus*). These lectures were collected around 1259–60 by Conrad of Austria under the title *Questions concerning [Aristotle's] 'On Animals'* (*Questiones super De animalibus*), for which we provided the first complete English translation in 2008.[6] Marking implicit approval of Albertus' educational innovation, the Dominican master general Humbert of Romans called on Albertus to work with other Dominican masters in theology to craft educational recommendations at the general chapter in 1259. To Humbert of Romans' dismay, this task was interrupted when Pope Alexander IV wrote to Albertus on 5 January 1260 and named him bishop of Regensburg. Albertus was consecrated during Holy Week in March 1260.

Albertus' new role as bishop consumed him. He worked feverishly over the next eighteen months to correct the problems of the diocese and likely had little time for scholarship. He returned to his 'Aristotle project' in earnest only after he travelled to the papal court in 1262 to beg the new pope, Urban IV, to relieve him of the episcopal responsibility. Urban IV asked Albertus to stay with the court in 1262, and it was during this period that Albertus returned to his consideration of the *Ethics*, wrote a treatise on Euclidian geometry (*Super Euclidem*) and likely continued his work on Aristotle's *On Animals* (*De animalibus*), using Michael Scot's translation from the Arabic and possibly William of Moerbeke's translation from the Greek, completed around 1260. Albertus' *On Animals* comprises nineteen books that gather together Aristotle's *History of Animals* (*Historia animalium*), *On the Parts of Animals* (*De partibus animalium*) and *On the Generation of Animals* (*De generatione animalium*). Albertus added his own discussion and a bestiary to expand the final product to 26 books, which we have also translated.[7] By early 1263 the pope had appointed Albertus to preach the crusade in German lands, and during this period, Albertus worked on a commentary to Aristotle's *Metaphysics*. In 1264 he took up residence at the Dominican priory in Würzburg and produced his works on Aristotle's *Topics* and *Sophistical Refutations* (*De sophisticis elenchis*). A few years later, he completed his examination of Aristotle's *Politics*.

From the middle 1260s Albertus returned his attention to biblical commentary, but only after he had completed his monumental paraphrases with commentary upon all of the works of Aristotle. The scope of this project is staggering. In most cases, Albertus' Latin texts of Aristotle were translated from Arabic exemplars and only very infrequently based on Greek originals. In order to master the Aristotelian texts, moreover, Albertus was compelled to become thoroughly familiar with the earlier Greek and Arabic commentators on Aristotle. Even though he did not know Greek or Arabic, Albertus was aware of deficiencies

Detail of Albertus Magnus in discussion with Averroes, miniature
in an edition of the Bible (Genesis to Ruth), S. Netherlands, c. 1430.
This introductory folio reproduces Genesis 1:1–12, and the panel
between Albertus and Averroes begins with the words 'Deus creator
omnium entium' (God creator of all beings).

in his received translations and consulted multiple translations
whenever possible in search of the best readings.[8] In this way
he sought to overcome the criticism of his contemporary Roger
Bacon that the Aristotle translations produced by contemporaries Michael Scot and Alfred of Shareshill (*Aluredus/Alfredus
Anglicus*) are so crude and difficult that 'no one can understand
them, but each one contradicts the other.'[9]

Albertus' Service to the Church in Cologne

After his regency in Paris, Albertus appeared more frequently in
public settings, making it possible to document his movements.
In 1252 he and the Dominican biblical theologian Hugh of St

Cher resolved a dispute between Cologne's archbishop Conrad of Hochstaden and the burghers of that city, and in that same year, Conrad issued or reissued privileges to Cologne's Jewish community. During the next two decades and more, Albertus frequently served as an arbitrator in legal disputes between Cologne's archbishop and its burghers.

In 1254, at the provincial chapter in Worms, Albertus was elected prior provincial of the German Dominicans, accepting responsibility for a religious order that was scattered over Switzerland, Austria, Belgium, the Netherlands, Germany, parts of France and even north to Riga in Latvia. The priors provincial were subordinate to the master general of the Order. As prior provincial, Albertus was expected to visit on foot – except in exceptional circumstances – all the houses within his province, which included more than three dozen priories for men and dozens more convents for women. The number of these houses continued to grow under Albertus, who in 1254 received into the German province a convent for Dominican women called Paradise at Soest.

Paradise at Soest had been founded in 1252 by the Hanseatic city of Soest, but Albertus has been considered its second 'founder' for having received it into the Dominican Order. It was Albertus who performed the 'clothing' ceremony, or investiture, for the women, visiting the nunnery probably in 1255 and preaching there. Despite a general perception that medieval women in religious houses received only the rudiments of education, over time Paradise at Soest acquired an extensive library that included not only biblical and theological texts, but medical treatises and herbals. The women there evidently shared Albertus' own interest in nature, and their library possessed a work sometimes ascribed to Albertus, the *Book on the Virtues of Animals, Trees, Plants and Species* (*Liber de virtutibus animalium, arborum, herbarum et specierum*), also known as the *Book on the*

Virtues of Plants, Stones and Animals (*Liber de virtutibus herbarum, lapidum et animalium*) or the *Experiments of Albert* (*Experimenta Alberti*). The text treats the 'virtues', or magical powers, of some stones, plants and animals, and its oldest Latin manuscript dates to about 1290. This very popular text often circulated with other short works attributed to Albertus with a similar focus under the title *The Book of Collections; or, The Book of Secrets of Albert the Great* (*Liber aggregationis seu liber secretorum Alberti Magni*). Isabelle Draelants, who published a critical edition of the Latin text accompanied by a French translation in 2007,[10] has identified 76 medieval Latin manuscripts of the work and 330 print editions before 1800 in Latin, German, French, English, Italian and Dutch. Frank Best and Michael Brightman published an edition and English translation in 1973 with the title *The Book of Secrets of Albertus Magnus of the Virtues of Herbs, Stones and Certain Beasts*. Although the work is probably not by Albertus himself, Draelants indicates that it likely emerged from a Dominican environment with close ties to Albertus. Its presence in the library at Paradise at Soest would support this view. Albertus continued throughout his life to support this convent and others, and at his death, Albertus left bequests of considerable size to support several Dominican convents, including St Catherine in Augsburg, where Albertus' own sister lived as a nun and where he also preached sermons in the vernacular.

From the number of observations of nature scattered throughout his works drawn from a widespread geographical region, it is clear as well that Albertus took his responsibility for visitation seriously. According to the late fifteenth-century *Cologne Legends* (*Legenda Coloniensis*), as Albertus walked to the Dominican houses throughout the German province, he carried no money but begged with his brothers for food, going from door to door, in imitation of apostolic perfection. According to Peter of Prussia's fifteenth-century biography of Albertus, the *Vita B.*

Alberti (c. 1485), in 1257 a German provincial chapter removed three Dominican priors because they had ridden on horseback and had not travelled on foot. The *Cologne Legends* emphasizes, too, Albertus' commitment to apostolic poverty by adding that he once ordered the body of a certain Dominican brother exhumed because at his death he had been in possession of three *solidi*.

In 1255 and 1256 Albertus presided over provincial chapters in Regensburg and Erfurt. He imposed on the Dominican prior of Minden as penance a fast of bread and water for five days, five masses and three other 'corrections' because he came to the chapter on horseback, contrary to the Order's custom. Albertus also attended the general chapter in Milan in 1255 and in Paris in 1256. Despite the pressure of his administrative duties within the Order, Albertus did not abandon his philosophical interests. These interests even benefited from his travels, for when he stopped for the night at Dominican houses, he was accustomed to using their libraries. It was during his office as prior provincial that he wrote his commentary on Aristotle's treatise *On the Soul* (*De anima*), and many of the animal descriptions found in his commentary on Aristotle's *On Animals* probably can be traced back to this period.

The Mendicant Controversy

It was also during his office as prior provincial that Albertus became embroiled in the conflict between secular scholars and mendicants in Paris that was stoked by William of Saint-Amour's *On the Dangers of the Last Times* (*De periculis novissimorum temporum*), which viewed the rapid growth of the mendicant orders with alarm. In under sixty years, mendicant friars had established over 1,000 houses in Europe, with four hundred in France alone. Friars also assumed leading positions in the church as inquisitors, bishops, archbishops, cardinals and even popes. Albertus Magnus would himself be consecrated as bishop of Regensburg in 1260. While their service to the church attested to the quality of the individual friars, it also marked a departure from the Order's explicit guidelines. At the same time, the growth of the mendicant orders led to the establishment of a growing number of urban schools for them. At Paris, as we have seen, mendicant theologians began to occupy chairs in the university faculty of theology.

In a reprise of the events of 1229, in April 1254 the Parisian watch arrested and beat four secular students and their servants, killing one and taking the rest to jail, where their bones were broken during a harsh interrogation. The university called for another strike, as it had done in 1229. In 1252 the secular masters sought to limit the Dominicans to only one rather than two chairs in theology, but the Dominicans agreed to participate in the strike only if they retained both chairs, which caused an outcry and prompted legal efforts to expel the friars from the corporate university body. At that same time, the Franciscan Gerard of Borgo San Donnino published his *Introduction to the Eternal Gospel* (*Introductorius in evangelium eternum*), which incorporates the proclamation of Abbot Joachim of Fiore (d. 1202), founder of the Order of San Giovanni in Fiore, concerning the advent of a third age. For Gerard, the Franciscan Order would introduce a new spiritual understanding of Scripture, and Gerard designated 1260 as the year for the opening of the sixth seal of the Apocalypse, signalling a period when the mendicant orders would come to replace the 'corrupt' secular clergy. The secular masters identified 31 heretical doctrines in this text and sent the list to Pope Innocent iv, leading Innocent to establish a commission to study it. His successor, Alexander iv, condemned the book and ordered it to be burnt. Gerard was ultimately confined to prison for life by the Franciscan minister general.

Pope Innocent IV sought to pacify the secular masters and issued a series of orders in 1254 that obliged the mendicant masters to submit to the demands of the university body and to respect the strike. In a serious blow to the mendicants, Innocent IV's bull *Etsi animarum* (November 1254) limited the rights of the mendicants to preach and perform sacraments without the approval of the secular clergy. But the pope died only weeks later on 7 December 1254, throwing all into confusion once more. William of Saint-Amour preached sermons that attacked the mendicants, while secular students fought with mendicants in the streets of Paris, requiring the royal guard to keep the peace.

William condemned Gerard of Borgo San Donnino's Joachimite ideas as a heresy circulating in the mendicant orders. Secular masters openly criticized King Louis IX, who supported the mendicants alongside new Pope Alexander IV. Alexander IV's *Quasi lignum vite* (14 April 1255) reinforced the friars' privileges both inside and outside the university. In response, the secular scholars called for the annulment of *Quasi lignum vitae* and refused to admit mendicants to the university at the start of the 1255–6 academic year. Feelings against the mendicants became so inflamed that during late summer 1255, King Louis IX had to send royal archers to protect the Dominican priory of St James in Paris. Although the Dominicans denounced William of Saint-Amour, he successfully defended himself before the bishop of Mâcon and before a Parisian gathering of some 4,000 clerics. In March or April 1256 William responded with his *On the Dangers of the Last Times*. On 27 June Louis IX had Pope Alexander IV order William's incarceration and the expulsion of his chief supporters from the university. Shortly thereafter, an investigation into *On the Dangers of the Last Times* at the papal court led to William's banishment.

Mendicant theologians sought in turn to defend their orders with treatises that attacked William of Saint-Amour. In late 1255 John of Fidanza, who earlier took the religious name

'Bonaventure' in recognition of his good fortune to study under Alexander of Hales in Paris, published his defence in *On Poverty and Renunciation* (*De paupertate quoad abrenuntiationem*). In October 1256, the same year in which he became a theology master in Paris, Thomas Aquinas published his own *Against Those Impugning the Worship and Religion of God* (*Contra impugnantes Dei cultum et religionem*), which is also a defence of the mendicant conception of poverty. Although the faculty strike was brought to an end with William's banishment, resentment between secular and mendicant scholars in Paris simmered for decades.

William's *On the Dangers of the Last Times* was intended for an audience of university-educated secular clergy and argued not only that the mendicant orders were guilty of heresy but that the Dominicans in particular were 'false preachers' whose appearance was a sign of the coming Apocalypse. He challenged the papal recognition of the mendicant orders that granted to them the right to preach everywhere, which undermined the authority of bishops, by appealing to scripture and established ecclesiastical and civil law. He even appealed to Pseudo-Dionysius' *On the Ecclesiastical Hierarchy* and *On the Celestial Hierarchy* – the very texts for which Albertus composed commentaries in Cologne – to argue that God had established only two orders in the Church: one composed of bishops, priests and deacons, and a second composed of monks, laymen and catechumens. He argued that there can be no third order for mendicant preachers and that only the bishops possess the right of preaching. All others are 'false preachers'.

William of Saint-Amour attacked another of the friars' privileges: the right to hear confession and administer penance. The Fourth Lateran Council of 1215 had required laypeople to confess before their parish priest once each year around Easter. One unforeseen consequence of the legislation was a dramatically expanded workload for local priests during a single week in the liturgical calendar, which made compliance nearly impossible in larger communities. The Fourth Lateran's Canon 10 attempted to address this problem by commanding that in cathedrals and other churches, appropriate men should be ordained to serve the bishop as assistants and coadjutors for hearing confession and imposing penance. Nevertheless, Bishop Robert Grosseteste's complaint that in England some priests wrongly delegated the task of hearing confession to their deacons suggests that local priests continued to feel burdened by the legislation. The increased workload was one factor that contributed to the use of mendicant friars as confessors, despite the opposition of some secular clergy. In letters from 1236–7 Grosseteste himself asked Jordan of Saxony, master general of the Dominican Order, and Elias, minister general of the Franciscan Order, for assistance from their friars to 'help in preaching God's word, hearing confessions, and imposing penances' because, he remarked, 'there are no assistants I know of for these and other responsibilities so effective as your friars.'[11] Although the friars who heard confession satisfied a real need, they did so by impinging on the traditional role of the secular clergy.

In contrast to the vow of individual and corporate poverty adopted by mendicant orders, William defended the vow of voluntary poverty found in stable Benedictine monastic communities and specifically identified Dominicans as harbingers of Antichrist. While many of his contemporaries shared his apocalyptic fears, they – like Caesarius of Heisterbach, cited earlier – typically had asserted that the 'seducers' and minions of Antichrist that threatened their world would arise among the Jews or barbarous peoples (for example, the Mongols that threatened Christendom from the East). But William insisted that the 'seducers' would not arise among Jews or Mongols, but from among Christians themselves.

In September 1256 Pope Alexander IV established a commission to examine *On the Dangers of the Last Times*. According to Thomas of Cantimpré, Albertus appeared then at the papal court in Anagni in response to a papal summons and was almost certainly consulted before *On the Dangers of the Last Times* was formally condemned on 5 October 1256. At the same time, Albertus presented a public refutation at the papal court of the Averroist doctrine of the non-individual character of the agent intellect, a refutation that he later codified in his *On the Unity of the Intellect* (*De unitate intellectus*, c. 1263).

Albertus was relieved of his responsibilities as prior provincial by the general chapter in 1257, and by August 1257 he appeared at Augsburg, Germany, where he preached a number of sermons. By spring 1258 Albertus had returned to Cologne, where he resumed his position as lector and regent of the *studium generale*. In 1259, during this third sojourn in Cologne, Albertus was appointed to a special commission by the fifth master general of the Order, Humbert of Romans (r. 1254–63), to define the course of study for the Dominican Order. This project, undertaken by Albertus and others (including Thomas Aquinas), determined not only the proper deportment of students and teachers but the weight to be accorded to philosophy and theology within the study curriculum. During 1258–9 Albertus also served as an arbiter in legal disputes between Cologne's archbishop Conrad of Hochstaden and the city burghers, or between Cologne and the city of Utrecht, and Albertus' name appears as a witness on several legal settlements.

At this stage of his life Albertus had already made an impact on Aristotelian studies, on the shape of medieval education and on various civil matters. He likely looked forward to remaining in one place and devoting himself to his students and his intellectual pursuits. Yet, once more, Albertus would subordinate his own desire in service to the Church.

FOUR

From Cologne to Regensburg and Back Again

Not long after his return to Cologne in 1258, Albertus' teaching career was again interrupted when on 5 January 1260, Pope Alexander IV appointed Albertus to the vacant bishopric of Regensburg (*Ratisbon*). The See had become vacant following the resignation on 11 May 1259 of Bishop Albert I, count of Pietengau, who had been the subject of a papal investigation in 1258 following accusations by the cathedral chapter of numerous crimes, or 'enormities'. A Rome consistory later added the charge of sodomy, although Albert I insisted that he was being persecuted by the papacy because he had previously supported Emperor Frederick II. Following his resignation, all charges against him were dropped.

Albertus Magnus' appointment was unwelcome news to Humbert of Romans, master general of the Dominican Order, who feared Albertus' loss to the Order, the threat to Albertus' own spiritual condition, and the interruption it would cause to Albertus' scholarly work. Humbert encouraged Albertus by letter to reject this episcopal appointment, which, by its very nature, would compel him to violate the rule and customs of the Order of Preachers. In the episcopacy, he would be bound again by those secular concerns he had voluntarily abandoned when he first entered the Order. Though as bishop he might reach a few lost souls, Humbert reasoned, by his teaching and example in Cologne, he could reach souls across Germany.

William of Saint-Amour too, we will recall, viewed the elevation of mendicants to episcopal office as a violation of their religious commitment. Such concerns did not, however, prevent a number of Dominicans from accepting high ecclesiastical office, including Hugh of St Cher (d. 1263), who had been made a cardinal priest in 1244; Pierre de Tarentaise, who reigned briefly as Pope Innocent V (d. 1276); and Jacobus de Voragine (d. 1298/9), who became archbishop of Genoa. According to the *Cologne Legends*, some thirty Dominicans who had been raised to the episcopacy attended the Second Council of Lyon (1274).

Despite Humbert's admonitions, Albertus submitted to the pope's desire and was consecrated bishop of Regensburg. By the end of March, Albertus had entered the city to celebrate Mass, returning to a city where he had previously served as a Dominican lector. The Regensburg diocese was virtually bankrupt and in scandalous condition, imposing on Albertus burdens Humbert feared would undermine Albertus' spiritual life and hinder his scholarly activities since an effective bishop must visit often the distant parishes of the diocese to ensure that they were properly served. Despite Humbert's concerns, during this period, Albertus completed his *Commentary to the Book of Isaiah*. He also began his *Commentary to the Gospel of Luke*, and an autograph of this work was once thought to have been archived in the Dominican library at Regensburg. Moreover, Albertus left the diocese in better financial condition than he found it, and his rough clothes impressed the local people as a sign of his humility. He also must have travelled widely to parish churches, earning a nickname that Weisheipl translated as 'Boots the Bishop' (*episcopus cum bottis* or *episcopus cum magnis sotularibus*), referring both to his coarse shoes and his travels on foot. The *Cologne Legends* insists that Albertus walked throughout his diocese with only a pack animal to carry his episcopal vestments and ornaments.

During his episcopacy, Albertus would have encountered an urban religious landscape in Regensburg with more churches and religious houses than most other German cities, with nearly two hundred churches, numerous chapels, four canonical houses and fourteen houses for religious men and women. Its famous Benedictine monastery of St Emmeram, incorporated within the city walls by the tenth century, possessed an extensive library that attracted scholars to the city. In the late eleventh century, the Irish monk Marianus had established a Benedictine *Schotten-kloster* there as one of many monasteries in Germany to house monks from Ireland and Scotland.[1] In Regensburg, the abbey of St Jacob of Regensburg became the mother house to *Schotten-klöster* in Erfurt, Vienna, Würzburg, Nuremberg, Constance, Eichstätt and Memmingen, and its abbot became the abbot-general for the congregation.

Regensburg was also one of the first German cities to host all four major mendicant orders recognized at the Second Council of Lyon: Dominicans, Franciscans, Carmelites and Augustinian Hermits. The Franciscans arrived first, taking up residence by 1221 at the church of St Salvator. The Franciscans produced the fiery vernacular preacher Berthold of Regensburg (d. 1272), with whom Albertus developed a personal relationship. By 1230 the bishop of Regensburg had granted the Dominicans the church of St Blasius at the opposite end of the city from the Franciscan house. The church of St Blasius is found today on Albertus-Magnus-Platz. Augustinian hermits took up residence at a small chapel in the city centre, immediately adjacent to the Jewish community's synagogue. There were also houses for religious women, whose number expanded dramatically with the arrival of the mendicants and included the Dominican convent of the Holy Cross (established in 1233) and Franciscan Poor Clares. The military orders were also present in Regensburg: the Teutonic Knights had a commandery in the city by the end of the first quarter of the twelfth century, and forty years later, there appeared a small convent of the Knights Hospitaller.

In Regensburg, Albertus also would have encountered another significant Jewish community, whose origins date to the tenth century. In the tenth and eleventh centuries, Jewish merchants brought luxury goods to the city. From Kiev and the Volga region they imported furs, horses, wax and metals, and they secured trading privileges in Regensburg. Although a Hebrew chronicle of the First Crusade relates that the Jewish community of Regensburg was forcibly baptized in the Danube and converted to Christianity during anti-Jewish violence in 1096, it had been allowed to resume its Jewish life by Emperor Henry IV (d. 1106), who regarded the forced baptisms as invalid and allowed the community to rebuild its synagogue.

Evidence from the first decade of the twelfth century attests to the economic importance of the community. Bishop Herman of Prague pawned five expensive *pallia* (that is, ecclesiastical vestments) with Jewish moneylenders in Regensburg for five hundred pieces of silver to pay a ransom for Duke Svatopluk of Bohemia (d. 1109), who was being held captive by Henry IV. Property records show that Jews and Christians lived as neighbours in the Jewish quarter, which was located within the old Roman walls for protection and had easy access to the Danube for trade. From 1182 a privilege from Emperor Frederick I allowed Regensburg Jews to trade in gold, silver and other metals, as was the established custom. The privilege was renewed by Frederick II (1216), his son Henry (1230) and King Rudolf I (1274). In 1210 the Jewish community purchased property from the Benedictine monastery of St Emmeram, which would become the site for the Jewish cemetery. In addition, the community purchased a property in 1225 near the Jewish school, likely for the construction of a new synagogue. There was a well house near the synagogue to which a *mikveh* (ritual bath) was probably attached. The only

wide street in the quarter was the Judengasse, which led north
to the cathedral and the stone bridge over the Danube. Even
though Albertus' episcopal successor in Regensburg, Bishop Leo
Thundorfer (r. 11 May 1262–12 July 1277), participated in a
provincial synod in Vienna in 1267 that ordered strict measures
to separate Jewish and Christian dwellings in urban centres, the
order itself is recognition that during Albertus' period of residence
in Regensburg there were numerous contacts between Jews and
Christians, including common use of bathhouses and public
houses. Benjamin Laqua even notes an agreement reached
between nearby Rohr Abbey and a Regensburg Jew, Gnelin, on
the construction, use and cleaning of a shared privy![2] Despite
repeated ecclesiastical prohibitions, Christians were employed
as servants in Jewish homes, and personal friendships existed
between Christians and Jews. Albertus' own exposure to the
Talmud may have grown as a result of contacts with Jewish
Talmudisti during his residence in Regensburg.

Excavations in 1995 of a central square in Regensburg, the
Neupfarrplatz, which is located within view of the Regensburg
Cathedral, revealed the level of prosperity of the medieval Jewry
in Regensburg. A treasure horde containing 688 gold coins that
had been buried in a cellar about 1388 was discovered, one of the
largest such finds in Germany. Economic prosperity was accompanied by Jewish learning, especially in the twelfth and thirteenth
centuries. The Tosafist Ephraim ben Isaac (d. 1175) and Rabbi
Judah ben Samuel he-Hasid (Judah the Pious, d. 1217) taught
at its famous Talmudic school. Judah, who likely moved from
Speyer to Regensburg circa 1195, became a leader in the Jewish
pietist movement in Germany known as *Hasidei Ashkenaz* and
is regarded as the principal author of the *Book of the Pious* (*Sefer
Hasidim*) that sheds light on its religious practices. Judah was
also a member of the *bet din*, or rabbinical court, and had extensive contact with other rabbinic leaders in Germany, Bohemia

and France. During Albertus' episcopacy, the prosperous Jewish
community in Regensburg attracted Jewish students to its school
from across Germany. After the Rintfleisch massacres of 1298
murdered thousands of Jews accused of ritual murder and of des-
ecrating the Eucharistic Host, the security of the community
began to erode, and by the fourteenth century, its economic and
intellectual vitality waned. Following the death of Emperor
Maximilian in January 1519, the Jewish community was expelled
and its synagogue was destroyed. After 1519, the stones of Jewish houses and buildings were exploited for the construction of
the present Neupfarrkirche, an evangelical Lutheran church
consecrated in 1542 on the Neupfarrplatz.

During his Regensburg episcopacy, Albertus' name appears
on numerous documents related to diocesan administration. His
episcopacy was brief, however. In the spring of 1261 and only
about a year after his consecration, Albertus set off for Rome to
plead with Pope Alexander IV to allow him to resign his See. On
25 May 1261 Alexander IV died, however, before Albertus had
reached him. Pope Urban IV was elected on 29 August 1261 to
succeed Alexander IV and allowed Albertus to resign his position, but apparently not until spring 1262.

From spring 1261 until spring 1262, Albertus remained in
Italy awaiting the pope's decision to release him from his episcopal burden. His movements for this year remain uncertain.
Henry of Herford's early fourteenth-century chronicle suggests
that once Albertus was released from the episcopacy in
Regensburg, he retained some sort of pension from the diocese.[3]
This information comports, too, with Albertus' own statement
in his last will and testament that an unnamed pope had provided a dispensation from his Dominican vow of poverty so that
he could possess personal property. After his resignation, Albertus
apparently remained at the papal court, which moved in October
1262 to Orvieto. During this period of relative inactivity, Albertus

continued to write. It seems certain that he was still at work on his commentary to Aristotle's *On Animals*. He also seems to have laboured during this period on a work related to Aristotle's *On the Movement of Animals* (*De motu animalium*) titled *On the Principles of Progressive Motion* (*De principiis motus processivi*). He may have completed his *Commentary to the Gospel of Luke*, which he had begun earlier in Regensburg. His treatise *On Euclid's Elements of Geometry* (*Super Euclidem*) and his paraphrastic commentary on the *Ethics* (*Ethica*) also date from this period in Italy.

From February 1263 until the death of Pope Urban IV on 2 October 1264, Albertus was once again tasked with ecclesiastical business. Although at least in his sixties, Urban IV appointed him as a papal legate to preach the crusade in Germany, Bohemia and wherever the German language was spoken. The pope, who before his elevation to the papacy had been patriarch of Jerusalem, commanded all prelates in Germany to provide Albertus with any necessary assistance to raise funds for a crusade to the Holy Land to defend its few remaining Latin possessions from the Mamluks. The call to the crusade was complicated, however, by political crusades within Europe itself that several popes had undertaken against Emperor Frederick II (d. 1250), his family – that is, his sons King Conrad IV (d. 1254) and King Manfred of Sicily (d. 1266) – and Hohenstaufen supporters. Urban IV relied on Dominicans to preach the crusade and conferred upon Albertus the authority to offer an indulgence to those who provided assistance for the crusade. By March 1263 Urban IV appointed the Franciscan Berthold of Regensburg to join Albertus in this commission.

Albertus did more than simply preach the crusade in Germany, however: he also served as vicar general of the archdiocese of Cologne to help resolve tensions between the city and its archbishop. His influence extended across Germany, moreover, and in May 1263 Albertus settled a dispute between Bishop Hartmann von Dillingen (r. 1248–86) and Count Ludwig III of Öttingen. By August 1263 Albertus witnessed a settlement between Archbishop Engelbert II (von Falkenburg, r. 1261–74) and the city of Cologne.

Following Urban IV's death in October 1264, Albertus' commission as preacher of the crusade lapsed. He continues to appear, however, as an arbitrator in numerous lawsuits in Germany. It is possible that Albertus dwelled with the Dominicans in Würzburg during 1264–5. By 14 July 1267 Albertus appears with Cistercian nuns at Burtscheid near Aachen to consecrate their chapel; on 4 August 1267 he consecrated an altar in Cologne, and on 29 April 1268 a Dominican church in Esslingen. By June 1268 Albertus appears in Strasbourg, where Pope Clement IV (d. 1268) had entrusted him to settle a dispute between its bishop, Henry IV of Geroldseck (r. 1263–73), and its citizens. Albertus' medieval chroniclers also indicate that at the invitation of Strasbourg's bishop, Albertus ordained a large number of priests there in 1268. In that same year, he consecrated a church for a leprosarium at Adelhausen, near Freiburg-im-Breisgau, where a Dominican cloister for nuns had been founded in 1234. By September 1269 he appeared in Basel to consecrate a Dominican church, but by 1270 he had returned as a lector to Cologne, where he would remain for the rest of his life.

This period following his release from the bishopric in Regensburg until his return to Cologne was also a time of intense literary activity, during which Albertus composed most of his biblical commentaries: on the Gospel texts of Mark, Luke and John, as well as on the Old Testament books of Jeremiah, Lamentations, Baruch, Ezekiel, Daniel, the Minor Prophets and – following his return to Cologne – Job, completed circa 1272 or 1274. It was also during this period that Albertus composed several works on systematic theology, including his *Summa of*

Theology (*Summa theologiae*, part one after 1268 and part two after 1274), a double treatise on the Mass (*Super missam*) and *On the Body of the Lord* (*De corpore domini*). He also prepared a written response to a list of 43 philosophical-theological problems (the *Problemata determinata*) that John of Vecelli (d. 1283), master general of the Dominican Order, had dispatched in 1271 to the three Dominican scholars Albertus Magnus, Robert Kilwardby and Thomas Aquinas, in search of orthodox solutions. Many of these arose from the effort to reconcile Aristotelian physics and Christian theology, producing numerous questions concerning the relationship of angels to the motion of heavenly bodies and their influence on the sublunar world.

Although after being consecrated bishop of Regensburg Albertus was no longer subject to the rule or jurisdiction of the Dominican Order, he continued to perceive himself as a Dominican brother at heart. Owing to his episcopal rank, however, after he returned to the Dominican priory of the Holy Cross in Cologne in 1270, Albertus performed tasks that demanded episcopal intervention, as well as tasks in support of the Order. In 1271 Albertus worked to resolve the protracted conflict between Archbishop Engelbert II and the city of Cologne, leading to a formal declaration of peace in April 1271. In 1272 Albertus' seal appears on a document that confirms a settlement between the monastery of Kampense and Gerhard of Cologne. During this decade, he consecrated churches in Antwerp, Utrecht, Nijmegen and Maëstricht, and consecrated altars in Vochem, Leuven and at Paradise at Soest. Albertus' assistance was also solicited by his former student in Cologne, Ulrich of Strasbourg, prior of the German Dominican province. It seems likely that in May 1274 Albertus attended the Second Council of Lyon. According to Peter of Prussia, Albertus spoke on behalf of Rudolf I of Habsburg (d. 1291), who had been crowned king of the Germans in Aachen on 24 October 1273. Rudolf still sought the support of

Pope Gregory x (r. 1271–6), however, who had convened the council. At its conclusion, the council recognized Rudolf as Holy Roman Emperor (after Rudolf made certain territorial concessions to the papacy), but Gregory x died on 10 January 1276, before the imperial coronation planned for 2 February 1276. In June 1275 Rudolf conferred upon Albertus the privilege to bestow the episcopal regalia upon bishop-elect Eberhard of Münster (r. 1275–1301), and on 4 July 1275, as noted earlier, Rudolf ratified the content of Pope Gregory x's reissue of *Sicut Judaeis*, which was presented to him under Albertus' seal.

Albertus' activity hardly abated between 1275 and his death in 1280. According to his medieval biographers, his seal appears on a letter of 2 June 1275 in which Archbishop Siegfried ii of Westerburg of Cologne removed ecclesiastical censure from the city of Cologne. As already mentioned, Albertus translated the bones of St Cordula to the Cologne chapel of the Hospitallers on St Valentine's Day, 14 February 1278, and he continued during 1278 to witness legal settlements. His medieval biographers attest that during the last few years of his life, however, Albertus' memory began to fail as his death neared.

From his Dominican 'family', Albertus selected a handful of individuals to serve as executors of his will: Konrad Gurli of Esslingen, the provincial of the Dominican Order in Germany from 1277 to 1281; Dietrich, the prior of the Cologne Dominican house where Albertus resided; and Albertus' sibling, Henry of Lauingen, who had followed Albertus into the Dominican Order and who was a Dominican prior at the Dominican house in Würzburg. In addition to these three, Albertus named as executors the Dominican brothers Godfrey the *physicus* (that is, either a physician or a natural philosopher) and Godfrey of Duisburg; the latter had long been Albertus' secretary and confessor, and claimed, after Albertus' death, to have received a miraculous vision of Albertus' glorification. Finally, Albertus had two Cologne knights attach their seals to the document to attest to its authenticity: Bruno Hartfust, the *procurator* who managed Dominican affairs in Cologne, and Daniel Judaeus, who was a member of the Cologne town council and a few years later became the city's *Bürgermeister*. Despite the name *Judaeus*, there is no evidence that Daniel was either a Jew or a recent Jewish convert.

Despite having taken a vow of poverty, in his will Albertus claims that an unnamed pope – perhaps Pope Urban iv (d. 4 October 1264) – had granted him a dispensation from the Dominican vow, probably about the time he was consecrated bishop of Regensburg, so that 'I am able to possess personal property of a temporal nature, and that I am able to dispense my possessions in accordance with the judgement of my free will and exactly as it pleases me.' Consequently, Albertus bequeathed a substantial gift to 'the brothers of the Cologne house, among whom I have stayed and taught for the greater portion of my life', assigning

> all my books to the common library; all my vestments
> to the sacristy; but all the gold and silver and gems that
> I possess which can be turned into cash should be used
> for finishing the choir of that same house, [the choir
> that] I founded with my own money and erected from
> its foundation up.

Albertus also designated a substantial number of monetary bequests in his will. In order to understand their size, one should be aware of contemporary currency, especially the 'Halle pound'. Halle (Saale, Germany) is located approximately 150 kilometres (90 mi.) west of Freiberg and approximately 450 kilometres (280 mi.) east of Cologne. Mines discovered there in the late twelfth century were producing about 20–25 tonnes of silver by the beginning of the thirteenth century. Albertus mentions Freiberg as an important source for the purest silver (DM, p. 181).

In his will, Albertus left the sum of 90 Halle pounds to be disbursed to three cloisters of Dominican nuns: St Mark of Würzburg (founded in 1245); St Catherine in Augsburg (founded c. 1245), where Albertus' sister lived as a nun; and Gotteszell in Gmünd, about 50 kilometres (30 mi.) east of Stuttgart, which was given to the Dominicans in 1246. It is difficult to establish a modern equivalent for 90 Halle pounds, but for the sake of comparison, in 1257 Count Thibaut v of Champagne and king of Navarre (d. 1270) made provision in his will for a gift of 20 pounds each to hospitals in Champagne and 10 pounds to the leper communities in the same locations. Albertus' gift of 30 pounds each to three cloisters was 50 per cent larger than the value of Count Thibaut v's bequest to individual hospitals and three times as large as his gift to individual leper communities. In his recent biography of Albertus, Hannes Möhle establishes the value of 90 Halle pounds as equal to 150 Cologne marks and determines that the average price of a house on the High Street – prime residential property – was only 33 Cologne marks.[4] In other words, Albertus' gift of 90 pounds could have purchased more than four or five homes in the most expensive part of town. Although such comparisons remain difficult, it seems clear that Albertus amassed a considerable fortune, which he bequeathed to Dominican communities in Würzburg, Augsburg, Gmünd and Cologne.

Not only did Albertus generously endow the Dominican house of the Holy Cross in Cologne, but he elected to be buried there. According to Rudolph of Nijmegen, Albertus himself chose the location for his sepulchre in the Dominican church and, even before his death, visited it daily to say prayers for the dead. After death, his body was carried in procession to Archbishop Siegfried II of Westerburg of Cologne and then buried in the choir of the church of the Holy Cross before the high altar. Albertus' entrails (*intestina*) were carried to the city of Regensburg, where he had reigned as bishop from 1260 to 1262, and were placed behind the high altar in Regensburg's cathedral, dedicated to St Peter. Construction of the present Regensburg Cathedral began in 1280, the year of Albertus' death, to replace the older *Niedermünster*, which burnt down in 1273.

While Albertus' death marked the end of his career, it also marked the expansion of his legacy. His work as a natural philosopher, which followed the long journey of investigations into nature that had begun some 1,700 years earlier, established his reputation as a pre-eminent natural scientist well into the modern era.

FIVE

Those Who Came Before

T he ancient Greek historian Herodotus reports (*Histories*, 1.74.2) that on 28 May 585 BCE, a solar eclipse occurred over what today we call Asia Minor and so terrified locals that it brought immediate peace talks between the warring Medes and Lydians. The event is even more interesting, Herodotus reports, because Thales of Miletus predicted it. This is the same Thales who, Aristotle says, knew the heavens so well that during one winter he determined that the next season would bring a bumper crop of olives, amassed a little capital, cornered the market on olive oil presses ahead of time and made a significant profit (*Politics*, 1259a). Thales had been taunted by the locals regarding the uselessness of philosophy and performed this financial wizardry to show that philosophers could become rich if they wished, but this was not what they cared about.

There is some scholarly debate about whether a solar eclipse could actually have been predicted at this stage in history, but the anecdote does give us our example of a man who can reasonably be thought of as the West's first natural philosopher, a type of natural scientist who was called a *physiologos* (investigator into nature or being) by the Greeks and who came to be known in Albertus' time as a *physicus*. The word *physicus* has its origin in the Greek word *physis*, which refers to the natural, inborn, orderly constitution of nature. Thales was always listed as one of the Seven Sages of Greece, and is reported to have studied, in addition to astronomy and weather, the basic element of things (he thought it was water), mathematics (he devised a way to measure the pyramids) and engineering (he reportedly directed the division of a wide river into two channels, making it easier to ford). Thus Thales is only the first historical example of a Greek passion to answer a simple, and yet quite difficult, question: 'What is the nature of all that is, and to what extent can we know it?' The search for the answer to this question gave rise to a tradition of inquiry that flowed, over eighteen centuries, to Albertus in a stream fed by many and various tributaries.

A glance at the recently published *Encyclopedia of Ancient Natural Scientists: The Greek Tradition and Its Many Heirs* offers a sense of the scope of the activity among the ancients in these areas. The book's admirable indices list hundreds of authors and their works, divided into the following categories, with the number of ancient authors writing in that category in parentheses: agriculture/agronomy (102), alchemy (56), astrology (96), astronomy (161), biology/botany/zoology (101), cosmology (65), encyclopedia (13), geography (246), lithica (mineralogy, 36), medicine (420), meteorlogica (meteors, rainbows and so on, 61), paradoxography (61), pharmacy (500), physiognomy (10) and veterinary medicine (41).[1] All these subjects are to be found in the natural science works bearing the name of Albertus Magnus.

We thus see that there is a strong parallel between those aspects of the natural world investigated in Greco-Roman antiquity and those studied in the Middle Ages by Albertus. The earliest of these investigators into such subjects are to be found not in mainland Greece, but in the area we know as Ionia, an area colonized by the early Greeks roughly corresponding to the western coast of modern Turkey and an early incubator for many aspects of Greek culture. Miletus, Thales' home, was a hotbed of philosophical speculation during the sixth and fifth centuries BCE.

Miletus lay at the mouth of the Meander River in what is now southwestern Turkey, near the small town of Balat. It lay south/southeast of Ephesus and the Greek island of Samos, and was about ninety minutes by car from modern Bodrum (ancient Halicarnassus) and the birthplace of Herodotus. Because of its location and natural resources, Miletus was soon eyed by the growing Persian Empire and became one of the flashpoints that led to the Greco–Persian Wars. Prior to this, however, a vibrant school of philosophy emerged that is known to us from the fragments of Anaximander and Anaximenes. As was true for Thales, neither of these thinkers drew a hard and fast line between studying what some today would call 'scientific' and 'philosophical' subjects, and what we know of their beliefs must be extracted from a handful of statements about them from other authors in later antiquity.

Ancient authors often state that Anaximander (d. *c.* 547 BCE) was Thales' student and successor. What we have left of his theories are as intriguing as they are vague. He believed that the 'boundless' (*to apeiron*) is both the principle (*archē*) and the elemental building block (*stoicheion*) of all that is. Anaximines (fl. *c.* 546–525 BCE) was born near the end of Anaximander's life and created a full cosmology in which the earth was the centre of the universe held aloft by *pneuma* (cosmic air or breath), which also served as the *stoicheion* of all things as it thinned or thickened, becoming, for example, fire and earth. Some of his beliefs even anticipate a theory of evolution, stating that the first animals were created in water and later migrated out onto dry land.

Another early school of philosophy that took a lively interest in the natural world was settled to the north of Miletus, at Ephesus. Heraclitus (fl. *c.* 500 BCE) offered fire as the primal element and believed that things constantly change, while Xenophanes (fl. late sixth century BCE) delved into the difference between true knowledge and mere belief. Many other names exist of those who were interested in the natural order of things, but we lack sufficient selections of their work to try to determine to what extent they actually studied individual elements of the natural world as opposed to concentrating on larger issues such as those just listed. Finally, Anaxagoras of Clazomenae (500–428 BCE) was well known for his investigations into natural science (eclipses, rainbows, meteors) and even posited that *Nous* (mind) was the basic force that put order on an otherwise-undifferentiated primordial matter.

The above philosophers/natural scientists are generally all put in a group called the 'Presocratics' in deference to the first great philosopher of ancient Greece whose thoughts and beliefs have been preserved for us through the works written by his disciples, Plato and Xenophon. These works do not depict Socrates as very interested in the natural world, and Xenophon denies any such study outright (*Memorabilia*, 1.1.11). In fact, apart from the times he served as a soldier outside the city, Socrates seems only to have left the walls of Athens twice in his life, as depicted in Plato's *Lysis* and *Phaedrus*. Nevertheless, in Aristophanes's famous play *The Clouds*, Socrates is depicted as a true *physiologos* who enters the stage suspended in a basket so that he might better study the heavens, puts wax booties on a flea so he can measure the length of its jump, and muses about whether gnats 'buzz' out of their backsides or their mouths. There are also some hints that in his youth he may have followed in the footsteps of the Milesians:

> When I was young, Cebes, I had a prodigious desire to
> know that department of philosophy which is called
> the investigation of nature; to know the causes of things,
> and why a thing is and is created or destroyed appeared
> to me to be a lofty profession; and I was always agitating
> myself with the consideration of questions such as these:

– Is the growth of animals the result of some decay
which the hot and cold principle contracts, as some
have said? Is the blood the element with which we
think, or the air, or the fire? or perhaps nothing of
the kind – but the brain may be the originating power
of the perceptions of hearing and sight and smell,
and memory and opinion may come from them, and
science may be based on memory and opinion when
they have attained fixity. And then I went on to
examine the corruption of them, and then to the
things of heaven and earth, and at last I concluded
myself to be utterly and absolutely incapable of these
enquiries. (*Phaedo*, 96a–b, trans. Jowett)

We see here Plato's Socrates listing and ultimately discarding
many of the areas of study that Aristotle, and eventually Albertus,
pursued equally alongside 'pure' philosophical endeavours such
as ethics, epistemology and metaphysics. The picture is, of
course, not quite as black and white as this, but it seems clear
that Socrates (d. 399 BCE) and Plato (d. 347 BCE) were less interested in studying the workings of the natural world than their
predecessors. It was Aristotle (384–322 BCE) who paved the way
for later philosophers such as Albertus to broaden their sense of
philosophical inquiry to include once more the study of the
natural world. But long before any such deliberations, there
existed a well-established and deeply entrenched set of beliefs
concerning nature and its wonders, viz. folklore.

It is important to stop and look at this orally transmitted
tradition as well, because it persisted throughout antiquity to
the Middle Ages and into the works of Albertus Magnus. Such
tales probably originated from what Albertus would call the
experti – 'experts', to be sure, but also implying, from the under-
lying Latin verb *experior*, those who had experienced something.

Such *experti* could include professionals like hunters, fishermen, animal breeders, beekeepers and the like, but also, and most importantly, travellers, mariners and tradesmen who brought back tales from foreign lands, either reporting things they themselves had seen or repeating tales they had heard. Not all they related was true, but it was almost universally believed and dutifully passed along with the trust that only oral tradition (or today's social media) can impart. Many of the animal tales and folk beliefs that appear in the works of Albertus and the encyclopedists of the twelfth and thirteenth centuries can be traced to such sources.

A goodly amount of such information entered the shared belief system of the ancients through the voyages of discovery the ancients undertook. Such explorers are often called geographers today, and indeed they did perform many of the same functions as modern geographers, but at the same time they acted as ethnographers, anthropologists and chroniclers of exotic flora and fauna. A flurry of this sort of activity occurred in the early fifth century BCE, and three voyages, two by Carthaginians and one by the Persians, can serve as examples. Hanno of Carthage is reported to have sailed out of the Straits of Gibraltar in the early fifth century BCE with a fleet of sixty ships and 30,000 men, women and children, probably intending to establish trading posts on the African coast. He headed west and then south along the western coast of Africa for a considerable distance. His report to his superiors was in Punic, but we have a Greek version of it that tells of volcanos, crocodiles, hippopotamuses and creatures his interpreters called *gorillai*, three females of which he skinned and brought the hides back to Carthage. At roughly the same time, Himilco of Carthage also exited the Straits of Gibraltar but turned east, hugging the west coast of Europe. He reports on native craftsmen and the ships we know as coracles. A contemporary Persian named Sataspes avoided a death sentence for rape by agreeing to circumnavigate Africa. He returned months later without completing his chore and was killed by King Xerxes I for his failure. Nevertheless, the tales he brought back, such as that of a dwarfish race dressed in palm leaves, caught the Persians' fancy. The list of such explorers is long, and ancient exploration hit its height when Alexander the Great opened up the East as far as India, and returning soldiers and sailors brought back reports of strange races and animals.

The point of this brief excursus is to indicate that while we have only bits and pieces of any written reports these explorers may have produced, their tales – and surely those of merchants – became part of the folkways of the times. Many such tales were repeated in writing by authors like Herodotus and Pliny the Elder (23/4–79 CE), and persevered until the time of Albertus. But we can be sure that Albertus also counted contemporary travellers – Crusaders, explorers, merchants and the like – among the *experti* from whom he extracted a treasure house of information and then had to pass judgement concerning its veracity.

It is because certain authors in antiquity began to write these orally transmitted beliefs down that we have the opportunity to study them. The earliest authors were travellers, some of whom travelled for mercantile or military reasons. We do not have extensive texts of these earliest *logographoi* (a vague term that means something like 'prose/story writers'), but between what we do possess and the indirect reports of their now-lost works, we get a sense of their penchant for reporting wondrous natural phenomena as a way of helping to define far-off places and races. The first extant ancient author to incorporate such interests into his work is Herodotus (c. 485–425 BCE), the 'Father of History', who chronicled the Greeks' victories over the Persians in the early fifth century BCE. Herodotus, born in Halicarnassus in modern Turkey, travelled a great deal in the East, investigating the empires of Persia and Egypt. In so doing, he literally and figuratively followed in the footsteps of those *logographoi* before him who reported not only what they saw and heard but, equally passionately, what they heard that someone else had seen or heard in far-off lands. Thus Herodotus glibly relates that no horse can stand the smell of a camel, that a crocodile cannot see underwater and that spear shafts are made from hippopotamus hides. India possesses ants the size of a fox that dig for gold; Arabia is home to flying snakes, whose skeletons he had seen; and there are sheep with tails so large that they have to be supported in carts. A surprising number of these beliefs endured the centuries to find their way into medieval texts.

Ctesias was a late fifth- through early fourth-century BCE Greek physician who served at the Persian royal court and reported back to credulous Greeks the marvels he saw or heard of in that vast empire. His writings are known mainly through the ninth-century summaries of Photius, but they reveal a lively interest in local fauna and marvels. We hear of wall-breaking elephants, lion-fighting dogs and the truly frightening *martichoras* (the later manticore), which had the body of a lion, the blue-eyed face of a man, the tail of a scorpion (complete with stinger), three rows of teeth and a row of spines that it could shoot like arrows. Ctesias first reported some of the fantastic races, like the Sciopods, that are found in Albertus' works. Likewise, we hear of gold-guarding gryphons; a small, dark red snake that lacks fangs but kills nonetheless by spitting; and a monstrous river-dwelling worm whose history we shall trace below.

There are thus many sources of information that existed side by side in the ancient world. Just as Albertus would do some fifteen centuries later, Aristotle sought to analyse the natural world and to present his findings in a coherent, organized fashion that would show the workings of nature. Born in Macedonia, he came to Athens at about the age of seventeen to study with Plato at his Academy and remained in the Platonic school at

least until the death of his teacher in 347 BCE. Thereafter he
moved towards the East, the area that had first spawned investigation of the natural world, and settled in Assos in Asia Minor,
which lies north of Lesbos. Having moved to Lesbos itself, he
turned his analytical mind to the abundance of marine life that
lay all around him, and the observations he made there would
lay the groundwork for large portions of his investigation into
the natural world. The works most associated with his investigations are *Investigation into Animals* (*Historia animalium*),[2] *On
the Soul* (*De anima*), *On the Parts of Animals* (*De partibus animalium*), *On the Movement of Animals* (*De motu animalium*),
On the Progression/Gait of Animals (*De incessu animalium*) and
On the Generation of Animals (*De generatione animalium*).

Aristotle breaks from the wide-eyed enthusiasm of the *logographoi* and relates in organized fashion the results of his close
observations of the natural world. Thus he rejects through silence
the belief that bees could be born from the carcass of a battered
ox and engages instead in long speculation as to the real method
of their reproduction. But he, as we will see in Albertus, was
also subject to the folklore of his day. Although he rejects as
nonsense the story that lionesses lose their uterus in giving
birth, he accepts the tale that Syrian lionesses give birth first
to five cubs, then four and so on, decreasing by one each year.
He expresses caution over Ctesias' *martichoras* and attacks
Herodotus' tale that certain fish breed by swallowing the milt,
but still believed that certain animals are produced by fire or
spontaneous generation.

Theophrastus of Eresus in Lesbos (c. 371–287 BCE) carried
on in the tradition of Aristotle and expanded his scope to
include the realm of botany. Theophrastus had been a younger
member of Plato's Academy, and after Aristotle left Athens, he
took over as head of the Lyceum founded by Aristotle. His works
show almost as catholic an interest in the natural world as do

Aristotle's. Diogenes Laertius, who wrote a work consisting of
ten books of lives of the philosophers, gives us a list of about
two hundred of Theophrastus' works (*Lives of the Philosophers*,
5.2.42–50). Those concerning natural philosophy include three
extant treatises: *On Weather*, *Inquiry into Plants* and *On the Causes
of Plants*, the latter two foreshadowing Albertus' *On Plants*. We
also have some fragmentary works that study such things as fire,
winds, storms, the senses, stones, fish, sweat, honey and odours,
as well as the names of some works whose loss is lamentable, such
as *On Land Animals*, *On Wine and Honey*, *On Juices*, *On Fruits*,
Opinions of the Natural Philosophers, *On the Heavens*, *Meteorology*,
On Vision, *On Those Living in Holes*, *On Biters and Strikers*, *On
Animals that Change Color* and *On Creatures Appearing in Swarms*.

When Theophrastus died, Alexander the Great had been
dead for 46 years, and the Greek world was firmly in what we
today call the Hellenistic Age. India, which had for so long been
a place of mystery, had been conquered and explored. The great
Library of Alexandria, built close to the time of Theophrastus'
death, was built to be a repository of all knowledge and focused
on acquiring in one place copies of as many books as possible,
making them available for study by the scholars who congre-
gated at the library. It was a scholarly age that tried to create a
standardized version of Homer's works and produced lexicons,
encyclopedic works and scholarly commentaries on literary works.
Predictably, a good deal of this activity centred on the natural
world, and, as is too often the case, most are known to us only
by being cited by later authors such as Aelian and Pliny (see
below). A few titles of such lost works will give a sense of the
loss: *Inquiry into Flocks and Herds* and *Inquiry into Birds* by
Alexander of Myndus (10 BCE–40 CE); *On Unusual Natural
Phenomena* by Archelaus of Chersonesus (c. 270–c. 180 BCE);
On Birds, *On the Rivers of the World* and *Collection of the Wonders
Happening around the World (Arranged by Locality)* by Callimachus

of Cyrene (*c.* 285–*c.* 245 BCE); and *Theriaka* by Numenius of
Heracleia (270–230 BCE), a work on poisonous animals and
antidotes.

The relative stability of the early Roman Empire also seems
to have encouraged such scholarship. Many authors are just
names to us, but one such name is telling. Didymus of Alexandria
(*c.* 63 BCE–*c.* 10 CE), nicknamed Chalkenteros, or 'Bronze Guts',
because of his capacity for work, turned out numerous works that
deal with animals among his alleged 3,500–4,000 titles. In Rome,
Nigidius Figulus Paulus, praetor for 58 BCE, anticipated Pliny the
Elder by writing on natural science. Grattius, a contemporary of
Ovid, following the lead of the Greek Xenophon some five centuries before, produced a work on hunting with hounds, the
Cynegetica (540 lines extant). Aemelius Macer (d. 16 BCE) wrote
an *Ornithogonia* and a *Theriaca*, and the too-often-forgotten
Mauretanian king Juba II (fl. last half first century BCE) wrote
widely on many subjects dealing with animals. He was well
received in antiquity and frequently cited, a reminder that not
all culture was found only in Rome.

The first century CE was a period of largely derivative but still
active scholarship. Pamphilius of Alexandria, essentially a lexi-
cographer, wrote an *On Plants* (*Peri Botanōn*) and a *Natural History*
(*Physika*, a term to be found in Albertus), preserving much that
was later to be of use to Aelian. At about the same time that
Alexander of Myndus published *On Animals* (*Peri zoōn*), *On
Fowling* (*Ornithiaka*) and *On Wild Beasts* (*Thēriaka*), while back in
Alexandria, Apion passed along enormously influential Egyptian
lore – the ultimate source for animal tales ranging from 'Androcles
and the Lion' to 'The Ibis Who Wouldn't Die'.

Better known and more frequently a source for later medieval writers are the encyclopedic works devoted solely to
natural phenomena such as Pliny the Elder's *Natural History*
(*Historia naturalis*), a massive encyclopedia in 37 books that

simultaneously benefits and suffers from its author's total and indiscriminate voracity. This is not the proper venue for tracing what we know of the lost authors he cites, but the interested reader is directed to Pliny's first book, where he lists his own sources. The list is impressive and gives us a sense of the wide appeal this sort of literature held long before medieval times. Influences from his work are frequently to be found in Albertus' *On Animals*.

Plutarch (d. c. 120) is best known for his biographies of famous Greeks and Romans, but engages in natural science in his *On the Cleverness of Animals*, *Whether Beasts Are Rational* and *Natural Questions*. Claudius Aelianus (Aelian, c. 175–235 CE), mentioned above, was born in Italy but wrote two works in Greek that include material from earlier authors, *On the Nature of Animals* (or *On the Characteristics of Animals* (*Peri zōōn idiotētos*) and the *Various History* (*Poikilē historia*).

Likewise, Seneca the Younger (d. 41 CE) is best known as a Stoic philosopher who wrote on living an upright life, but near the end of his life, he produced eight books of the *Natural Questions*, six of which are extant. The work covers a wide array of natural-philosophical subjects ranging from the four elements to meteorology, from winds to earthquakes and other natural phenomena. His work seems to have had little influence on Albertus.

The thirst for such books grew, and each generation mined the works of those who had gone before. The veterinary medicine tradition also has its place with authors such as Pelagonius and Vegetius. Much evidence of such works will be noticed in *On Animals* when Albertus speaks of various cures for horses, hounds and birds of prey.

Finally, compilers such as Solinus, who wrote an epitome of Pliny about 200 CE, and Isidore of Seville (c. 560–636) did much to bridge the gap between antiquity and the Middle Ages,

passing along unquestioningly whatever they found in earlier
sources. Isidore's *Etymologies* (*Etymologiae*) is frequently cited
for his etymologies of animal names found in book twelve. These,
though commonly incorrect, are still useful in pointing out what
were felt to be the salient points of an animal's nature. For example, he derives *haedus* (young goat) from *edendo* (eating). A few
other predecessors deserve to be mentioned. Albertus cites two
of the most prominent ancient physicians fairly often, Galen
and Hippocrates. Hippocrates of Cos was most likely contemporary with Socrates (d. 399 BCE) and is widely considered the
greatest physician from antiquity, and doctors have historically
taken the Hippocratic Oath as an ethical guide to practice.
Curiously, while there are many Hippocratic treatises, none can
be confidently attributed to the man himself. Albertus knew of
Hippocrates and cites him frequently in his section of *On
Animals* (DA, 1.126–67; SZ, vol. I, pp. 93–108) that is concerned
with physiognomy, calling him Hippocrates of Cohy (DA, 1.167;
SZ, vol. I, p. 108), making him a contemporary of Philemon,
whose work on physiognomy is known to us only from Latin and
Arabic translations from the Greek. Far from being Hippocrates'
contemporary, Philemon wrote in the second century CE. Loxus
(third century BCE), another physiognomist, is frequently cited
in the same section on physiognomy in *On Animals*. In addition
to physiognomy, we find the influence of the ancient veterinary corpus in Albertus commonly when treatments for dogs
and horses are discussed (DA, 22.31–4; SZ, vol. II, pp. 1460–63).
Vegetius (*Mulomedicina*, late fourth century CE) and Pelagonius
(*Ars Veterinaria*, end of fourth century CE) are the most important of Albertus' predecessors in this field, and he cites Vegetius
on several occasions.

To what extent was Albertus directly familiar with such
sources? The question is not subject to a facile answer, but a
search of his works reveals over forty ancient authors cited by

name. For example, Anaxagoras and Theophrastus, mentioned above, appear about forty and fifty times, respectively; Democritus (b. 460–457 BCE) over two hundred; and Plato over 1,200 times. The authors cited by name include mathematicians (Euclid, Pythagoras), medical writers (Hippocrates, Galen), philosophers (Aristotle, Plato, Theophrastus), poets (Homer, Solon, Virgil) and handbooks of a more practical nature (Vitruvius, Palladius, Vegetius). Albertus had to rely on Latin translations of Greek authors, and often the reference to an author came to him second-hand, being quoted by an author like Pliny. Some Latin authors, such as Ovid, Lucan and Seneca, are actually quoted, however. The presence of some less well-known authors such as Apuleius, Dares Phrygius and Lucan reminds us not to think of the thirteenth century as totally cut off from knowledge of ancient authors.

Late antiquity presents other authors such as Ambrose (d. 397), whose *Six Days of Creation* (*Hexaemeron*) began to add a strong religious viewpoint to the narrative of natural science. But it was the emerging *Nature Inquirer* (*Physiologus*) that was to have the most impact. It began as a collection of descriptions of some forty animals and a few stones but grew rapidly after that and was first written down, probably in Alexandria, by an anonymous author between the second and fourth centuries CE. Here Greek, Roman, Egyptian, Hebrew and Indian lore is gathered, blended and given moralizations for the Christian community. The gold-digging, camel-pursuing ants of Herodotus (*Histories*, 3.102–5) have become the two-faced ant-lion, and the beaver's tactic of self-castration to avoid capture is now symbolic of man's need to cast off the temptation of the flesh.

The work's popularity was unprecedented, and versions soon appeared in numerous languages, including Armenian, Syriac and – most importantly for its contribution to the medieval authors on natural history – Latin. The Latin *Physiologus* contributed directly to the massive medieval bestiary tradition whose works also incorporate all that had gone before. Versions of the *Physiologus* vary in length and content. Some are illustrated profusely, others poorly. Some are extremely religious, others somewhat sceptical. But they all had an immense influence on the Middle Ages, especially the twelfth century and the early part of the thirteenth, when there was an explosion of interest in animal lore and the possibilities it offered for moralization and sermon writing. It was at about this time that the *Physiologus* tradition morphed into that of the bestiary tradition. A bestiary takes the information the *Physiologus* provides and mixes in various details from authors such as Pliny the Elder, Isidore or Rabanus Maurus (d. 856 CE), whose *On the Nature of Things* (*De rerum naturis*) consists of 22 books that draw on many earlier authors to create an encyclopedia of all knowledge.

Bestiaries range from small to large and can treat up to 120 animals. Some assemble the animals in groups (for example, terrestrial, winged or marine creatures), while others employ a rudimentary alphabetical system wherein all the A's have their own section, and so on through the alphabet. Within this larger grouping, however, alphabetization is haphazard. Many bestiaries are illustrated, and some, such as the Aberdeen Bestiary and the Northumberland Bestiary (*c.* 1250–60), are lavishly illustrated.

This brings us, finally, to the medieval writers for whom animal lore was indispensable. The thirteenth century is notable for its interest in natural science, especially that found in the encyclopedic works of several authors such as William of Auvergne, Alexander Neckam, Arnold of Saxony (*Arnoldus Saxo*), Vincent of Beauvais and Bartholomew the Englishman (Bartholomaeus Anglicus). Bartholomew was a Franciscan whose monumental *On the Properties of Things* (*De proprietatibus rerum, c.* 1240 CE) had a wide influence in the field. Organized into nineteen books,

Adam naming the animals, miniature from the Northumberland Bestiary (c. 1250–60).

it attempts to cover all aspects of our existence, ranging from God and the angels down to birds, fish, animals, plants and stones. Standing firmly on the shoulders of all who had gone before, these authors now began to have access once more to Aristotle's natural philosophy and, as in Albertus' case, would often include their own observations.

Books 22–6 of Albertus' *On Animals* are organized as a bestiary, and his entry on the weasel displays both the benefits and dangers resulting in the long literary tradition we have discussed here. Albertus says it is a 'sort of a long mouse' (*mus longa*), repeating the etymology of Isidore, but goes on to say it really resembles the marten more than a mouse, citing its dentition as one proof, which implies close observation of the animal, dead or alive. He further distinguishes two genera of *mustela*, noting differences in their size and colouration. This is followed by a flawed version of Pliny stating that the weasel loses its life (*vitam*) if transported to the island of Proselena. But Pliny actually claims that the weasels there never cross a road (*viam*).[3]

Further difficulties arising from receiving information so removed from its original sources and corrupted by the process of translation, often from Greek to Arabic and then Arabic to Latin, are readily seen in *On Animals*. In this work, Albertus cites Herodotus without knowing it, for the name has come down to him as Brocotoz and Eradytis, who, he thinks, was a poet. 'Eradytis' originally stems from Aristotle, who cites the philosopher Heraclitus, and, indeed, Michael Scot offers *Eraclitus*. Yet 'Eradytis the Poet' harkens back to Albertus' own 'Aradotus the Poet', even though Michael Scot also reads *Eraclitus* here, faithfully rendering the original Aristotle. Sometimes Albertus is aware of the problems since, for example, he states that Protagoras is 'corruptly' called Abrokaliz by some. In the very next paragraph, however, he offers as a source Pitagoras, where the original Avicenna and Aristotle texts cite no one in particular.[4]

A few other examples will show the perilous nature of the texts that made their way to Albertus. We have marked the text to reflect Albertus' *post illa* style in which he inserts his own comments directly into his received text. The editor of *De animalibus*, Hermann Stadler, faithfully marks his edition to reflect this process. Following his text, Albertus' received material is printed here in bold-faced type, while Albertus' additions are printed in regular type.

First, a case of simple textual corruption is found in DA, 1.18. Here, very early in his work, Albertus is discussing ways in which animals differ according to their actions. But one is surprised to find Albertus' text saying:

> **Comparatio etiam haec fit in membrorum actione:**
> **sicut** discrepant elefas et equus in hoc quod **elefas**
> **pugnat aure sua, et capit** et tenet hoc quod impugnat,
> **nare** sive naris promuscida: quod non facit equus aure
> et nare sua.

> Comparison is also made with respect to the activity
> of the members. Thus the elephant and the horse
> differ in that the elephant fights with its ear [!] and
> it seizes and holds what it attacks with its nose, called
> its trunk. This is a thing the horse does neither with
> its ear nor nose.

If one reads just what is in bold, we see that Albertus' received text says, 'Comparison is also made with respect to the activity of members, as when an elephant fights with its ear and seizes with its nose.' This statement, so odd on the face of it, causes Albertus to interpolate heavily into his received text, trying to explain away a seeming impossibility and calmly making it clear that this is a thing no sensible German horse would ever think of doing. What has occurred is an obvious copyist's error in which *nare* (with its nose) was misread as *aure* (with its ear), and Albertus has done his best to cover up for his received text.

Let us move next to the second example, where we trace the history of the somewhat-unpleasant *hahane* and its outrageous eating habits:

> HAHANE – This is a sea animal more gluttonous than all other sea creatures, which is said not to have a separate and distinct stomach. It is a predator and all its food is converted into fat. Thus its stomach swells out beyond all reason. When this animal fears danger, it folds its skin and fat over its head, hiding its head like a hedgehog. If the thing causing the fear should remain for a long time, it is sustained by eating part of its own flesh until the danger should go away.
> (DA, 24.11, no. 17; SZ, vol. II, p. 1664)

There is no hint that Albertus harbours doubts about the existence of such an improbable creature, but for a modern reader, the challenge is immediate. Where and how did such a tale arise? Stadler suggests Aristotle HA, 571a28f., but there is nothing in this passage parallel to our passage, save a casual reference to fat. The real answer lies in the tortuous path that the text has followed on its way to Albertus and by the fact that the Arabic translator probably had the Greek read aloud to him as he worked.

The initial two letters in 'ha-hane' represent the Greek article *hē*, 'the'. Since Albertus received his Greek via the Latin translation of an Arabic translation of the Greek, there had been ample occasions when a scribe, listening to a person recite the text, might have allowed his ear to make the article part of the actual noun. In Aristotle's HA, 591b, the habits of three fish, the *kestreus* (a mullet), the *sinodōn* and the *channa* (a perch), are being discussed:

> The grey mullet is the greediest and most insatiable
> of the fishes, hence its stomach is distended and when
> it is starved it is in poor condition. When frightened, it
> hides its head thinking that it is hiding its whole body.
> The *sinodōn* too is carnivorous and eats the cephalopods.
> Often both it and the *channa* extrude their stomachs while
> chasing the smaller fishes, because the stomachs of fishes
> are next to the mouth and they have no gullet.

Here we find the needed form *hē channē*. And looking a bit before and after, we find the strange attributes of Albertus' *hahane* neatly arrayed. We have the greediness and the distended stomach in the mullet, followed immediately by the head-hiding also as a trait of this mullet. The general lack of a true stomach is discussed at the end as an attribute of all fish. Somehow, over the years and as the text passed through many copy houses and many languages, two of the original fish in the passage dropped out, and all the traits became subsumed under the Greek 'hē channē', now written as a single name, 'hē hannē'.

One trait, however, and this the oddest, seems unaccounted for. What of the *hē hannē*'s ability to live off its own flesh when in danger? The answer lies in another type of error commonly found in the text received by Albertus – simple mistranslation of the Greek original, probably by the original Arabic translator. At issue are two specific quasiscientific phrases: *sarkophagei* and *malakia*. *Sarkophagei* literally means 'eats flesh', but in Aristotle it equates to our 'is carnivorous'. *Malakia* literally means 'the soft ones', but in Aristotle is tantamount to the name of a genus and indicates 'molluscs' or 'cephalopods'. The translator, not knowing this, has been more literal. Still thinking of the just-mentioned head-hiding, he has rendered the whole as follows: 'when it is frightened it hides its head and eats its own flesh and its soft parts.'

A final example reflects the changing pronunciation of Greek over the years as it moved from the classical pronunci-ation towards the modern pronunciation. This is not always a benign change, as in this case, where it presents us with lobster claws with lips. The words in bold were added by Albertus to the text he received:

> The lobster, however, eats small fish. When it is at
> the bottom of the sea in rocky locales, it takes them
> in with the two lips **of its hand** and leads them to its
> mouth, broken into two parts, just as the crab does.
> (DA, 7.20; SZ, vol. I, p. 594)

This is a fascinating corruption of Aristotle's original at HA, 590b26, where the crayfish is said to perform this action with its double claw (*tē dikroa chēlē*). However, the Greek for 'lip' is *cheilos* and its plural is *cheilē*, which in the more modern pro-nunciation would be pronounced identically with *chēlē*, 'claw', both being pronounced 'cheelee'. Faced with lips on crabs, which Albertus knew did not exist, he did the best he could with his received text and adds the phrase 'of its hand', perhaps thinking the 'lips' might refer to the serrated edges of the claws.

Albertus was fully aware of such problems. He complains in the following three examples of odd Latin words that had come to him:

1 If there should cling to the mare's young the thing called
   the *ycomenez* . . . the mares lick it with their tongue
   and eat it. Women who cast spells use this, when they

can get it, to produce certain chants for incantations
with which they arouse parents to love their infants.
Aristotle corruptly calls these chants 'proverbs', but
the fault is not the philosopher's, it rather belongs to
the one who translated his book into Latin. (DA, 7.115;
SZ, vol. I, p. 638)

2 This bird lives by hunting sea fish, but it sometimes comes
   to the streams near the sea. Its eggs are five in number
   and it is in heat the whole span of its life, beginning to
   copulate at the age of four months. This account is more
   probable than the first, which was given according to
   Aristotle, whose book in our lands is in many ways less
   than it should be.[5] (DA, 8.79; SZ, vol. I, p. 701)

3 We are using the word 'roof' here for a shell in which
   shellfish are enclosed, even though the use of 'roof' is
   improper. But Aristotle used this word before us for
   'shell' and we therefore use it too. (DA, 13.112; SZ,
   vol. II, p. 1038)

The process of textual transmission can resemble the parlour
game commonly called 'Telephone' where the first person is given
a short text to read and then must relate it to the next person
without looking at the text. The second tells the third, the third
the fourth and so on, until the final person relates the story out
loud and all marvel at how much it has changed in the retelling.
Consider these tales of three enormous creatures living in the
Ganges River as related by Albertus (the Latin spelling is his):

1 Unde et in Gange fluvio in quo *anguillae* magnae sunt,
   vermes quidam esse dicuntur qui *bifurcata crura* anterius
   habent sicut cancri qui longitudinem habent sex
   cubitorum et corripiunt elefantes et mergunt eos.
   (DA, 24.8, no. 2).

Some also say that in the Ganges River, where
there are huge eels, there are certain worms that have
bifurcated front legs like crabs and attain a length
of 6 cubits. These seize elephants and drown them.
(sz, vol. II, p. 1660)

2 Caeruleum est nomine et re caerulei coloris *animal
   aquaticum* quod Ganges fluvius nutrit, et habet *brachia
   duo* longitudinis cubiti unius, valde saeva, quibus
   ad portum fluminis magnas bestias rapit et trahit in
   profundum. In nostris autem aquis hoc animal non
   invenitur. (DA, 24.26, no. 38)

The *caeruleum* is blue both in name and fact. It is
an aquatic animal which the Ganges River supports.
It has two arms, each quite fierce and each 2 cubits
long. It seizes large beasts with these at the mouth
of a river and drags them to the bottom. This animal
is not found in our waters. (sz, vol. II, p. 1677)

3 Platanistae ut dicit Plinius belluae sunt marinae quae
   Gange fluvio Indiae nascuntur et in mare veniunt et
   rostrum habent delfini et caudam habent sedecim
   cubitorum longitudinis. Hiis sociae sunt *beluae* quas
   stacias vocant, *brachia bina* habentes quibus tanta inest
   fortitudo, elefantes in aquam intrantes infestent et
   eis promuscidas abrumpant. (DA, 24.49, no. 99)

According to Pliny, *plantanistae* are sea monsters
which are native to the Ganges River in India and
which also go out to sea. They have the snout and
tail of a dolphin and are 16 cubits long. The monsters
which are called *staciae* are their companions and
have bifurcated claws, in which there is such force
that they attack elephants entering the water and
rip off the elephants' trunks with these arms.
(sz, vol. II, p. 1696)

These three animals have a long history dating as far back as Ctesias himself. Ctesias, as preserved in Photius, tells us that in India there is a worm (*skōlēx*) 6 cubits in length that has two teeth only, one above and one below. It comes out at night and can carry away even a camel. It can be caught with an iron hook, and when dead, the locals drain liquid from it that can burn trees and animals alike. A very similar tale is found in Pliny (*HN*, 9.46), where he describes the *platanista*, a 16-cubit-long creature with the tail and beak of a dolphin. He states further that one Statius Sebosus describes a worm in the same river that has two gills (*branchiis binis*). The worms are called the *caerulei* (blue) because of the colour of their face. It is so strong that it seizes the trunks of elephants coming to the river for a drink and drags them into the river. Solinus (52.41), who, as we have seen, wrote a digest of Pliny's work, distorts some of Pliny's account. In Solinus' version, the worms of Sebosus become eels named *caerulei*, and they have two arms instead of gills (*brachia* for *branchia*) and are 6 (not 16) cubits long, probably reflecting a misreading of XVI as VI.

Isidore of Seville (*Etym.*, 12.6.41) gives the *caeruleus* only one line but manages to give the creature thirty feet, perhaps misconstruing its original length. He also has dropped any mention of the eels. Thomas of Cantimpré (*ThDNR*, 6.42), one of the likely sources for Albertus' bestiary, gives an account based on Pliny. He mentions the *platanistae*, but there is no mention of the *caerulei*. In fact, in his version, the beast is now called the *statius*, which in the original Pliny is the author's name from whom he took the account of the creatures. Thomas retains the arms that were once gills, and the elephants still come to the river for a drink. This brings us to Albertus' three entries. In the first, he keeps the eels and worms separate, but the *brachia bina* of predecessors have become *crura bifurcata*, 'forked legs'. The second passage correctly keeps the name *caeruleus*, but instead of coming for a drink (*ad potum*), the elephants now come down to the port (*ad portum*). The third entry returns us to the *platanistae* introduced by Pliny. If we take Pliny's *platanistae* as reflecting Ctesias's original unnamed river creatures, we have an unbroken line of garbled animal lore that changes as it passes from author to author over the course of sixteen centuries. Albertus, however, was not the only medieval scholar to transmit and even to magnify ancient lore. Many of Albertus' contemporaries took what was a rather unorganized flow of information and sought to collect it in once place where it could easily be consulted. In the thirteenth century they gave rise, then, to the age of the encyclopedists.

SIX

Albertus and the Encyclopedists

The thirteenth century saw many authors interested in the world of nature and natural science. Some of these authors are identified as medieval 'encyclopedists', even though the term 'encyclopedia' did not appear in English until the sixteenth century. Nonetheless, during the thirteenth century, several large texts were written in Latin and in the vernacular that sought to assemble the sum of contemporary knowledge for a nonspecialist audience. Among the most influential Latin encyclopedias are Alexander Neckam's *On the Natures of Things* (*De naturis rerum*), Thomas of Cantimpré's *On the Nature of Things* (*De natura rerum*), Bartholomew the Englishman's *On the Properties of Things* (*De proprietatibus rerum*) and Vincent of Beauvais's massive *Greater Mirror* or *Four-Fold Mirror* (*Speculum maius* or *Speculum quadruplex*). All these deal with the things of nature or the nature of things: that is, with all the elements surrounding human beings, whether found in heaven or on earth. They deserve the name 'encyclopedias' because their contents are arranged under several rubrics and summarize diverse fields of knowledge, such as theology, astronomy, mathematics, biology and daily life.

The medieval predecessors to these thirteenth-century encyclopedias, like Isidore of Seville's twenty-book *Etymologies* (*Etymologiae*) or Rabanus Maurus's modestly titled *On Everything* (*De universis*), sought to make available to a wider audience the wisdom of the Bible and of the fathers of the Church in one accessible collection demonstrating the hand of God in the natural world. By the thirteenth century, however, the 'golden age' of the medieval encyclopedia, the encyclopedias began to emphasize the natural laws and principles at work in the world around us. Certainly, God remains in the background as the author of these laws, but the encyclopedias increasingly turn their gaze upon the foreground, aided by the rapid diffusion of works on nature by Aristotle, and by medieval Arab and Jewish authors made available in Latin translation. The introduction of this new knowledge expanded the horizons of scientific learning, which contributed to the emergence of the medieval encyclopedias. In turn, the encyclopedists assembled their sources for a large popular audience: for nobles, princes and others with intellectual interests who had neither the time nor the training to explore the sources themselves. The growth of this audience depended, then, on thirteenth-century social and economic change: on the appearance of more densely populated urban centres in which universities were established, and upon the desire and need for knowledge not only in an expanding clerical class but among educated laypeople.

To satisfy their audience, the encyclopedists had first to organize their materials. Unlike modern encyclopedias, their works were not intended to serve as mere reference works, in which one can locate a general article on individual topics that have been arranged alphabetically. Instead, the medieval encyclopedists expected their readers to explore the whole of the text, just as they hoped to provide a window onto all things capable of being known. Their principle of organization was typically indebted to Plato and Aristotle, then, and introduced a philosophical rather than biblical division of the world.

Arnold of Saxony (*Arnoldus Saxo*), who also refers to himself at times as *Arnoldus Luca*, composed one of the first thirteenth-century encyclopedias, a brief anthology titled *On the Flowers of Natural Things* (*De floribus rerum naturalium*, composed *c.* 1220–30). It organizes its material in five books: (1) On Heaven and Earth; (2) On the Natures of Animals; (3) On the Powers of Precious Stones; (4) On the Universal Power (in all things having matter and form); and (5) On Morals. The influence of Aristotle's zoology and biology is especially evident in books two and four, which Arnold knew through Michael Scot's recent translation of Aristotle's *On Animals*. Although Arnold mentions several ancient authors (such as Pythagoras, Seneca, Cicero and Sallust), these mentions are easily eclipsed in number by Aristotle. In the second book alone of *On the Flowers of Natural Things*, Arnold cites Aristotle 99 times. By contrast, across the whole of his book, one can count on two hands his references to Plato.

A second and far more popular encyclopedia is Bartholomew the Englishman's *On the Properties of Things* (*De proprietatibus rerum*). Unlike Arnold of Saxony, who may have been a Dominican friar, Bartholomew had joined the Franciscan Order, and almost all that is known about him is gleaned from Franciscan chronicles. According to the *Chronicle of Jordan of Giano*, which covers the years 1207–62, in 1230 a provincial chapter of the Franciscan Order decided to split the German province into two: the Rhineland region (*Alemania*) and Saxony (*Saxonia*). Two English friars – John (*Johannus Anglicus*) and Bartholomew (*Bartholomaeus Anglicus*) – were dispatched to organize the province of Saxony. In 1231 Bartholomew became a lector at the provincial study centre, or *studium*, in Magdeburg, where he gave basic instruction in theology. The more able Franciscan students might be sent from there to the *studium generale* in Paris. In 1247 Bartholomew was elected minister provincial of Austria, which had split as a separate province from Saxony between 1232 and 1237. In 1262 Bartholomew

The Four Elements, the seven Planetary Spheres and the sphere of the
fixed stars, engraving from Albertus Magnus, *Philosophia naturalis* (1506).

returned to Saxony as minister provincial and died in that post
in 1272.

It was in Magdeburg that Bartholomew completed his *On
the Properties of Things* (c. 1245), an encyclopedia of science and
theology in nineteen books – a number that symbolizes uni-
versality, since it represents the sum of the twelve signs of the
zodiac and the seven planetary bodies of the medieval universe
(the Moon, Mercury, Venus, the Sun, Mars, Jupiter and Saturn).

Although Bartholomew's first book treats God and his second
examines the nature of angels, in the remaining seventeen books
Bartholomew most often turns his attention to this world below.
For example, book four investigates the four elements (earth, air,

fire and water) and their corresponding bodily humours; book five
explores human anatomy; book six treats the various ages of man;
book seven treats human illness, medicine and the role of physicians; book nine looks at the seasons of the year; book eleven
treats meteorology (wind, rain, snow and lightning); book twelve
investigates birds; book thirteen the nature of water, pools, rivers
and lakes; book fourteen, mountains; book fifteen, the diverse
geographical regions of the world; book sixteen, precious stones
and metals; book seventeen, plants and medicinal herbs; book
eighteen, various animals (beasts, serpents, domestic animals and
insects); and book nineteen examines sensible qualities (odour,
taste, colour and more). Despite its size – 1,190 chapters spread
over 1,261 pages in the 1601 Frankfurt edition – we can conclude
from the number of extant manuscripts that *On the Properties
of Things* was widely read. It offers its readers a coherent, well-
organized compilation. It also has a practical utility, especially
because of its extensive discussion of illness based on medical
authorities such as Hippocrates, Galen, Isaac Israeli, Constantine
the African, Haly Abbas and more. From the beginning of the
fourteenth century, moreover, it would be translated into numerous vernaculars, including French, Spanish, Dutch and English.
Equally important, Vincent of Beauvais read this text alongside Thomas of Cantimpré's *On the Nature of Things* (*De natura
rerum*) when he compiled his own massive and more comprehensive *Greater Mirror* (*Speculum maius*), which is roughly ten
times larger than Bartholomew's work.[1] Bartholomew's encyclopedia draws not only upon theological authorities (for example,
Ambrose, Augustine, Pseudo-Dionysius the Areopagite, Bede,
Gregory the Great, Rabanus Maurus and Remigius of Auxerre),
but upon Islamic natural philosophers (Alhazen, Al-Ghazali and
Avicenna), and especially upon Aristotle or Pseudo-Aristotle.

The next thirteenth-century encyclopedist is Thomas of
Cantimpré. Although much of the information we have about

his early life is speculative, it does seem well established that he was born into a rural noble family in Brabant and that his father had followed King Richard I of England on the Third Crusade. In 1217 Thomas entered a religious order, the Canons Regular of St Augustine, at the abbey of Cantimpré (near Cambrai). In 1223, while still at the abbey, he was ordained a priest. By 1232 he had joined the Dominican Order in Leuven and for the next thirty years devoted himself to hearing confessions, a role for which mendicant friars like Thomas of Cantimpré were specially trained.

Thomas was sent in 1237 to the Dominican priory of St James in Paris to study, where he, like Albertus, became involved in the controversy that resulted in the burning of the Talmud. From Paris, he returned to the Low Countries and reappeared in 1246 as subprior in Leuven. By 1250 he had travelled to Cologne, where he studied under Albertus Magnus alongside other distinguished Dominicans, including Thomas Aquinas. A first redaction of his encyclopedic *On the Nature of Things*, on which Thomas laboured from 1228 to 1248, consists of nineteen books like Bartholomew's *On the Properties of Things*: books one and two treat human anatomy; book three investigates the 'monstrous' human races located in the East; books four through nine treat animals (birds, marine monsters, fish, snakes, worms and insects); books ten to twelve discuss plants, herbs, trees and their medicinal properties; book thirteen, waters; books fourteen and fifteen, stones and precious metals; book sixteen, the seven celestial regions; book seventeen, the spheres of the earth and the seven planetary bodies; book eighteen, movements of the air and wind (meteorology); and book nineteen, the four principal elements (earth, air, fire and water). A second redaction adds a twentieth book treating solar and lunar eclipses. The work survives in at least 147 manuscripts from the thirteenth to sixteenth centuries, attesting to its widespread popularity.

Bartholomew the Englishman never cites Thomas's *On the Nature of Things*, although this is not proof that he was unfamiliar with it. Vincent of Beauvais, however, who was also a Dominican, does cite explicitly Thomas's encyclopedic work. What about Albertus Magnus? Thomas of Cantimpré was Albertus' student in Cologne, and they clearly shared an interest in the natural world. Although Albertus' general approach to nature is more investigative and empirical than Thomas's, scholar Pauline Aiken demonstrates conclusively that Albertus is heavily dependent upon Thomas's encyclopedia for the last five books of Albertus' own 26-book commentary *On Animals*. Many medieval and early modern readers of Thomas's *On the Nature of Things* clearly recognized this, which led them to draw the erroneous conclusion that Albertus, whose fame far outshone that of his student Thomas of Cantimpré, must be its author.

Monk contemplating the heavens, miniature in Thomas de Cantimpré, *Liber de natura rerum* (c. 1280).

Not surprisingly, then, many of the 147 manuscripts of *On the Nature of Things* attribute the work incorrectly to Albertus Magnus. Even Jacob of Maerlant, a poet and younger contemporary who produced a modified translation of Thomas of Cantimpré's *On the Nature of Things* in Flemish under the title *Der Naturen Bloeme* (*The Flowers of Nature*), attributed the work to Albert of Cologne (Albertus Magnus).

According to modern conventions, one might be inclined to think that Albertus Magnus plagiarized the work of Thomas of Cantimpré by including in his own book substantial, unattributed material from Thomas's earlier work. But medieval authorial conventions were different than ours, and it was quite acceptable to 'borrow' material, especially from near contemporaries, without identifying them by name. In the same way, Thomas of Cantimpré includes in his own work large extracts lifted verbatim from earlier authors. For example, book one includes a condensed version of the fictional *Letter of Aristotle to Alexander* and borrows heavily from William of Conches's twelfth-century *Dialogue on Natural Philosophy*. This is not to say that Thomas never names his authorities: he frequently cites by name Aristotle, Pliny, Solinus, Ambrose, Basil the Great, Isidore of Seville and his own contemporary Jacques de Vitry. He also cites Galen (from the work of the late eleventh-century Benedictine Constantine the African) and the Arab authors Alfraganus, Albumasar and Averroes, probably known to him through Michael Scot's translations from Arabic. Nonetheless, since Thomas's explicit purpose is to unite in a single volume the wisdom of the ages, he and other thirteenth-century encyclopedists often include material from other authors without identifying them. Equally frustrating, Thomas includes material from sources that he only identifies opaquely. One such source that Thomas and Albertus Magnus both cite, but which modern scholars have struggled to identify, is the work of one *Experimentator*.

The last thirteenth-century encyclopedist we shall mention is the Dominican Vincent of Beauvais (d. c. 1264) and his massive *Greater Mirror*.[2] For approximately twenty years, from 1240 to 1260, Vincent devoted himself to this work. According to the late fifteenth-century *Cologne Legends* (*Legenda Coloniensis*), Vincent 'assembled everything capable of being known in four volumes'. The work underwent several redactions, revisions and expansions. By 1250 Vincent planned to divide the work into four parts: a *Speculum naturale* on natural history, a *Speculum doctrinale* on the arts and sciences, a *Speculum morale* on virtues and vices and a *Speculum historiale* on human history from creation to his own day. Vincent dedicated an early version of the work to the French king Louis IX (r. 1226–70), who, having learned that Vincent was preparing a substantial work to epitomize all that can be known, gave Vincent a large sum of money to produce a copy for him. In 1245 Vincent presented to the king a copy of the first half of the *Speculum historiale*.

Although the work is known as the *Greater* or *Four-Fold Mirror*, referring to its four parts (natural, doctrinal, moral and historical), modern scholars acknowledge that Vincent never completed his *Speculum morale* and that the work of that name ascribed to Vincent was instead produced by an early fourteenth-century Franciscan. Of the other three parts, the *Speculum historiale* was the most popular and was especially useful to mendicant preachers, who turned to it for historical information that included even the early years of the Dominican Order itself.

When Vincent began this encyclopedia, Aristotle's treatises on natural philosophy and metaphysics were still banned in Paris because they seemed to endanger certain well-established Christian doctrines, including the teachings that God created the universe out of nothing (*creatio ex nihilo*) and had endowed each individual human being with an immortal soul. In 1231 Pope Gregory IX had reaffirmed that Aristotle's works on natural science were forbidden to Parisian scholars until purged of error. By the time Albertus Magnus had become a regent master at the university in Paris (1245–8), attitudes towards Aristotle had begun to change and scholars turned to purging his writings of error. Albertus sought to introduce *all* of Aristotle's work to the Latin world, and he cites Aristotle abundantly in his work on creation, the *Summa de creaturis*. Vincent includes portions of Albertus' *Summa de creaturis* in a second redaction of the *Speculum* and even incorporates into the *Greater Mirror* some of Albertus' work on falcons from book 23 of his *On Animals*.

As Aristotle's philosophical work spread among Parisian scholars, the scope of the *Speculum* expanded dramatically. In response, Vincent introduced a new feature absent from earlier encyclopedias: searchability. By introducing various devices like a table of contents, chapter and section headings (often employing coloured inks to make them stand out), and marginal notes or guides, Vincent sought to produce a work that would enable the reader to find what they seek with greater ease. Although these devices fail to provide the ability to 'google' the *Greater Mirror*, and even though Vincent did not alphabetize entries or materials within each book like a modern encyclopedia, his new finding aids – which had also recently been introduced to Bible manuscripts in Paris – nonetheless represent a significant advance that help explain its popularity.

Just as Vincent of Beauvais used the work of Bartholomew the Englishman, Thomas of Cantimpré and Albertus Magnus for his *Greater Mirror*, so Albertus, in turn, used the encyclopedias of both Thomas of Cantimpré and Vincent of Beauvais for his own work. Should we include Albertus among thirteenth-century encyclopedists? We surely can in the sense that Albertus' intellectual interests extended to all the areas of human wisdom and were therefore 'encyclopedic' in nature. Not long after his death, therefore, Albertus was known as the *Doctor universalis*, or 'Teacher of Everything'. But Albertus was not merely a compiler. He was himself an original thinker who sought to extend the boundaries of human knowledge through his own scientific observations of the natural world, even if many later readers used his works as reference materials.

SEVEN

Albertus and the Experts

From the fifth century BCE, written stories concerning exotic animals from far away had been passed from author to author, usually accepted as truth. Tales such as the report of giant worms swimming in the Ganges or the one-footed race of the Skiapods are as old as Ctesias, and innumerable 'facts' concerning the natural world made their way from Pliny, through Solinus and into the *Physiologus* and the bestiary tradition, ultimately becoming fixtures of the Middle Ages, believed with the same fervour some people today have for Bigfoot or the 'fact' that porcupines shoot their quills. The natural-history works of Albertus Magnus, however, are notable for their readiness to question hoary traditional tales whenever they seem to contradict his personal observations, common sense or those he considered experts in a given field. Albertus indicates his more scientific approach in his commentary on the Pseudo-Aristotelian *On Plants*:

> Of those things which we will propose some we have
> proven ourselves through experience; others we report
> according to the opinions of those we have ascertained
> do not readily say anything unless it has been proven by
> experience. For experience alone provides certainty in
> such matters for the reason that in particular natures a
> syllogism cannot be applied. (*De veg.*, 6.1.11, pp. 339–40)

Albertus proposes, then, that his own experience and the experience of experts must guide an investigation of nature. Although the certainty of a deductive syllogism (such as, 'All men are mortal; Socrates is a man; therefore Socrates is mortal') is not possible from observations of individuals, Albertus contends that, nonetheless, given certain suppositions or assumptions about nature, natural philosophy can not only lead to knowledge that is highly probable but will even achieve a level of certainty of its own. For this reason, he is notable in his time for challenging stories that had come to him from the ancients.

Pliny, it will be remembered, contains pseudo-facts he found in numerous works now lost to us. Some of these sources, such as Ctesias, are known for their fanciful stories of exotic animals and plants, and as a result are subject to Albertus' scepticism and even scorn. When discussing Pliny's heron called the *monoculus* (one-eyed), he first uses logic to refute it, saying that nature distributes other 'parts' to animals in pairs: two nostrils, two lips, two ears and so forth. Going further, he states, 'To be sure, this Pliny says many things that are entirely false and in such matters his words should not be given consideration' (*DA*, 23.21; *SZ*, vol. II, p. 1556). Albertus commonly adds personal observations to refute Pliny. For example, in refuting beliefs held by Pliny 'and others' that no one had ever seen a vulture's nest since they really lived elsewhere and only migrated into 'our areas', he says that he had seen many nests in the mountains that lie between Trieste and Worms, adding the additional fact that Worms had a constant stench about it arising from the carcasses vultures bring there. In the same passage, he contradicts the belief that vultures do not copulate, claiming that such behaviour had been observed many times in these same areas. Pliny's claim that nightingales do not sing when sitting on their eggs is also rebuffed through personal observation. Albertus also supplies a personal observation to refute Pliny's report of a

northern eagle incubating its eggs by putting them in a fox's
pelt facing the sun. Again, he is quite specific, saying that he
had never seen this behaviour in Livonia (south of Estonia and
east of Latvia). It is clear that Albertus visited Livonia: as early
as 1256 Pope Alexander iv had urged the German Dominicans
to expand throughout Prussia and Livonia, and the anonymous
Cologne Legends (*Legenda Coloniensis*) reports that Albertus visited Dominican houses there while he was prior provincial
(1254–7).[1]

While Albertus often gives credence to Avicenna (d. 1037),
he also contradicts him. Albertus describes Avicenna as among
'the finest of philosophers', and Albertus' natural philosophy
borrows heavily both from Avicenna's *Canon of Medicine* and
Book on Animals (*Abbreviatio de animalibus*). Nevertheless,
when Avicenna relates the old belief that hares have clefts on
their hindquarters resembling vulvas, growing a new one annually, Albertus carefully contradicts the Persian, clearly basing
his view on close examinations of the animal. Even Aristotle
is not immune from correction. Albertus' enormous respect for
Aristotle notwithstanding, he remarks that since Aristotle was
only human, he could err like anyone else. Although Aristotle
claims that moles have no functioning eyes due to an imperfec-
tion or flaw that occurs at their birth, Albertus contends that if
this were true, then nature would be constantly erring, and that
is clearly unacceptable. He counters in modern-sounding terms,
saying that since it lives primarily underground, it usually has no
need of eyes but nature provides a thin skin over the eyes for the
times it emerges into daylight.[2]

Albertus commonly takes time to refute false folk beliefs,
and the language he uses is quite informative. The false belief is
commonly prefaced with terms like *dicitur* (it is said) or *quidam
dicunt* (some say). A great number of the refutations are based
on personal observation using phrases based on the Latin stem

exper(t)-, which indicates personal knowledge or experience. Thus we commonly see phrases such as *expertus sum* (I have experienced), hear that a fact has been proven or disproven *experimento* (through experience or trial) or are told that the story comes from one or more *experti*. In *On Animals*, he tells us that he studied badgers frequently and the belief (cited in Thomas of Cantimpré's *On the Nature of Things*) that their legs are not of equal length is untrue (DA, 22.49; SZ, vol. II, p. 1475); that magpies do not moult when dead; that the cuckoo does not sometimes turn into a hawk and then back again; that ostriches do not incubate their eggs by sight, although they occasionally might glance over at the eggs; that cranes do not have a stone in their stomachs that they vomit up when flying; that wolves do indeed bark; and that he never had experienced wasps losing their stingers during winter.[3]

This is not to say that Albertus is always correct. When discussing the beaver, he tells us that beavers are common in some parts of Germany, Slavic lands, Poland, Prussia and Russia. Some of his comments indicate that he observed the animal, yet he misidentifies *castoreum* (still the name of the musky secretion they exude) as the testicles themselves; incorrectly claims they eat fish; and retells the tale that solitary, wandering beavers are sometimes enslaved by native beavers, put on their backs, loaded up with wood and dragged from the trees to the water, like a kind of animate sledge. He says this explains the beavers he has seen who have 'hairless backs' (DA, 7.50–51; SZ, vol. I, pp. 607–8). Thomas of Cantimpré (ThDNR, 4.14.22f.) has the same story, citing the *Experimentator* as his source, and versions are found in other authors such as the twelfth-century Gerald of Wales (*Journey through Wales*, 2.3) and Bartholomew the Englishman (*De prop.*, 18.28). Some bestiaries (for example, Harley MS 4751 fol. 30r, second quarter of the thirteenth century) have a parallel story, claiming that one badger will hold a stick in its mouth and lie on its back. After other badgers have loaded its belly with dirt, two badgers grasp the stick and drag the badger-wheelbarrow away. To his credit, Albertus does scoff at the beliefs that beavers never take their tails out of water and that during winter months they force otters to swim around their tails to keep them from becoming immobilized by ice (DA, 22.40; SZ, vol. II, p. 1468).

Most notably, Albertus conducted experiments to test certain beliefs. We are not using the term 'experiment' as it is used today, referring to a carefully controlled test producing results that can be reproduced. Albertus, as we will see, conducted his experiments once and did not do follow-up experiments to explore alternative reasons for the results he obtained. It is better to think of his actions more as the testing of a concept or fact rather than as actual experiments. The following examples are chosen because the Latin text contains some form of the Latin root *experi-*, which implies first-hand knowledge. In some cases, Albertus uses a more complete phrase: *probavi(mus) experimento/per experimentum* (I/we have proven this through experience), as if differentiating his personal involvement in the experience.

Albertus was quite interested in moles, commenting on their diet and that he had seen them hunt from underground (DA, 22.143; SZ, vol. II, pp. 1538–9). As we have seen above, he investigated rationally Aristotle's belief that their lack of eyes was an inborn flaw in the animal. But this was insufficient for Albertus:

All viviparous animals, however, do have eyes except for the mole . . . It sees nothing at all *and when it comes out of the earth it merely wanders about. I have tested the following by firsthand experience. The skin on its head over the places for its eyes is smooth, thin, white, and is so entirely closed that it lacks any hint of a division. When I delicately*

cut into this I found nothing at all of the dark of the eye or
of the matter of eyes. I found rather some flesh that was
moister than it is elsewhere. Now this was a freshly caught
mole, so much so that it was still squirming. (DA, 1.140;
SZ, vol. I, p. 98)

Apart from the disquieting portrayal of vivisection, the *post
illa* style is revealing, for Albertus inserts into his received text
everything in italics in the passage above. At another time,
curious about the fact that oil in which a scorpion has died was
said to be good for a scorpion bite when mixed with vinegar,
he tests it. He placed a scorpion under oil, and it only died on
the 22nd day, all the while walking around on the bottom of
the container. To test a received belief about the cicada (possibly the cricket), he states that he and his associates decapitated
one and it continued to sing for a fairly long time. He discusses
the salamander's supposed ability to withstand fire and to produce a kind of fireproof wool, dismissing the latter as a natural

Salamander in a miniature from a Franco-Flemish Bestiary (c. 1270).

accretion on the walls of forges sold by itinerant peddlers under the name 'salamander wool'. The product today is called iron wool, rock wool or mineral wool, and is used for insulation and soundproofing. One cannot be sure, but the story may have arisen from salamanders seeking the warmth of forges on cold days. Likewise, spiders were thought to be fairly fireproof, since spiders were thought to have a cold, wet make-up like the salamander. Albertus tested the theory, putting a spider on a piece of glowing, hot iron, and reports that 'it lay there a long while before it twitched and felt the heat of the burning', but in the same passage notes that he held a small candle up to another spider and the light went out.[4]

Albertus submerged a wax vessel in sea water to show that this does not produce fresh water and stopped up the entrance to a woodpecker's nest with an almond to demonstrate the strength of its beak. An illustration in the Millstatt Bestiary (Landesmuseum für Kärnten, VI.19 fol. 99r) shows a man feeding horseshoes and nails to an ostrich, and the Caius Bestiary (Gonville and Caius College Library MS 384 604 fol. 174r) shows an ostrich holding a horseshoe in its mouth. The latter was created circa 1180–1220 and is thus an example of the belief, common in Albertus' era, that ostriches eat iron. To test this belief, Albertus informs his readers, 'I have often spread out iron for several ostriches and they have not wanted to eat it. They did greedily eat rocks and large, dry bones that were broken into smaller pieces.' The ostriches in question could have belonged to Emperor Frederick II, who had ostriches in his travelling menagerie. On other occasions, Albertus drew the wrong conclusions. He smeared honey on a wall to see if the pests that are found in beehives are born from the honey. When he came back and saw over a hundred *vermiculos* (small insects or, more likely, larvae) in the honey, he felt he had proven this instance of spontaneous generation, apparently not considering the possibility that

the *vermiculi* were the result of insects laying eggs on the honey.
Neither did he try the experiment by smearing the honey in a
sealed container or room.[5]

In another passage, Albertus shows caution. He reports that
there are certain birds that always fight one another because
they are natural enemies, and moreover:

> This same sort of abhorrence exists between the feathers
> of the eagle and goose, for one eagle feather joined to
> many goose feathers consumes them. I have tried this
> myself [*expertus sum*] on their wing feathers and it might
> be the same for the other feathers of these birds. It is said
> to be the same for wolf hair and sheep's wool, but I have
> not tried this myself. (DA, 8.27; SZ, vol. I, p. 678)

It is clear that Albertus, amid all his ecclesiastical work and
travels, always found time for personal observation of nature
and that he trusted his own experiences over ideas held by the
ancients and what he calls the common folk (*vulgus*). Moreover,
it is equally clear that he was a patient observer. His observations, sometimes of many individuals over long periods of time,
led him to refute the idea that kingfishers moult their skin once
a year; to verify that the magpie and crow eat other birds; and
to know that swallows teach their chicks to turn around and
defecate outside the nest. He tells us that the age-old belief that
turtledoves are monogamous is false, a fact he could only have
ascertained through long-term observation. The birds are not,
in fact, absolutely monogamous, but socially monogamous,
which means that a pair stays faithful during one breeding
season but may have different partners in another. Albertus
remarks, too, on parenting among birds. He claims to have seen
'a male crane throw a female crane to the ground and kill her'
because she had taken her chicks away from him. Moreover,

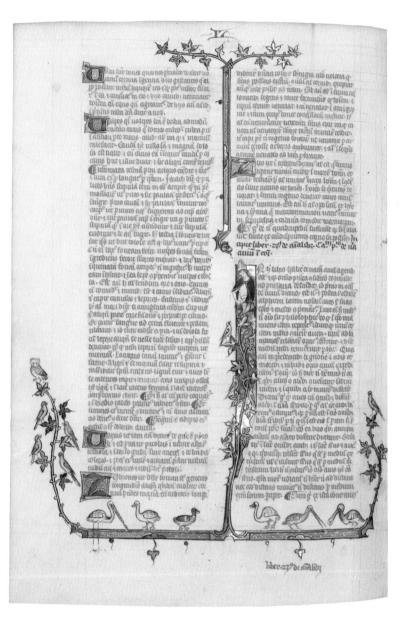

Folio from the beginning of book 23, 'On the Nature of Birds',
in Albertus Magnus, *De animalibus* (14th century).

Albertus adds, 'This occurred in Cologne, where there are domesticated, breeding cranes.'[6]

Albertus was especially interested in the many raptor birds that lived in his area, and, in fact, almost half of the 84 pages devoted to birds in book 23 of *On Animals* is devoted to birds of prey. Robin S. Oggins offers an excellent review of Albertus on falcons and hawks, including his sources.[7] This interest is not surprising, since falconry was an important subject of study during the thirteenth century. The work of a certain Moamin/ Moamyn deals with the diseases of falcons and hawks, and had been translated into Latin from Arabic by Theodore, a philosopher at the court of Frederick II. A Latin and Old French translation of a work attributed to one Yatrib was also in circulation. Another influential work was attributed to Dancus Rex, whose identity is unknown, but who cites the work of Roger, king of Sicily. Finally, the thirteenth-century polymath Frederick II, king of Sicily and Holy Roman Emperor, composed *On the Art of Hunting with Birds* (*De arte venandi cum avibus*), which meticulously lays out all aspects of the capturing, training and keeping of birds of prey. Dated to around 1247–8, it does not, however, seem to have been utilized by Albertus in his own studies on falconry.[8] Albertus does cite Frederick's falconer, but we know that the king had over fifty falconers. He also cites the letter of 'Aquila, Symachus, and Theodotion, men of very ancient times, written to Ptolemy, king of Egypt' (DA, 23.103; SZ, vol. II, p. 1618), an apocryphal document of his time. As one would expect, Albertus also went directly to the *experti*, that is, falconers themselves, and relied on personal observation as well.

Albertus observed that the sparrowhawk is a solitary hunter and does not hold live birds beneath it to keep warm. He visited a golden eagle's nest for six years in a row to check the number of eaglets it produced annually, watching as someone was lowered on a rope of great length while others above shot arrows and threw stones to keep the eagle from attacking the intrepid observer. Apparently, Albertus convinced professionals who dealt in the trade of snatching young birds of prey from the nest for sale to falconers to undertake the dangerous task. He seems to have had a number of such professionals whom he consulted to help flesh out his own theories. The most notable of these was a man who lived in isolation high in the Alps and was a most experienced falconer (*expertissimus falconarius*). This expert informed Albertus that ropes let down to a peregrine falcon's nest could be as long as 90 metres (300 ft) and explained how peregrines feed their chicks and teach them to become self-sufficient. Albertus had seen so many falconers at work that he lists three major ways to catch wild falcons and evaluate the usefulness of each, two based on personal observation and a third told to him by the Alpine hermit.[9]

Several factors led Albertus to be particularly interested in birds of prey. Most notable, perhaps, is his personal experience with them. In a detailed account he reports that, when he was hunting as a young man, wild falcons struck birds the dogs flushed. The falcons received one bird each as a reward (DA, 8.110; sz, vol. i, p. 716). Beyond giving us a sense of Albertus' social status in his youth, the passage marks the beginning of a lifelong interest in raptors. He likewise tells of watching a swan battle an eagle for two hours high in the air until the eagle was finally victorious and landed with the swan. He backs up his account's veracity by saying it was also witnessed by his associates (*socii*) and that their servant (*famulus*) ran up to snatch the swan from the eagle.

Other passages reflect Albertus' tendency to seek out experts and question them for information. Swabian fowlers told him they once came upon a very old, blind goshawk. Wondering how it managed to stay alive, they hid in the bushes and observed young goshawks coming with a catch that they served to the old bird. The fowlers, Albertus adds, are trustworthy (*fides*), a comment he often provides to show that a particular source is to be trusted and may imply repeated interactions. Fowlers also told him that the best goshawks came from Sweden and Latvia. His own observations include well-trained falcons who would enter houses, even flying over the dinner table, coming and going as they wished. During the hunt, they would fly free, without jesses, and return whenever the falconer called. He combines his own observations with those of fowlers to determine the different ways hawks and eagles teach their young to hunt and how they then drive them off to seek their own territories. Albertus even tells us that he himself caught a vulture, adding modestly that it was slow at the time because it had just gorged itself (DA, 23.144, no. 113; SZ, vol. II, pp. 1653–4).[10]

Albertus applies many of the same methods to his reports concerning hunting and fishing. He personally observed how wolfhounds taught their young, running ahead of the young ones and detaining the wolf if they lagged behind. A close look at another passage demonstrates the extent to which Albertus, through the use of the *post illa* style, amplifies the text he received from Michael Scot's translation of Aristotle. The received text from Aristotle's *On the Generation of Animals* (781b) reads as follows: 'For this reason, dogs which track down hares have a good sense of smell.' Finding this account wanting, Albertus expands it to read:

For this reason, *noble, small* dogs, which track down hares *and other wild creatures using an odor trail,* have *a nose that is well exposed and short,* and they have a good sense of smell. *The claim that dogs with long noses have a good sense of smell does not hold up at all as it is found false by experience* [per experimentum]. (DA, 19.23; SZ, vol. II, pp. 1343–4)

Albertus does not tell his readers whether the 'experience' is his own, that of masters of the hounds, or an author of a veterinary text, but it certainly emphasizes his preference for hands-on experience. When Albertus narrates a method of hunting a deer, the details are those that an experienced hunter would give. One man puts a leaf under his tongue and imitates the sound of a fawn to draw out an older deer. If the older animal's ears are pointed forwards, it detects the trap, but if the ears are laid back, it goes towards the sound, only to be taken down with an arrow or spear. According to Stadler, who prepared the early twentieth-century edition of Albertus' *On Animals*, Albertus is the first naturalist to describe this process.[11]

Albertus shared a preference for personal experience over received wisdom with Frederick II, the author of *On the Art of Hunting with Birds*. Frederick II (d. 1250), like Albertus, maintained an active life as a scholar while fully devoted to other pursuits. In Albertus' case, these pursuits centred around his religion; in Frederick's, it was a total absorption with the politics of his day. By the time he wrote his treatise on falconry, he had been many things: king of Sicily, Italy and Germany, Holy Roman Emperor, and even, after leading the Sixth Crusade in 1228, king of Jerusalem. He had made his court a centre for learning by bringing in translators fluent in Latin, Arabic and Hebrew who helped introduce scientific works, including those of Aristotle, to the West. Among these learned men were Michael Scot and the Jew Judah ben Solomon ha-Kohen. When his resident scholars were unable to satisfy his thirst for knowledge, Frederick, who himself had become fluent in Arabic, wrote to other scholars, including the Iraqi mathematician Kamāl al-Dīn ibn Yūnus and the Andalusian Sufi philosopher Ibn Sab'in. The arts also flourished at Frederick's court, especially in developing a type of poetry that had wide influence on later Italian poets.

Frederick himself was an active scholar, speaking many languages. He almost surely penned or dictated *On the Art of Hunting with Birds*, and he personally edited and corrected the Latin text of Moamin, doing so during the siege of Faenza in 1240–41. Just as Albertus had the nickname *Doctor universalis*, a contemporary styled Frederick *Stupor mundi*, 'The Wonder of the World'. According to the late thirteenth-century Franciscan chronicler Salimbene Di Adam, Frederick II repeated an experiment first attempted by the Egyptian ruler Psammetichus (670–610 BCE) and reported by the historian Herodotus. Psammetichus sought to discover the original language of humankind by having infants raised by a mute goatherd, away from any human speech, in order to determine their 'natural' language. Although in the later fifteenth century, King James IV of Scotland conducted the same experiment, leading him to conclude that Hebrew is our primordial language, Frederick's experiment evidently did not achieve any result. According to the nineteenth-century historian Frederic W. Farrar, Frederick's 'little unfortunates died for want of lullabies!'[12] The failed experiment remains a testimony, nonetheless, to Frederick's inclination to credit experience and observation while rejecting fanciful tales from days gone by. In the fragmentary preface to *On the Art of Hunting with Birds*, he states:

> For this reason we do not follow the prince of philosophers
> [namely, Aristotle] in all cases, for he rarely or never
> experienced hunting with birds, whereas we have
> constantly delighted in and practiced it. In his book
> on animals he says that certain ones say something,
> but perhaps neither he himself nor the ones saying that
> thing ever actually saw it. Certainty does not arise out
> of hearsay [*Fides enim certa non provenit ex auditu*].
> (Prologue 1, 1, 24f.)[13]

Although there is no hard evidence that Albertus had any direct interaction with Frederick, he does cite his falconers frequently, and we may surmise that he visited Frederick's menagerie as it travelled throughout Italy and even into Germany.[14] Frederick took the menagerie with him whenever he travelled, and, as Ernst Kantorowicz says, 'Apart from administrative officials, High Court judges and the Saracen bodyguard, a complete menagerie was in his train, that brought people crowding in from miles around.'[15] It is hard to imagine Albertus passing up an opportunity such as this, for the menagerie included camels laden with burdens from the East, leopards, lynxes, apes and wild predators such as bears, panthers and lions. Other animals, such as peacocks, buzzards and all sorts of raptors and dogs, added to the spectacle, as did the great number of servants from the East who led them. The emperor even possessed a giraffe, ostriches, Indian parakeets and the quite novel sight of an elephant with a wooden tower on its back.

The giraffe abounds in *On Animals*, appearing under several names. The *camelopardulus* is a variant of the common name for the animal in antiquity, using the names of the camel and leopard. Albertus says it is from Ethiopia and has a ruddy colour. He does not specifically equate it with the giraffe. Citing Pliny (*HN*, 8.27.69), Albertus elsewhere (*DA*, 22.16; *SZ*, vol. II, pp. 1449–50) discusses the *anabula* that the Arabs and some of the Italians call the *seraph*, adding the fact that 'during our own times and in our area the Emperor Frederick possessed one of these.' The name *seraph* is a version of the Arabic *zar(r)âfa*, and it has been suggested that *anabula* is ultimately derived from *nabun*, which Pliny tells us is Ethiopian for giraffe. Finally, Albertus describes the *oraflus*, once more equating it with the *seraf*. His description of the *oraflus*, which closely resembles that of Thomas of Cantimpré, accurately describes a giraffe and tells us that the Arabs call it a *seraf*. Albertus' description is close to that of Pliny, but also differs from it in several places. Surely it is possible that Albertus saw one in Frederick's menagerie.[16]

Frederick's elephant was given to him by Malik al-Kāmil Nasir al-Din Muhammad (1180–1238 CE), a nephew of Saladin and sultan of Egypt, and Frederick sent the sultan a polar bear. Albertus inserts a story into his text that is also found in Thomas of Cantimpré that an unnamed elephant threw a donkey over a roof. Albertus adds that the donkey was fully laden (DA, 12.195; SZ, vol. II, p. 969). This might sound like an apocryphal folk tale, but Brunetto Latini, Dante's teacher who appears among the Sodomites in the seventh circle of hell, marvelled at the same tale, which occurred in Cremona. Unfortunately, we know of no passage in which Albertus claims to have seen Frederick's menagerie, but the likelihood is strong.

Fishermen were also a target for Albertus' inquiries, and they gave him details on various methods of catching fish. One passage (DA, 4.79; SZ, vol. I, p. 472) is worth quoting in full, as it shows the range of *experti* Albertus employed, the varying degrees of trust he put in them and the details he extracted from them:

An indication of their [fishes'] hearing is that we often see them flee a sound, loud voices, and the noisy clash of oars on ships. When fishermen hunt them, therefore, they move their oars lightly. Avicenna says that he has seen a certain genus of fish come to the sound of a bell and when the sound stopped, they went away.[17] In our lands it is known by all the men on the Flanders sea and that of Brabanicia [Brabant] and lower Germany that a most beautiful but bony fish, called the *vint* [shad] in the language of the inhabitants, comes in a school to the sound of chimes, cymbals, or small bells. Around the end of spring, in May, the fishermen spread a rope over the water and tie little bells to it. When they ring, this fish comes along with a school of its genus and goes into the nets.

It is interesting that Albertus lists the proofs that fish can hear in the order in which he values them. First is personal observation ('we often see them'), followed closely by evidence from fishermen. Avicenna's opinion is given next, but without either Albertus' confirmation of his statement or the usual language used when contradicting false statements.

Fishing with hooks was naturally a mainstay, used to take burbot in deep lake waters and fish that dwell at the bottom of the ocean. Albertus is at some pains to demonstrate that fish have the senses of hearing and smell without having external organs for these purposes, and in so doing, he imparts several strategies used by fishermen in his day, expanding on those in the received Aristotelian text. For example, when Aristotle claims that roasted meat is an excellent bait, Albertus adds that this is known *per experta* (from experiences). He also inserts into the same text the fact that barbels (freshwater carp) are caught by the use of a carcass or by hanging crab meat from the back of a boat, and a statement that in the sea of Flanders and Germany the fish called a *spyrinch* by the locals but a *stent* by others, while tasty for humans, drives away all other fish, even large ones. We hear also that eels are taken on hooks baited with things like frogs, insects and fish parts. An interesting comment suggests that fish discern only extreme colours and that hooks should not be dyed with these colours, indicating perhaps the use of artificial lures. Ice fishing is even hinted at when Albertus tells us that ice covering ponds and fishponds is pierced in order to allow the fish to breathe. Nets, of course, were used; and then, as now, the herring 'in the waters off of France, Great Britain, Germany, and Dacia' were caught by enormous nets, but only after the massive schools had split into two following the autumnal equinox. Albertus also claims first-hand experience in seeing an unusual method for catching barbels in Germany above the Danube. After the autumnal equinox, the fish take up residence in cracks in (retaining?) walls and between stones, doing so in such numbers that many can be caught by hand.

Albertus even notes the use of the trident for large sea fish and in the Danube to catch sturgeon, a fish that can grow too large to hunt by hook or net. But perhaps most interesting is the evidence for the use of various sorts of fish traps, some used in the fishponds that were so necessary during the 140 to 160 days a year when Catholics were forbidden to eat meat. Most common is the *gurgustium* or *sporta*, which appears to be a wicker trap, perhaps a one-way affair like a lobster trap. *Muscilliones* (crane flies?) were said to be almost irresistible to fish and were used as bait on traps. Another, ingenious method involves digging a trench on the bank near a stream and covering it with grass and wood. When the ditch is connected to the stream, the fish enter it seeking calm waters and are easily taken. Albertus, in the same passage, also describes the use of a weir. Although his language is a bit vague, a weir traditionally consists of a series of poles or stones designed to channel the fish into a certain area that can then be fenced off.[18]

It is somewhat surprising to see a lengthy section on whales. First, he relates that a whale had been captured in Frisia (between the mouths of the Rhine and the Elbe) and had yielded eleven large jars of oil, stating that he had seen both the jars and the oil itself. Next, he speaks of another that had been captured in the vicinity of Holland whose head yielded forty jars of oil, and, since he does not offer a personal comment, this was perhaps a story related to him. When a whale was stranded in Frisia, the locals secured it with ropes, attaching them to rocks and buildings, only to lose the ropes when the whale broke loose. Eventually, it beached again and was captured. His detailed description of open boat whaling is one of the most vivid passages in *On Animals*. Whalers ventured out into the ocean in fairly small boats and harpooned the whale with a lance either thrown by a hunter or shot from a crossbow. The description of the lance is meticulous, and that of the whale's struggles is as bloody as anything written by Herman Melville. Although, as Friedman points out, Albertus' section on whales and whaling owes much to Thomas of Cantimpré and Thomas's sources, this does not detract from the fact that the detailed information had to come through whalers themselves.[19] In the same paragraphs, Albertus denounces the widespread belief that a whale could be so large as to be mistaken for an island by sailors who land on it, build a fire and are then shaken off. Stories of this *aspidochelone* are found in *Physiologus*, bestiaries and the *Voyage of St Brendan*, but Albertus says that he had not been able to verify from fishermen the existence of whales as big as the ancients describe, adding that he *has* verified, however, that butchered whales can yield between 150 and 300 cartloads of bone and flesh. A bit later, he refutes a belief that males mate only once, after which they grow so fat that they equal an island in size, saying, 'Those with experience do not tell such tales.'[20]

We see Albertus here at his best, carefully weighing received tradition against personal observation and the opinions of *experti*. But immediately following this section, he repeats, without negative comment, an incredible tale about the walrus, which he calls a 'hairy whale'. Walruses sleep so soundly when hanging onto rocks with their tusks that hunters can sneak up on one, pierce its hide and slide a rope through the opening without waking the walrus up. The ropes are tied off onto rocks, stakes or trees, and the fisherman withdraws to a safe distance and hurls rocks from a sling at the beast. It awakens, tries to flee and in the process skins itself. The wounded, often skinless animal is then easily caught and dispatched. The skin, he tells us, is very strong,

fluctuantes maris ūn mgūt uf: ad mferos nō em mcipien
tib: ſi pfeilantib: premium promittitur·

Sea creature (belua) in a miniature from the Northumberland Bestiary
(c. 1250–60).

used for lifting huge weights, and is always for sale in the markets
of Cologne. The passage must be put in the 'fantastic' category,
for walruses do not sleep this way and are not hunted in this way.
They are social animals and rest or sleep in groups on ice floes
or rocky islands. They certainly would not tolerate a rope to be
passed through their skins without waking up. The attributed
sleeping posture is a misunderstanding of the fact that walruses
use their tusks to haul themselves out of the water, hooking the

tusks on the ice and then working their flippers up onto the solid surface. But, as Albertus' comment on the Cologne markets shows, they were hunted sufficiently to give Albertus some *experti* from whom he could have sought verification of the tale, although he makes no explicit reference to them. Directly after the story, he sums up the entire whale section by saying, 'These, then, are the facts which we have experienced concerning the nature of whales. We are passing over the things which the ancients wrote, since they do not find agreement among the experts.'[21]

Throughout *On Animals* and in other works, Albertus frequently makes comments alluding to Germany and surrounding areas. Often it is to make garbled animal names accessible to his readers. Consider this passage where Albertus is trying to identify what has come to him as the *ankatynos*:

> There is another animal which the Greeks call the
> *ankatynos* but which Avicenna calls the *katiz*. In our
> lands it eats chickens and is their enemy. In French
> it is called the *fissau*, but the Germans call it the
> *illibezzus*. It is an animal with a long body, like a
> greyhound, when it is a pup. (DA, 8.51; SZ, vol. 1, p. 688)

The *ankatynos* is a corruption of Aristotle's (HA, 612b10) *iktis*, a type of marten that was often kept in antiquity as a pet, and *fissau* refers to the European polecat, which is a type of ferret. *Illibezzus* is probably the forerunner of modern German *Iltis*. Other identifications include *crapa*, modern German *Krebs* for 'crab', or *orhun*, a predecessor of the modern German *Auerhahn*, the capercaillie. It is noteworthy that Albertus will often mix Latin and German names for a local animal:

> This deceiving bird seems to be, in our lands, the one that
> we call the *warchengel* [butcherbird] in German. This one

preys upon the small songbird which we call the *vinco*
[finch], but which certain Latin grammarians call the
scicendula, giving it an onomatopoetic name in imitation
of its song.

To give but a few examples, we see the German words *wisent*
for the extinct animal of the same name, *gemeze* for the modern
German *Gämse* (the chamois) and *elent*, which Albertus gives
for the Latin *equicervus*, the European elk, which is actually a
type of moose.[22]

As indicated above, Friedman argues that these sorts of
inclusions were inserted by Albertus from material taken from
Thomas of Cantimpré without acknowledging him.[23] This may
well be true in some instances, but the sheer number of the 'in
our lands' comments leads us rather to believe that Albertus
was trying to both make his received texts more accessible to
his contemporary audience and provide evidence of his own
observations and experience.

It is difficult to read Albertus' works on natural history and
not take away a mental image of a Dominican friar squatting
in a field, intensely gazing at something passers-by cannot see.
Albertus' curiosity was boundless, and no matter the official
tasks at hand, he would invariably take the time to stop and
observe the wonders of nature or interview those who knew
about them. Many examples of this behaviour have been given
above, but adding to these will give a better picture of the scope
of the interests the *Doctor universalis* pursued.

Such a survey raises some intriguing issues. The first is the
extent to which Albertus took field notes. Did he keep writing
materials with him when he went out to study nature? Did a secretary record his observations? Did he organize what he had seen
each night? No creature, however lowly, was beneath his attention.
His description of the spider in his bestiary (DA, 26.7–8, no. 2;

sz, vol. II, pp. 1742–4) contains many first-hand observations. The following passage speaks to the number of times Albertus must have stood patiently, observing local spiders:

> Spiders sometimes carry the eggs with them at all times in a little pouch, as does the spider we said lies in wait in a hole in the ground. When it carries its eggs it looks as if it were made up of two globes, one white and one black, for the eggs are very white. Other spiders, however, sometimes keep the eggs in their mouth, sometimes under their chest, and sometimes separate from them. I have personally seen all these ways. (*DA*, 26.8; *sz*, vol. II, p. 1744)

A second passage comes from a lengthy interpolation into his received text and is thus based on his own observations:

> Now it is reasonable that, due to its coldness, a spider has cold venom. But it is nevertheless more venomous in proportion to how venomous the animals it sucks on are. It is therefore commonly said that the bite of all spiders is more venomous in the autumn, because by then it has sucked on many venomous animals over the course of the summer and these have been incorporated into it. A spider, however, does not only suck on those things it hunts, but it also sometimes sucks larger animals to which it clings, much as *gusanes* or lice cling to those they suck. Thus a spider is often seen to lower itself on a thread from above, to pierce a toad or a serpent with its tongue, and to suck on it. It sometimes also pierces humans this way when it wishes to suck moisture from them. There is also another genus of aquatic spider. These do not weave at all but rather stand on top of

the water with their feet and run swiftly over it, seizing small flies that alight on the water. (DA, 8.139; SZ, vol. I, p. 729)

Albertus' comments on deer antlers leads one to believe he kept notes on antlers he found in the forest. He studied their substance, finding it porous, especially so when the deer is old, and he compares the antler's materials to the *radix cornu*, the 'root of the horn', which seems to be the keratin that covers the bone that lies at the core of the horn of other quadrupeds. By stressing that these are antlers the deer have shed of their own accord and that were found *in situ*, he emphasizes that he did not content himself with looking at trophy antlers mounted on walls. Elsewhere, when trying to determine how many 'branches' (modern 'points') deer grow, he admits he does not know, but notes he had seen one rack with 22 points. Another antler that he found under some leaves disproved the belief that they shed their antlers in the water.[24]

Barnacle geese hanging from branches by their beaks, miniature from the Harley Bestiary (c. 1230–40).

We have seen above that Albertus sometimes apparently made special side trips to observe certain phenomena or consult with various experts. This is certainly the case concerning birds of prey, but at other times, he seems always to have stopped what he was doing to observe things of interest. He speaks of studying a pheasant that had landed 'between a sage and a rue plant' when it was tired out from flying and uses the experience to shore up his observation that these birds do not migrate out of their region but move from forest to forest instead.

Albertus' friends and companions were not immune to his compulsion to study nature as he encountered it. Barnacle geese (*barliates*) were widely believed either to be born by hanging from trees and taking nourishment from their sap or to spring out of rotten logs found in the sea. Albertus scornfully condemns the belief: 'now this is entirely absurd for, just as I have said in preceding books, I and many of my friends have seen them both copulate and lay eggs as well as nourish their young.' The bird in question is the brant goose (*Branta bernicla*), and Edward Heron-Allen has thoroughly treated its legend.[25] Several factors might have contributed to the story that it arises through spontaneous generation. Heron-Allen and Maaike van der Lugt point out that the story seems to have originated in such northern countries as England, Ireland and Scotland.[26] The brant goose does not winter in these lands and migrates at high altitudes, flying south to the Wadden Sea, on the southeast edge of the North Sea, where they nest. Thus these northern locals did not have the same opportunity to see them mating as Albertus did. They inhabit brackish water, and this fact also helps explain the legend. Actual barnacles found on driftwood exhibit appendages, which resemble feathers and with which they obtain food. Since the geese were found in that same environment, the connection was there for the credulous to make. The hanging on trees may have arisen from seeing logs with barnacles on them, but Albertus will have none of this in the face of personal observation. Similarly, he refutes on the basis of personal observation the story that the heron weeps blood from the pain it incurs during mating (DA, 23.20, no. 5; SZ, vol. II, p. 1556), claiming that he has often seen the birds mating and laying eggs. Albertus had much to say about domestic birds as well, but we reserve this discussion for Chapter Eight.

Another, somewhat surprising indication of how Albertus' curious nature and his wide travels intersect is the number of times he seems to have interacted with men and women alike concerning medical matters. He spoke with, and undoubtedly examined, wisdom teeth that had erupted in a twelve-year-old girl and an eighty-year-old man. He personally saw a man who had lost all the hair on his head, which was now 'shiny as a mirror', and another who had two passages in his penis, one for urine and one for sperm.[27] Some of these encounters were rather intimate. As a Dominican, he had taken a vow of chastity, and his interactions with women, even as bishop of Regensburg, would have been quite limited, so he undoubtedly relied on other 'experts' such as midwives for anecdotal evidence. For example, in his *Questions concerning [Aristotle's] 'On Animals'*, he reveals information that he learned during confession attesting to a surprising interest in female sexuality:

It is well known that when a woman is stroked on her breasts and belly, this arouses her then for intercourse and, although she may hide the fact, she burns then like fire. And this happens for the reason that her testicles [that is, ovaries] located in the womb hang down on certain nerves and cotyledons coming from the breasts and the belly. Thus, when the breasts are touched the sperm is driven out of them and they pour it out into the womb. This effusion into the womb arouses a soporific

warmth in her, just like water cascading over limestone.
For this reason, women particularly desire intercourse
then. Therefore at that time, because of the vehemence
of the desire, they secretly urinate and emit sperm and
sometimes cleanse themselves. Therefore, crafty suitors,
as I heard in confessions in Cologne, tempt women with
this kind of trick and touch. (*QDA*², p. 411, our italics)

The reader will find many other similar examples in Chapter
Nine, where we also deal with the bounds surrounding confession, but this one example demonstrates well Albertus' hierarchy
of credibility: highest is information gleaned from personal experience and observation; second is that of the *experti* and people
whom he deems trustworthy; third is the more trusted authors,
such as Avicenna; and the lowest level is reserved for folklore
and fanciful tales, which his naturally cautious mind placed in
the 'must be proven' category.

EIGHT

Albertus and Everyday Life

O ne unexpected benefit of Albertus' insatiable curiosity is that it gives us many glimpses into everyday life in thirteenth-century Germany and its environs. Cologne's location on the Rhine had made it an important trading town from the first-century BCE Roman settlement called Colonia Claudia Ara Agrippinensium, and Albertus' Cologne possessed many markets. The main *Haymarkt* initially attracted farmers and their goods, but after it was moved into town, it grew to a length of 1 kilometre (0.6 mi.), spurring the formation of other markets such as a butter market, beer market, meat market and more. During Albertus' lifetime, the town even set up its gallows in the Haymarket. The market is still celebrated in modern times at the *Mittelaltermarkt* of Cologne by a group that re-enacts the markets of 1399 CE, displaying products such as clothes, leather-work, jewellery and falcons alongside entertainers such as jugglers and musicians.

We have seen that the raw products of the cobblers in Augsburg attracted a multitude of ravens, and we must imagine that cobblers of Cologne exhibited their shoes and boots in the markets as well.[1] Albertus tells us that shoes made from the hide at that place on an ass's back where loads are placed are very sturdy, allowing the traveller to traverse even rocky terrain with no discomfort. In fact, he says, they grow harder over time and eventually become too hard to wear. Given the fact that

Dominicans were forbidden from travelling by conveyance and were directed to travel on foot, this passage surely seems to reflect Albertus' own experience with such footwear.[2] In discussing the hide of the hippopotamus, his received text points out that 'the thicker part . . . furnishes the soles of boots', and to this Albertus adds, 'The thinner part [furnishes] the laces of their bindings.'[3] Was the skin of this exotic animal actually for sale in his Cologne? He clearly states that walrus hides, also very tough, were on sale in Cologne, and straps made from them were used for lifting heavy objects, perhaps connected to a great wheel within which a bear walked to provide the power to draw water from wells or lift heavy stones to the top of walls under construction, a sight Albertus had seen himself (DA, 22.145, no. 107; SZ, vol. II, p. 1541).[4]

As a Dominican and then a bishop, Albertus naturally had limited choices as to his attire. According to Rudolph of Nijmegen's biography, only after Albertus' death did Godfrey of Duisburg see him, in a vision, clothed in noble vestments and garments covered with jewels – a metaphor for the glory Albertus receives in heaven. Albertus leaves us a few insights, nonetheless, into the fashion of his times. Items of clothing were surely for sale in the markets, and Albertus knew rather a lot about the raw products that went into making them. For example, when speaking of a certain shellfish (the perna), he notes that 'it is known by the yellow and red fleece within its shell which is very valuable and from which precious ornaments for clothes and veils are made.' The perna probably refers to Pinna nobilis, a bivalve that reaches up to 45 centimetres (1.5 ft) in length and lives exclusively in the Mediterranean. The 'fleece' is the byssus, often called the beard, by which the shell attaches itself to the sea floor. These fine filaments, often dyed yellow with lemon juice and spices, have since antiquity been spun into ultrafine threads and then made into cloth called 'sea-silk'. It also is clear that Albertus knew about silk production, speaking of it in his bestiary entries under the animal names *bombex* and *lanificus*. He says that the terms are interchangeable but gives each its separate entry. He speaks of its larval stage and the fact that it produces fine silk when it eats mulberry leaves, and says that eating lettuce leads it to produce inferior silk. He accurately describes the larva's pupal stage wherein the larva spins yellow or white silk from its mouth and stresses that any other colours are artificial. He even describes the adult mating cycle and how, as is still done today, the female's eggs are collected on white cloth and put aside for the entire winter, to be brought out into the direct sunlight in the spring. The *varius*, a type of squirrel, has its place as well: 'its colouration is delightful and its pelt is exceptionally useful in the ornamentation of clothes.' So, too, the otter 'is dusky in colour but its pelt has a shininess to it, which is why the trim on clothes is made from it'. Further, 'Those who take delight in their clothes are decorated with [the ermine's] pelt' (DA, 22.101; SZ, vol. II, p. 1452). Not only does Albertus comment on clothes available for sale, but he provides some insight into their production. He briefly describes women at work weaving cloth on a loom (DA, 15.15; SZ, vol. II, p. 1091) and mentions that weavers use sea urchin skins on the upper portion of the loom (DA, 19.30; SZ, vol. II, p. 1347). It is interesting that the former passage concerning the women is an updating of Aristotle's *On the Generation of Animals* (717a36f.), which describes weaving on an upright loom where the warp threads are held taut by stone weights.[5]

Fantastically, Albertus also suggests that as a sign of its capacity for instruction, 'the ape learns to stitch cloth together', and with this craft, 'an ape makes a tunic.' Albertus does regard the ape or monkey as so receptive to instruction that it 'immediately imitates what it sees' and seems capable of performing many human tasks – so much so that he recommends raising a

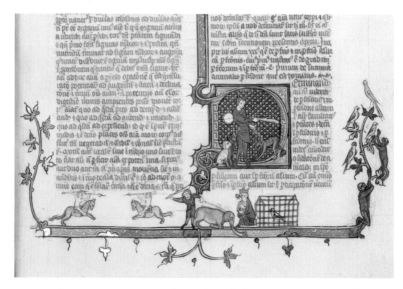

Scenes of training a monkey and an elephant, miniature from Albertus Magnus, *De animalibus* (14th century).

dog, 'the most easily taught animal', in the company of a monkey so that the dog will learn from it how to do many human tasks. Might Albertus have seen a monkey someone had trained to imitate the motions of weaving?[6]

Fish Markets

Certainly there was a fish market in this city on the Rhine, and Albertus speaks of dishonest fishmongers who take the heart out of a living salmon and, since they know the heart beats the longest outside the body of all fish, place it near the fish for sale, giving the impression that all the fish for sale are equally fresh. The fishmongers also probably sold byproducts of their fish to other manufacturers. After a discussion of the glues made from the hides of cows, sheep and goats, Albertus mentions that an even better glue is made from the bladders of fish, especially sturgeon and cod. In turn, those who produced the glue would sell it to carpenters and those who made furniture, such as the craftsmen who made footstools from the antlers of elk. It was probably also used by those who made the brushes for combing flax or human hair.[7]

Cologne's *Biermarkt* has a special connection with Albertus. In 1212 Emperor Otto IV gave permission to levy a tax called the *Bierpfennig* (Beer-Penny) on mills and beer for a period of three years. In 1238 Emperor Frederick II bestowed the same privilege on Cologne's archbishop Conrad von Hochstaden. During the Great Arbitration of 1258, discussed above, Albertus, as one of the arbiters, was instrumental in persuading the archbishop to share the *Bierpfennig* revenue with the city government for a period of ten years. It is a bit curious that the only mention of beer in *On Animals* is as an ingredient in a poultice used to treat sores on a horse (DA, 22.66; SZ, vol. II, p. 1486).

Jewellers told Albertus about their use of the so-called hyena stone, reportedly found in that animal's eyes, and he also knew about necklaces and knife handles made from the thick part of certain seashells. When he describes the varying densities of teeth, he notes that the teeth of elephants and whales are made of solid bone and can be sculpted or engraved. It is likely that such products were sold as ecclesiastical art (even as luxury book covers) or for personal adornment. He likewise describes the methods goldsmiths use to make gold and silver easy to draw into threads in order to decorate shields. Albertus' interest in and knowledge of the minerals of his homeland are displayed in his *On Minerals*. Albertus outlines his methodology for this study, admitting that despite intense searches in various parts of the world, he had not seen the entire *On Minerals* of Aristotle but had to content himself with excerpts. In fact, this work is spurious and appears in manuscripts attached to translations of Aristotle's *Meteorology*. To compensate for his inability to obtain the complete 'Aristotelian' work, Albertus says:

Therefore, I shall state, in a manner which can be
supported by reasoning, either what has been handed
down by philosophers or what I have found out by my
own observations. For at one time I became a wanderer,
making long journeys to mining districts, so that I could
learn by observation the nature of metal.

As will be seen below, Albertus is referring to a period in his life,
apparently when he was fairly young, when he toured Germany
'as an *exul* [wanderer/exile]', visiting several mining and smelting sites.[8] When Albertus visited mining works, he would talk
to miners (*fossores*) and smelters (*depuratores*), and we know the
names of several mining districts he visited: the mines of
Rammelsberg near the mines of Goslar in the Harz Mountains
and now a UNESCO World Heritage Site; Lübeck in far northern
Germany; Freiberg, 'Free Mountain', mining silver; and a place
he calls *mons aeris* (Copper Mountain, *Kupferberg* in German).
Wyckoff believes Albertus may also have visited the so-called
Cologne Pits near Ems and the Lüderich mines that produced
lead and lay near Cologne.[9] Both these areas were probably
under the control of the archbishopric of Cologne, and the
Lüderich mine may have provided income for Conrad of
Hochstaden's renovation of Cologne Cathedral. Albertus' close
observations offer insights into the mining of the time, such as
the fact that in Germany he had seen selenite produced in such
quantities that carts were full of it and that he had seen it in
France as well, probably in the quarries at Montmartre, near
Paris, or the fact that there were deposits of jet along the Baltic
Sea in eastern Prussia.[10]

The sheer number of jewels on the Shrine of the Three
Kings in the cathedral at Cologne, discussed above and as seen
in Chapter One, reminds us of the heavy trade in precious
jewels that existed in Albertus' time, and Albertus' *On Minerals*

grants insight into the jewellers' and metalworkers' craft and trade. For example, we find that when gold is drawn out into very thin sheets, it can be woven in with silk, inserted into pictures as gold leaf or used by bell makers mixing tin with copper to give the finished product a deeper sound. Pearls, of course, were widely used in jewellery, and Albertus reports that while the best are from India, Germany does have its own from areas along the English Channel. In fact, he tells us, he 'had ten pearls in [his] mouth' during a single meal that included oysters. Craftsmen shared information on the smelting of silver and the making of brass, while jewellers are probably the source of the statement that jasper is best when it is set in silver. Albertus also tells us how steel is made so hard that it can serve as an engraving tool for gems. Just like the mendacious fishmongers mentioned above, it seems that counterfeiters used an arsenical compound called *falcones* to whiten copper in order to pass it off as silver.[11]

The markets of Cologne surely dealt in foodstuffs. We have dealt in Chapter Seven with the information on hunting and fishing found in Albertus, but he also regularly speaks of the eating habits of the time. It is not surprising that most of this information comes from the casual comments Albertus interjects into the bestiary section of *On Animals*, for here he is less bound by any received text. It is also notable that Albertus offers far more comments on birds and fish as human food than he does on quadrupeds.

In the *Questions concerning [Aristotle's] 'On Animals'*, however, we learn that people who gulp their food have a shorter lifespan, and the reasons why some people who eat more are thin while others who eat less are fat: 'Indeed, people eat incomparably more at a sitting in cold places than in warm ones. Thus, one Pole or German eats more in a single day than a Lombard or a Frenchman does in four.'[12]

In *On Animals*, Albertus often comments at the end of an entry on that animal's use as food. The entry on the thrush offers a fine example. The thrush 'sings in the spring, and has a varied song and good flesh, fit to eat', while others, like the snipe, are 'sweet to eat'. We find that the medieval population of his time enjoyed dormice as much as the Romans did, and, like the Romans, the people of Carpathia and Bohemia set out vessels for the dormice to hibernate in over the winter, only to be harvested later, perhaps being served with roasted chestnuts and eggs. He probably spent some time interviewing cooks, for to Aristotle's discussion of the qualities of broths made from fatty animals, he adds those made from cow and – unexpectedly – dog, while elsewhere he tells us that wild hares are best cooked in an oven or a pan. Albertus even gives us a sense of local cheese manufacturing when he says that the milk from animals that have a row of breasts on their belly is not fit for cheese making. He also describes a cheese that is called 'one-and-a-half' (*sexqualiter*) because it is made with equal parts of goat's and cow's milk, and speaks of various items used to curdle the milk, such as rennet, fig juice and a red flower that grows in the high fields and has downy fibres. When the flower is dried and mixed with milk, it makes a fine coagulant. In all likelihood, this is *Silybum marianum*, known also as milk-thistle. Albertus also reminds us that 'wine, milk, and beer . . . are both food and drink.' Cologne was (and is) famous for its wines, and Albertus discusses the production of 'formic wine', which took its name from the Latin word for ant, *formica*, because it was first chemically isolated using crushed ants, who use the acid as a form of defence. Wine does contain some formic acid on its own, but Albertus says that putting the staves of the barrel over an ant mound will impart to them a sharp taste, which in turn is passed on to the wine itself. He even expounds on the properties of various kinds of water. Albertus inserts the fact that there is water in Sicily that is so acidic that people there use it in place of vinegar and that in Germany many places have astringent water (*aqua acris*) that they used to make laxatives.[13]

The young did not escape the medieval table; the chicks of a magpie, skinned and eaten, were said to sharpen one's eyesight, and those of the rook are 'fit to eat' if similarly treated. The flesh of the swan is tough, and the crane should be left to age before it is plucked, a process known today as 'hanging', wherein the taste of birds like pheasants or quail is enhanced. Eating certain other birds may have consequences: eating a jackdaw will cause your head to itch.[14]

Because of his travels, Albertus experienced both freshwater and saltwater fish from such diverse places as Germany, France and Italy. Thus he points out that the Italians do not hunt dolphins but the Germans do, with the result that dolphins help Italian fishermen, but flee from Germans. Likewise, Albertus tells us that the *murena* is present in the waters of France and Germany. Three types exist in eastern Germany, one of which is a lamprey that has nine spots, and its flesh, while tasty, is unhealthy unless it is pickled in hot spices and strong wine.[15] The mullet is tasty, but eating it can come with consequences:

> When eaten it diminishes the sexual drive and dulls the eyes, and one who eats it often reeks of fish. If this fish is killed in wine and if this wine is drunk, it takes away the desire for wine.

And one must be cautious in the choice of sea anemone:

> One is quite small and is good for the health, especially when its moisture is dried out. For this reason, people hunt it in wintertime and eat it salted during the summer as a guard against the heat. The other is large and spotted

with white. This one carries disease and is the undoing of anyone who eats it.

He advises us that the flesh from the back of the *huso*, likely a sturgeon, is comparable to veal and that from its belly to pork, and that a sturgeon's liver is so sweet as to be cloying.[16]

We have spoken in Chapter Seven about the lore Albertus learned from hunters and fishermen. We will turn next to agriculture, husbandry and hunting with birds of prey. Albertus presumably had ready access to farmyards, and it appears that he investigated them thoroughly. The issues surrounding the copulation, hatching and rearing of chickens especially intrigued him, and much of the information he reports would have implications on anyone trying to maximize the survival rate and control the male/female proportions in the flock. For example, Albertus takes up the issue of whether an egg's shape can be a sign of the sex of the hatchling. Aristotle had stated that long, pointed eggs produce females and rounder eggs produce males. Michael Scot's translation, however, states the opposite, and this was the 'Aristotle' that came to Albertus. Complicating the issue, Avicenna reports that males are produced from rounded, short eggs and hens from the sharp, pointed eggs. Albertus first says that the fact that his version of Aristotle got it wrong was due to improper copying and not to the actual words of the great philosopher, and he points to Avicenna to back up his beliefs. Moreover, he says his own experience supports Avicenna's version as more accurate than that passed along by Michael Scot's translation. It is interesting that this debate still elicits lively discussions on the Internet, even though science has shown that there is no correlation between egg shape and the chick's gender. It is clear that Albertus took the time to study the eggs and track the gender of the hatchlings, perhaps doing so by interrogating the farmers. Further, when discussing Aristotle's report that some eggs can be incubated artificially by being buried in the warm ground of Egypt, he adds a contemporary method consisting of putting the eggs in warm vessels covered in warm tow.[17]

As had Aristotle, Albertus expresses a recurring interest in the effects of castration on humans and domesticated animals, adding several graphic details to Aristotle's description of the process in calves and sows, bringing to life some of the realities of medieval farming. He particularly studied the effect castration had on roosters. He notes with surprise that a rooster sometimes takes over the care of chicks if the hen dies and that the rooster becomes softer of voice and ceases to copulate until his parenting chores are finished. In the same passage, he claims to have confirmed visually that capons (castrated roosters) do the same thing and elsewhere adds that he had seen cases of capons plucking their chests and rubbing them in nettles. Sitting on the chicks soothes the itching, and the capon delights in becoming a surrogate mother. Then, as now, domestic chickens attracted a plethora of predators: weasels (*mustela*), the 'stinker' (*putorius*, a mustelid, probably the European polecat, *Mustela putorius*), foxes and cats. The *putorius* and fox were especially harmful, tearing the throats out of chickens without eating them.[18]

He even refutes the story that partridge hens conceive through the air by referring to the copulation of domesticated partridges, 'which I have watched with my very own eyes'. We are told that wild ducks came in two colour patterns, and he carefully differentiates between the males' and females' plumage patterns. Domestic ducks, presumably kept for feathers, eggs and meat, are white, ash-grey or a combination of the two. Duck flesh is more tender than that of geese, which were another source of feathers, eggs and meat, and Albertus is quite thorough in treating the genus, carefully describing four wild types he had personally observed, as well as domestic geese, one of which, he claims, was more than sixty years old. As he often does, Albertus considers the edibility of the animal and says the flesh of geese is 'usually cold and dry, hard and melancholic, and indigestible', so much so that one wild goose caught in 'our lands' was boiled for three days straight but could not be rendered edible. He else-where speaks of the egg-laying behaviour of peacocks and cranes, getting his information for the former from 'one who is very experienced with the bird' and stating of the latter that 'there are domesticated, breeding cranes.' Since the crane migrated yearly out of Germany, keeping a domesticated population made sense. Umberto Albarella and Richard Thomas argue per-suasively that although herons are not particularly tasty, their presence on the banquet tables of the wealthy served as a status symbol indicating a certain level of wealth and privilege.[19] Further, the heron was a prime target for fowlers and their birds. Another bird that served as a social marker was the swan. Albertus notes that domesticated swans have their wings cut off at the first joint to prevent their flying away, a process that stops the birds from leaving and presumably keeps the muscle tissue tenderer. Yet Albertus declares that swan flesh is dark and tough, a fact that apparently did not prevent the swan from adorning the tables of the wealthy and being a prime target for fowlers.[20]

When discussing the generation of bees, Albertus states: 'I have already investigated a beehive *experimento* [at first hand]. There I found many which were partly larvae and partly bees that were beginning to form from the *gusanes* [worm-like larvae]' (*DA*, 15.43; *SZ*, vol. II, pp. 1103–4). This is an excellent description first of the larval stage of the honeybee and then of its pupal stage, and it only seems possible if Albertus had cut open part of a beehive in order to study it – or, more likely, watched as a beekeeper did it.

According to Albertus, the *alches/elent* was apparently domesticated by some and could be ridden in one day 'as far as a horse can be ridden in three' (DA, 2.22; SZ, vol. I, p. 295). The usual translation for *alches* is 'elk', which can lead to some confusion. For Americans, an elk is a very large deer with pointed horns. The European elk, *Alces alces*, is the Old World version of the American moose, whose horns are flatter and wider, and is not an animal one normally thinks of as able to be ridden. Yet a search of the Internet will yield modern pictures of people riding them, and rock drawings from Russia, dating to the end of the Stone Age and the beginning of the Iron Age, do show moose in halters bearing riders on their backs.

In the same book, Albertus gives a fairly long description of the *bufletus*, a term commonly used by medieval authors to refer to the European bison or wisent (*Bison bonasus*). Yet Albertus' description does not fit this animal:

> This one is tamed and a ring is placed in its nostrils by
> which it is led around. It has many wondrous properties.
> Its body is black with but few hairs, so much so that it has
> almost none on its tail. Its head is small compared to the
> size of its body and its horns are small, almost like those
> of the domestic goat. They sometimes hang down near
> its neck toward the inside of its chest and sometimes are
> erect. It is strong and pulls the load of almost two horses.
> It has short legs that are very thick and strong, and
> the cheese made from its milk is very solid and earthy.
> (DA, 2.30; SZ, vol. I, p. 299)

This animal is clearly the Italian Mediterranean buffalo (*Bufala Mediterranea Italiana*), which is the source of buffalo mozzarella so prized today, and which Albertus would have known about from his visits to Italy. It closely resembles the African water buffalo and may have been imported to Italy as early as the sixth or seventh centuries.

Finally, we come to the matter of veterinary medicine. In the bestiary section of *On Animals*, Albertus has lengthy sections devoted to the care, feeding and curing of dogs, horses and birds of prey, three animals that were vital for many aspects of the culture but were especially part of the lives of the nobility. In doing so, he is once more following an ancient tradition. There is evidence of veterinary medicine in the Code of Hammurabi (d. 1750 BCE) and on Egyptian papyri of the Twelfth Dynasty, dating to around 1850 BCE. Xenophon, a student of Socrates, wrote three works that are relevant to the history of veterinary medicine: *On Hunting, The Art of Horsemanship* and *The Cavalry Commander*. Each of these contains the same sort of information that interested Albertus, but none is a work devoted to veterinary medicine as such. For this, we turn to Greek works such as the *Corpus hippiatricum Graecorum*, an early Byzantine collection of excerpts from largely fourth-century CE Greek authors on treatments for horses, mules and donkeys. Latin provides us with three treatises that deal with treating equids that were ascribed to Chiron, Pelagonius and Vegetius, whose dates range from the

Buffalo farm in Capaccio Paestum, Italy, 2019.

late fourth to the mid-fifth centuries CE. Although there seems to be no evidence that Albertus used these sources directly, he is clearly part of the same tradition and, as is his wont, he relied heavily on the experts who cared for these animals.

Albertus' section on dogs is found in book 22 of *On Animals*, and he begins by stipulating that since dogs have so many uses for humans, it seems proper to 'pass on the skill by which noble dogs can be had, nourished, and cured if they are sick' (DA, 22.27, no. 16; SZ, vol. II, p. 1458). He begins by speaking first of hounds and then of greyhounds, listing the traits one should look for in selecting the most noble examples of the breeds and then enumerating the special diet newborn dogs should be fed at different points in their first year of life. He speaks of the specific talents of various breeds for service as watchdogs, bird dogs, trackers and the like. He ends by listing 'cures' for canine diseases, many of which appear also in Pliny and aim to cure things like impetigo, scabies and 'leprosy'; heal wounds; and eliminate vermin.

In listing cures for worms that arise on injured dogs, he says that expert hunters state that all such worms die if freshly dried yellow lavender is hung from the animal's neck. And one who is 'especially experienced' said that the plant, ground and put into drink, was equally effective for oxen and horses. After the worms are gone, one should smear the wound with butter made in the month of May, which encourages the dog to lick the wound. Some of the treatments have modern parallels. Small 'ladies' dogs', he says, almost always die of constipation and should be fed oatmeal or oat bread. Modern veterinarians often prescribe additional fibre for small dogs, whose anal glands are prone to swell, blocking efficient emptying of the bowels. In a very strange passage, Albertus relates without hesitation the following:

> The dog is by far the most easily taught animal. They therefore learn the mimetic works of actors. If anyone

Folio from the beginning of book 22, 'On the Nature of Animals', in Albertus Magnus, *De animalibus* (14th century).

should wish to find this out for himself, let him take a dog
born out of a vixen or from a fox, if that can be done. If it
cannot, let him take a red dog from among those that are
his watchdogs and let him accustom it while it is young to
keeping the company of a monkey. For with her he becomes
accustomed to do many human things. And if he should
have intercourse with the monkey and the monkey should
give birth to a dog, that dog will be the most praiseworthy
of all for games. (DA, 22.30; SZ, vol. II, p. 1460)

Albertus elsewhere allows that hybrids can exist, the most
obvious example of which is the mule, and he certainly knew of
wolves breeding with dogs. But this sort of story is rather outside
his usual comfort zone, and one would expect it to be prefaced
by 'some say' or 'it is said', his usual disclaimers. Further, in an
earlier discussion on hybrids, he correctly states that

animals which are similar in species and genus naturally
intermingle through copulation. In addition to these
there are those whose nature is close to, though not
exactly in, the same species, and this is so especially
for those which do not have a great difference in shape
and size and which are alike in the length of time their
pregnancy lasts. (DA, 16.130; SZ, vol. II, p. 1226)

He then lists the fox, dog and wolf as examples of this tenet but
reiterates the monkey and dog story, saying that 'this is seen
sometimes.' Other examples represent 'the opinion of some',
including the ancient belief that the mating of female dogs and
tigers produces the tall hunting dogs of India. Albertus is clearly
placing the monkey and dog story with sounder examples of
hybridism. There is one possibility for this seeming lapse on his
part, namely that he is repeating a story that aims to account for

the appearance of baboons, perhaps especially the Hamadryas baboon, *Papio hamadryas*. This animal has a face with a canine-like muzzle, and, while a true monkey, it travels on all fours like a dog. Indeed, the ancient Greek word for baboon is *kynokephalos*, 'dog head'. We shouldn't be excessively critical of Albertus here, for an Internet search on the terms 'monkey dog hybrid' will lead a curious reader to an astonishing number of doctored photographs and to articles that still proclaim the possibility of such a hybrid.

Albertus devotes many more pages to equine care than he does to that of dogs. A fair amount of Albertus' text shows a clear link to the work of Rutilius Taurus Aemilianus Palladius. Palladius wrote in the late fourth to mid-fifth century CE, and his *Work of Agriculture* (*Opus agriculturae*) was well known in the Middle Ages and used as a practical manual for all aspects of work on the farm. He also wrote *On Veterinary Medicine* (*De veterinaria medicina*), which contains very detailed remedies for a wide variety of equine complaints.

As he did with dogs, Albertus begins by listing the most desirable properties of horses, breed by breed. He lists four types of broken – that is, not wild – horses in his lands: war horses, also called chargers (*bellici*, *dextrarii*); palfreys (*palefridi*); race-horses (*curriles*); and workhorses (*runcini*). The first two types, for example, should not be castrated, and while workhorses do most of the heavy jobs, Albertus admits that other horses are often used for such chores as well.

Albertus then describes the horse's diet and moves on to a list of over thirty diseases, conditions and injuries, each with appropriate cures. There had been a strong tradition of written manuals on equine medicine in later antiquity, but these works seem to have had limited direct effect on practical medieval horse medicine. Rather, Albertus mostly relies on an anonymous *Book on the Treatment of Horses* (*Liber de cura equorum*) and was probably familiar with the work of Jordanus Ruffus, a soldier in the stables of Frederick II.[21] Many, if not most, of the cures Albertus mentions entail the application of poultices consisting of herbs and substances such as soot, honey, spiderwebs, lard, butter and quicklime. Other treatments offer insights into the equipment that must have existed to control large animals and to the harshness of some of the methods used. For example, to treat an unnamed disease whose symptoms seem to approximate those of foot-and-mouth disease, Albertus says the following:

> The cure for this consists of first scraping away the ulcerousness and stickiness from beneath the tongue. Afterward, mix two spoonsful of soot and one of salt, grind well, mix with one bulb of garlic, and rub the spot with the mixture. After this, cut the two veins which are beneath the tongue and, on the fourth or fifth day, bleed the horse from the neck vein in proportion to its strength. (DA, 22.59; SZ, vol. II, p. 1482)

Bleeding a horse seems to have been a regular treatment, and Albertus gives directions for the amount to be bled and the position and frequency of the process. In a discussion of how to clear dead tissue from a horse's wound, he recommends a mixture of quicklime, seashells, salt and deer horn, all ground fine and mixed with lye or urine, specifying that the urine of a virgin boy works best. To cure itching in a horse, take the intestines of a young chicken, put them in the horse's mouth and, holding its head upright, force the horse to swallow them.

We have discussed above the intense interest Albertus had in birds of prey, and it is fitting that his discussion of falcons in the bestiary section of *On Animals* is located under the rubric 'falcon', for, Albertus says, 'We call every bird of prey used in hawking a falcon.' Thus this wide-ranging section includes all

types of raptors, forming a separate unit within the discussion
on birds. He divides the discussion into 24 chapters, within
which he describes what he feels are ten genera of noble falcon,
three of ignoble and two of mixed traits. Chapter Eighteen is
devoted to cures of goshawks, and he cites William the Falconer
as his source. Most of the text, however, parallels the text of a
certain Dancus Rex, a supposed king of India. In fact, most
manuscripts of Dancus pair it with the work of William, the
falconer of King Roger, who has been identified as Roger
(Ruggero) II, king of Sicily from 1130 to 1154. It is thus most
reasonable to believe that these works were Albertus' source.
Chapter Nineteen adds additional veterinary information
'according to the falconer of the Emperor Frederick'. Chapters
20–24 branch off into various types of hawks and other
raptors.[22]

Throughout, Albertus offers very pragmatic advice for training a falcon to hunt and how to adjust its diet for different
situations. The range of treatments for the birds is as impressive
as the various maladies that affect them. We hear of sneezing
fits, different kinds of gout, constipation, mange and itch, swol-
len feet, lost talons, lung disease and more. In addition to the
expected potions and poultices, some cases call for cauterization
near the eyes or the severing and cauterization of a blood vessel
near the bird's head. Since the birds were rather expensive and
represented the investment of a good deal of time in training,
some of the cures are fairly elaborate:

> If it should be that it has *bulsus* (that is, it is infirm in
> the lungs), take one ounce of crushed orpiment and nine
> pepper seeds, crush them together, and serve them to the
> falcon with warm meat. Another way is to take three
> pieces of lard, such as a falcon can swallow, and dip them
> in honey. Next, sprinkle iron filings over them and place

them in the falcon's gullet. Do this for three days and
serve it nothing else at all. On the fourth day, take a small
pig and get it very drunk with strong, clear wine. Then,
once it is drunk, warm its chest at a fire. When it is well
warmed, strike its chest so that the blood ascends to the
chest and is mixed with the wine. Then kill the pig and
immediately dip the chest that is still warm into goat's
milk. Feed the falcon for three days with such food and
it will be healed. (*DA*, 23.86; *SZ*, vol. II, p. 1604)

Falconry may have been the sport of the wealthy, but Albertus
is equally interested in passing along what we might call 'household management' for the less well off. For example, we learn
that when one of the many storks making their nests on German
chimneys ejected one of its young, the common people believed
it was paying a sort of rent to the owner. But beyond doubt, the
majority of household management passages deal with the problem of vermin invading the living spaces of humans. Many of
these passages can be traced back to ancient authors, but their
frequency still speaks to the prevalence of these pests in medieval
Germany. To prevent moths in clothes, one should wrap them
in lion's skin, a fact that may have come to Albertus from an
Arabic source. Mosquitoes were no less of a problem in Albertus'
time than in ours, but repellents differed greatly, including fumi-
gation with elephant dung and horsehair attached to the door of
a house. While these treatments were probably folk remedies,
Albertus offers a practical and more modern-sounding remedy:
canopies made of netting. Moreover, while many factors play
into what attracts mosquitoes, the amount of carbon dioxide a
person exhales is a primary factor, and Albertus correctly states
that 'they follow the moist spirit that animals exhale, especially
that of humans. This is the reason that, late in the day, they fly
in the air directly over the heads of those that are sweating.'[23]

At this time, long before chemical repellants, fleas were a great problem, and Albertus reports many ways to rid a house of the pests. One can keep them off a dog by smearing the dog with olive oil (*DA*, 22.34, no. 16; *SZ*, vol. II, p. 1463). Using Pliny without citing him, Albertus states that people say that cuckoo's earth, taken from the spot where one hears the bird's call for the first time and sprinkled in a given place, will stop fleas from breeding there. Another passage, citing Avicenna and folklore ('some say'), contains a list of efficacious substances such as bitter gourd, blackberry juice, goat's blood and cabbage or oleander leaves. A final flea repellent makes a certain amount of sense, namely the use of hedgehog fat. Take a salted hedgehog and boil it, skimming off the fat. Smear the fat on a stick, put the stick in a flea-infested spot, and the fleas will throng to it, whereupon you should toss the stick outside. At first glance rather fatuous, this method may be based on the fact that hedgehogs are plagued by fleas. It follows by homeopathic logic that its fat might also attract them. Lice, like fleas, were thought to be spontaneously generated and, also like them, were a grave nuisance to the medieval world. Even today, body and head lice are quite difficult to eradicate, but at least the treatments have improved. Albertus claims that 'many have found by experience' that a concoction of stavesacre, mercury, oil and butter or lard kills lice when it is smeared on a cloth and carried with a person's clothing. Or the clothing could be treated by fumigating it with a mixture of mercury and lead sprinkled on a coal fire. This undoubtedly killed the lice while also imperilling the health of those carrying out the procedure. Other pests preying on humans included bedbugs that lived in cracks in the wall near beds and ear-invading centipedes. A somewhat more unexpected problem arose from frogs that, at the onset of winter, 'enter people's homes and sometimes creep into a fold in one's garment over the groin or belly'.[24]

Albertus is a source for many other types of pest-control devices. Sulphur mixed with wild marjoram, ground and scattered over an anthill, will drive the insects out. Stag's horn, ground and used as a fumigant, will drive out poisonous insects, as will storax resin, except in the case of the *multipes* (centipede or millipede), which likes the smell so much that it can be lured into a jar with it and captured, clinging to it so tightly that even if split in two it does not relinquish its hold. It is, however, repelled by the smoke of fleabane. If all else fails, one can follow Pliny's advice and burn ass's lung to cause all vermin to flee a house. Mice and rats, of course, were virtually an uncontrolled problem, not only for the damage they did to stores of food, but, as would soon be alleged in the Black Death of the fourteenth century, for carrying infected fleas. Albertus says they eat seeds, bread and cheese, trying each cheese in turn until they find their favourite. Effective mouse poisons include yellow arsenic worked into a paste and a mixture of lead oxide, hellebore and flour.[25]

NINE

Human Sexuality, Gender and Race

Albertus shows great interest in the details of human sexuality, but this is not merely a prurient interest. Neither was he writing a medieval *Joy of Sex*. Rather, as a bishop, he was charged to hear confessions. As mentioned previously, since the Fourth Lateran Council (1215), laypeople were required to confess at least once each year, around Easter. To accommodate them, not only did bishops and their parish priests hear confessions, but so too did specially trained members of the mendicant orders. These were charged with interrogating laymen and -women to elicit a comprehensive list of their sins, including – and especially – sexual sins like adultery, fornication, incest or sodomy. Confessors were also charged with correcting married partners who engaged in sexual intercourse during prohibited times on the Church calendar or who did so solely for pleasure and not for the purpose of procreation.

Not only did Albertus provide instruction on the Church's teachings via the confessional, but from it he received insights into sexual practices. For example, confessions may have provided him anecdotal information regarding auto-stimulation and common contraceptive practices. Certain animals, Albertus notes, especially desire sexual intercourse: these are 'especially woman and the mare'. Only mares and women desire sexual intercourse after becoming pregnant, and lustful women are said to 'whinny' like mares. Albertus adds, 'I, moreover, have seen a lustful woman who told me with her own mouth that she exposed herself in similar fashion to the wind and took great pleasure in catching up wind in her uterus.' The woman who described this behaviour to Albertus 'with her own mouth' likely did so in confession.[1]

Folk recipes for aphrodisiacs also existed: 'if wolf's penis is roasted in the oven and sliced, and part of it is chewed, it immediately arouses desire for intercourse.' Or one might need an antaphrodisiac:

> If someone mixes the right testicle of a wolf with nut oil and gives it to a woman to put in her vulva with a bit of wool, it will take away from her the desire for intercourse, even if she is a whore.

Other recipes promote conception:

> They say also that if equal amounts of the bile of this animal [the gazelle], the semen from the testicles of a fox, pepper, and the seed of garden rocket are taken to equal the weight of an *aureus*, and two ounces of honey are added, and an electuary is made from this, and a woman holds it in wool, she will conceive when she lies with her husband.

Here Albertus avoids endorsing such treatments by citing 'some people', but elsewhere, he may also name a source without endorsing the account. For example, following Avicenna, he cites the otherwise unknown philosopher Symerion, who says that the bite of a certain spider – perhaps the wolf spider – will produce an erection. Still, in an age when pregnancy could readily lead to death, its prevention could be desirable. Elsewhere,

Albertus notes that after intercourse, pregnancy may be avoided 'if the woman immediately rises and moves about or leaps, or if she should urinate', causing the male's sperm to slip out of her womb.

Although Aristotle's authority seems to recommend this, Albertus often is critical of similar claims, even when he records them, and indicates as much with the important qualifier (or disclaimer) that 'some people say' or 'it is said'. For example, he notes that 'if, after her period, a woman drinks hare rennet for three straight days, *some people say* that it prevents conception' (italics ours). This does not imply his endorsement. In the same way, Albertus records folk recipes that act as love charms. Some people say that 'if a man's penis is anointed with' the dung of the animal called *algazel* in Arabic (likely a gazelle) 'and if he has intercourse with his wife this way, she will always adore him'.

Physicians examining a woman for blockages in the womb that prevent conception, miniature from Albertus Magnus, *De animalibus* (14th century).

Similarly, 'when the bile [of a wolf] is mixed with rose oil and is smeared on someone's eyebrows, he will be beloved by the women when they go walking with him.'[2]

Albertus also had an abiding medical interest in the details of sexual intercourse. He affirms that frequent intercourse and frequent male ejaculation will have a deleterious effect on the human body, 'emptying' it of its moisture, leading to untimely death. He cites as authorities Avicenna and Constantine the African (d. before 1099), a Benedictine monk who composed the treatise *On Intercourse* (*De coitu*) and produced Latin translations of Arabic medical works. Both Avicenna and Constantine proclaim that 'those who engage in a great deal of intercourse die the quicker for it' (*DA*, 22.8; *SZ*, vol. II, p. 1444). Averroes's commentary on Aristotle's *On the Causes for the Length or Brevity of Life* (*De causis longitudinis et brevitatis vite*) makes the same point. The very influential *On the Secrets of Women* – a work that for centuries was accepted as Albertus', but was likely produced perhaps by one of his students – explains that this drying out is the reason that males generally do not live as long as females. Albertus states that the brain can be desiccated this way, and its dryness then may cause baldness. Conversely, 'Baldness', Albertus opines, 'never afflicts eunuchs' (or *castrati*, that is, those boys who have been castrated). But 'those who enjoy sexual intercourse too frequently go bald quickly, since coition dries out and cools the body.' Similarly, 'those who copulate a great deal sense an emptiness of the brain and their eyes become sunken.' In his *Questions concerning [Aristotle's] 'On Animals'*, Albertus illustrates these effects with an anecdote:

> Clement of Bohemia told me there was a certain
> hoary old monk who approached a certain beautiful
> mistress and just like a starving man he demanded
> her 66 times before the striking of matins; the next

day he fell down and, on the very same day, was dead.
And because he was a noble, his body was opened up
and his brain was found to be entirely evacuated, so
much so that nothing more of it remained than the
size of a pomegranate and, similarly, his eyes were
destroyed. Nature marvels at this, although it seems
to be consonant with reason. This, then, is an
indication that intercourse particularly evacuates
the brain.[3] (*QDA²*, p. 268)

It is remarkable that here Albertus does not condemn the old
monk on moral grounds. Instead, he records the monk's excessive sexual activity to establish a medical claim, based on
empirical evidence gathered from a postmortem inspection. It
is unlikely that this procedure was a true dissection or autopsy.
Rather, Albertus notes, the monk's body was opened 'because
he was a noble', referring to an increasingly common practice of
removing from noble persons certain organs for local burial,
while the bones would be returned to their homeland. Katharine
Park calls this practice 'division of the corpse', stating that it was
most commonly used for north European royalty and aristoc-
racy. In fact, the custom was sometimes referred to as the *mos
Teutonicum*, 'the German custom'. Pope Boniface VIII banned
the practice in his bull *Detestande feritatis* (27 September 1299).[4]
This practice of organ 'repatriation' became more frequent
towards the end of the twelfth century, especially for Crusaders
killed in battle. The custom was also followed for religious fig-
ures. Five days after the English bishop of Hereford, Thomas of
Cantilupe (the last medieval English Catholic to be canonized
as a saint), died in Italy on 25 August 1282, all his organs save
the heart were removed and buried locally. Once the flesh was
boiled off, his bones were returned to England and buried at
his own cathedral in Hereford, whereas Thomas's heart was

delivered to the monastic church of Ashridge, founded by
Edmund, Earl of Cornwall. The opening of the noble monk
mentioned above seems to have been a similar procedure.

Albertus confirms in *On Animals* the link between too-
frequent intercourse or ejaculation and its effects upon the
brain, remarking that 'when excessive sperm has been emitted,
it especially weakens the brain and those members near it.' It
was Hippocrates (d. c. 370 BCE), Albertus relates, who postulated
that semen descends from the front of the brain through veins
behind the ears that extend to the male member. This is allegedly proven by the claim that when these veins are cut, men can
no longer deliver sperm for intercourse. Albertus tends to agree
that the sperm originates in the brain but describes the theory
of the 'spermatic veins' behind the ears as 'implausible' and not
in accord with experience. This Hippocratic notion helps to
explain, however, the belief that excessive intercourse 'empties'
the brain. Albertus' fellow Dominican Vincent of Beauvais likewise notes that because excessive intercourse evacuates the
brain, it also damages eyesight. Michael Scot agrees and adds
migraines and baldness as side effects. He adds that excessive
urination following coition will have a doubly desiccating effect,
resulting in illness or death. Life is especially dependent upon
moisture and heat, just as a seed without moisture and warmth
will not germinate and a plant will not grow. Since blood is a
principal humour and source of moisture in the human body,
one can better appreciate Albertus' remark that 'women perform
an abortion by being bled often, especially beneath the ankle
on the inside part of the foot.' Although phlebotomy was an
essential medieval medical practice, during pregnancy it can
cause a miscarriage or abortion.[5]

Albertus also evaluates various theories for determining the
sex of a foetus. He rejects entirely a view attributed to the second-
century medical authority Galen that males are formed when

Initial and border from the beginning of book sixteen, 'In What Way the Male and Female Are Principles of Generation', depicting various animals copulating. From Albertus Magnus, *De animalibus* (14th century).

the power of the male's sperm is dominant and females are formed when the power of the female's sperm is dominant.

The notion of female sperm requires some explanation. In his *Questions concerning [Aristotle's] 'On Animals'*, Albertus asks whether females produce sperm. The question itself points to a disagreement between philosophers and physicians, and between the followers of Aristotle and those of Galen, concerning the female's contribution to the foetus. Albertus attempts to reconcile the opposing positions. Like Galen but unlike Aristotle, Albertus opines that both males and females produce 'sperm'. For Albertus, during coition, females emit a white humour or 'sperm' that, together with the menses, provides the matter which will receive Aristotelian form from the male sperm, when the male and female sperms unite during intercourse. Albertus rejects Galen's attribution of agency and a formative role to female sperm, however: female sperm represents, then, a material substrate that must be 'in-formed' by male sperm.[6]

For Aristotle, matter is a passive principle that must receive properties – shape, dimensions, tangible qualities and so on – from an active, formal principle, just as clay receives shape and form from a potter. Aristotle identifies the male with the active generative power, whereas the female womb is a passive vessel containing material awaiting form. For Albertus, however, the female sperm is not a bare potentiality capable of receiving any form whatsoever. Since it already exists before it receives the male sperm, it possesses certain properties that establish a 'confused beginning of form' and a disposition for a *specific* form: that is, a woman's sperm can receive form from a male's, but not from a dog's. As a material principle, female sperm plays *some* role in conception, but Albertus treats it as having a purely secondary role, whereas the male sperm imparts form and determines foetal development. This is clear from his statement that

although that which comes from the woman is like the
sperm of the male in colour, nevertheless it is not alike
in power. For it is watery and thin, *more fit to be formed
into a young than to form one.*[7] (italics ours)

Although Galen believed that a child's sex is determined
according to whether the power of the male or female sperm
prevails in conception, Albertus claims that its sex is determined entirely by the male sperm. While a woman has a fluid
analogous to male sperm, hers does not have an active and
formative power. Consequently, 'the opinion of the unskilled
crowd of physicians which says that the woman has the causal-
ity of the moving principle in generation, because the fluid
which she ejects during the pleasure of intercourse resembles
sperm, is false.' Instead, Albertus insists, the proper cause of sex
differentiation is found in the complexional heat of the male
sperm. The male (and male sperm) is 'hotter' and therefore is
disposed to produce a male rather than a female, since females
have a colder, phlegmatic complexion. It is precisely the female's
colder complexion that makes it impossible for her to produce
a true sperm, since 'females have only a weak heat, and this is
why there is insufficient power in the female to generate sperm.'
The female, as we have seen, produces something *analogous* to
male sperm, with the result 'that there can be sperm in a female
in some manner, and this is when the heat is kindled in them'.
But her sperm is deficient in power.[8]

How is a woman's deficient heat kindled to produce female
sperm? A hot climate can be a contributing cause, just as intercourse and its energetic movements may also 'heat' the body.
The two factors are related since, Albertus remarks, 'humans
in warm lands are stimulated to coition more.' The more one
engages in intercourse, the more heat is produced. This is not
always a good thing, since a dry heat is a desiccant. Albertus adds

a peculiar ethnographic detail, however, related to the production of female sperm:

> Sperm like this is found more often in black women, who have sex more than all other women, and more than white women. Because black women [*nigrae*] are hotter and particularly dark [*fuscae*], they are the sweetest for sex, as lechers say.

Similarly, Albertus affirms that the bodies of Black Ethiopian women are made more flexible by the hot climate in which they live, so that they 'easily give birth, although due to dryness and weakness, they do not easily conceive'. Although such language and reductive stereotypes are unacceptable today and rightly deemed racist, Albertus' comments relate to his discussion of sexual differentiation and foetal development. For the Galenists, female sperm is a formative agent, just like male sperm. When its quantity in the womb exceeds and overpowers that of the male, a female will be produced. Contrariwise, when there is more male sperm, then a male will be produced. The active role of female sperm provided a simple explanation for foetal sexual differentiation. This theory of female sperm also helped Galenists explain apparent reproductive anomalies. If the female sperm is not an active agent, then how can one explain a child's resemblance to its mother more than its father? For medieval Galenists, the answer lay in the dominance of the female sperm at conception. Michael Scot provides an example that can be traced back to Aristotle: a certain white woman had intercourse with a Black Ethiopian and gave birth to a white daughter, whereas a Black woman had intercourse with a white man and gave birth to a Black son. How can this be? The explanation, Michael Scot alleges, is that the female sperm overpowered the male's to produce progeny more like the mother than the father (*Lib. phis.*, 1).

This is unsatisfactory for Albertus since he endows only the male sperm with an active, formative power. But Albertus' doctrine also faces certain difficulties. First, if only the male has active agency, why does nature produce females at all? Why are not all progeny male? Second, how can he explain an instance in which the child resembles the mother and not the father? Or neither the father nor the mother?

To answer the second question first, Albertus attributes such resemblances not to female sperm but to the power, or 'accidents', of imagination. For Albertus and for medieval psychology generally, imagination is an important mental faculty and a 'place' all its own, much different from the idea of making things up that the word 'imagination' evokes today. Images from our sense experience are imprinted upon the interior imagination, as one might make an imprint upon wax with a stylus. In this way, when the object of experience is no longer present, we can bring that object to mind again by invoking the image. But as sense experience of the external world imprints itself on the imagination, so too imagination can reciprocally influence and imprint on the body. This is readily illustrated by human sexual behaviour: the mental image of an absent lover, Albertus insists, is enough to cause sexual stimulation, an erection and nocturnal emission. Similarly, 'the recollection of intercourse arouses desire for it, for an accidental trait of the soul changes the body greatly.'

Not only does imagination, as a faculty of the mind or soul, generate a response in one's own body, it may also pass on its 'power' through the sperm to a foetus. For example, 'a certain king once imagined a black monstrosity during intercourse and made mention of this to the queen while he was having intercourse with her. The fetation, when born, was monstrous and black.' Albertus provides other examples in which a woman's imagination is active during coition:

For it is said – and it sounds extraordinary, although it may be part of nature [*licet sit physicum*] – that an offspring often resembles what the woman imagines or what falls into her imagination at conception. In this way, Avicenna says, a certain woman, owing to this, gave birth to a dwarf. But this would only be the case if the imaginative power ruled the generative power in some way, and so too for the others.

The power of imagination in these two cases helps explain characteristics in the offspring absent in the parents. The theory of female seed alone offers no solution. Neither does the theory that only the male sperm is an active power. How, then, does one account for the anomaly? Albertus turns again to the power of imagination:

> The imaginative power leaves its impression on the natural power because it is superior to and dominates it.

Pregnant woman with the foetus sucking its thumb, miniature from Albertus Magnus, *De animalibus* (14th century).

> Thus the entire body is altered by various imaginings . . .
> various types of imagining cause a change in every part
> of the body.

Elsewhere, moreover, Albertus cites Aristotle to support the
fact that such anomalies may be due to 'the grandfather or the
greatgrandfather and yet no part of their seed is in it. Further,
this similarity is sometimes traced to one who existed many
generations ago.'

Such reproductive anomalies were poorly explained by a
theory that only the male's sperm possesses a formative power.
Imagination adds an additional causal agency, but one that, for
Albertus, is especially associated with women. It is the woman's
imagination in these cases that seems to overcome the natural
or generative power of the male. This sense that the woman is
especially susceptible to the power of imagination is made clearer
in a remark from Albertus' student Thomas of Cantimpré: 'for
they say that the nature of women is such that whatever they
look upon or imagine when they conceive in the extreme heat
of desire will affect the appearance of the child.'[9]

Is Nature Male?

We asked above, if only the male sperm has active agency and
formative power, then why does nature produce females at all
and not only male progeny like itself? Albertus offers a reply in
his commentary on Peter Lombard's *Sentences* (written 1243–9)
where he remarks that Aristotle had insisted in his *On Animals*
that 'specific nature never intends a woman, but that a female
is rather a flawed male.' More specifically:

> A female . . . is caused from the corruption of some
> natural principles, because nature intends a perfect work,

which is the male, and this is why Aristotle says that 'a
female is a flawed male' just like a crooked tibia [is flawed].

While females are the result, then, of 'corruption of some natural
principles', females are clearly necessary to nature, since without
them there could be no generation or procreation:

> Nonetheless, the female does not exist outside the natural
> course of universal nature, [but is created to be] an aid to
> the man for generation, seeing that were she not necessary
> for generation, nature never would produce a female.

Albertus explains further in his *Questions concerning [Aristotle's]
'On Animals'*:

> Nature is of two types: universal and specific [*natura
> particularis*]. Universal nature intends to conserve the
> entire universe and its parts . . . to conserve the species.
> But a species of animals cannot be conserved without
> the generation of individuals, and a female as well as
> a male are required for this generation.

If nature were only concerned with the reproduction of
individuals, she would always produce males. But since she must
also attend to the perpetuation of the species, females are necessary. Nature produces a female not only when suitable material
is not present to produce a male, but when the male's complexional heat is inadequate to overcome the female's complexional
coldness, resulting in sexual differentiation:

> As has been well shown in previous parts of this
> investigation, male's sperm, which is formative and
> factive for a fetation, always aims to . . . produce a

male unless it is hindered by some flaw which corrupts the instrument with which it works, and this flaw is heat. Or it may be hindered by the intractableness of the material which it forms and makes, this being the humour.

Either, therefore, when the male's sperm is inadequately 'heated' or when the material provided to the sperm for formation is intractable,

> it forms a female lest the work of nature be rendered totally useless. Although she does not generate as such, she is still a helper to the male and necessary for the purpose of generation just as the passive is necessary for the active and just as material underlies works of art. This is why too we have said in the *Physics* that the material desires form as does the female the male and the ugly the beautiful.[10]

Since the male alone is active, nature is inclined to produce only males, except when the male's power is 'hindered by some flaw', namely by intractable material or by an insufficient heat. When the male's sperm is 'cooled', then, it may produce a female, fulfilling nature's secondary intention. Albertus acknowledges, therefore, the influence of concomitant causes for determining the sex of the foetus. The Galenic doctrine that male sperm deposited to the right side of the womb will produce a male is of itself an insufficient explanation. Albertus appeals to experience to refute this notion and explains that 'the opposite is sometimes found to occur, namely, that a male is on the left side and a female on the right.' This has been demonstrated, Albertus claims, by dissection (*anatomia*). In the same passage, Albertus remarks that male and female twins have been found 'many times' in one and the same part of the womb, which would not occur if males are formed only on the right side and females only on the left.[11]

In the same way, Albertus criticizes those who claim that a male foetus arises when the male's sperm comes from his right testicle, but a female when it comes from the left. They attempt to prove this by experiment: they will tie off the right testicle to show that 'if copulation then occurs, a female will be generated from this sperm', but when the left testicle is tied off, 'then a male will be generated' (*DA*, 18.12; *SZ*, vol. II, pp. 1286–7). They also claim that males who do not have their right testicle generate only females, and those who do not have their left generate only males. Michael Scot insists that this has been proven 1,000 times by experience (*Lib. phis.*, 7.2). 'But this is not true,' Albertus proclaims, 'for I myself saw one with his right testicle amputated and after the castration he first sired a son and then a daughter. Therefore', Albertus concludes, 'what they say about the right and left side as the causes of sexual differentiation amounts to nothing at all' (*DA*, 18.12; *SZ*, vol. II, pp. 1286–7).

It is not simply the location to the right or left that determines the foetus's sex. Heat and cold are principal determinants. The theory that argues for the right or left determination is not entirely wrong, Albertus remarks, but only because typically the right side is hotter and the left side colder. Therefore, he gives only qualified support to the right/left beliefs of his contemporaries. Albertus acknowledges that experience seems to confirm this, remarking that he had seen a woman 'who had always borne daughters because, after lying with her husband, she would lie on her left side. When instructed to lie on her right side after relations, she began to produce sons and from that time on bore many of them' (*DA*, 9.101; *SZ*, vol. I, p. 813). But this evidence obscures the truth, namely that 'the proper cause of masculinity is the sperm's heat', whereas a female will result from complexional coldness (*DA*, 9.101; *SZ*, vol. I, p. 812).

Initial and border from the beginning of book nine, 'On the Principles and Origin of Human Generation', revealing women with multiple foetuses during pregnancy. From Albertus Magnus, *De animalibus* (14th century).

Just as Albertus rejects as insufficient the Galenic doctrine that male sperm deposited to the right side of the womb or arising from the right testicle will produce a male, he also rejects a Galenic theory (shared by Michael Scot) that divided the womb into seven chambers: three on the left, three on the right and one in the middle. According to this model, males develop in the chambers on the hotter right side, females on the cooler left side, and hermaphrodites are formed in the middle chamber. Michael Scot also appeals to this model to establish the limits for multiple births. If the male sperm is sufficiently abundant to distribute itself to all seven chambers of the womb, then seven children can be generated at once, but not more: three males, three females and one hermaphrodite. Albertus defends instead a Hippocratic model in which a human womb has only two chambers, rejecting the attempt to explain multiple births by assigning each foetus to one of the seven different chambers in the womb. Instead, Albertus develops an alternative theory that proposes that twins are produced when the male's formative power divides the sperm – provided that a sufficient quantity is available – and creates more than one foetus in the womb (that is, twins, triplets and so on). Sometimes this material does not divide completely, however, resulting in conjoined twins. Likewise, sometimes the membrane in the womb that would normally separate twin foetuses will rupture and create conjoined twins. Among animals, he mentions that he had himself seen 'a two-bodied goose. Its bodies were joined only at the back and it had two heads, four wings, and four feet, and it went in whatever direction it turned itself.' Albertus is likely the first medieval author, moreover, to provide an anthropological report of conjoined twins. He introduces a report from credible witnesses of conjoined human twins:

Further, many worthy of trust have related to us that they have seen such a man who was in fact two men joined at the back. One was rash and wrathful while the other was gentle. They lived more than twenty years and after one had died the other lived on until he himself died from the putrefaction and stench of his dead brother. Sometimes, though, they have one heart and they have other multiple members as a result of abundant material.

Albertus identifies excessive movement during sexual intercourse as another cause for both twins and conjoined twins:

> Sometimes there arises one with a body doubled above
> or below, as occurred in the one that was born with
> two heads, and from there each one's neck and back
> continued as two bodies, and below one body was
> evident. At another time, however, one was seen
> that was born in an opposite way, who had four legs,
> and one continuous body appeared on the upper part,
> which happened without a doubt from the division
> of the spermatic [matter] in the womb. The birth of
> twins who are found born in one cell of the womb
> occurs in this way as well; for there are some women
> and some animals that delight overmuch in intercourse,
> and in that delight the womb is moved, when the sperm
> is poured in upon her sensory nerves, and during that
> motion the sperm is divided. If the semen coalesces
> in a foetus, then twins arise when the entire division
> is completed. If the division is not completed, but the
> sperm is branched, as it were, then animals arise that
> are double-bodied either below or above, or even in
> the middle according to the manner in which the
> sperm is divided. And for this reason some are found
> with two penises, others with three or four arms, and
> so too for other variations of the middle of the body.[12]

Although Albertus attempts a scientific, technical explanation for twin births and for conjoined twins, his explanation does not avoid the contemporary moral censure, also found in literary works, that the female's excessive pleasure causes motion in the womb and division of the sperm. Albertus' Aristotelian text notes that multiple births are especially common among women in Egypt, who often bear three or four young at once. Albertus adds an ethnographic slur that 'Egypt must be accounted a wanton nation.' He does not apply the same judgement to German women, despite his fantastic claim that 'a physician, a truthful man and an expert, told me that a certain noblewoman in Germany has given birth to sixty children, five each time.' Despite his general opinion that women in the northernmost clime have difficulty conceiving, he makes an exception for German women: they conceive easily, even if they only give birth with difficulty. Perhaps this statement represents a compromise with Bartholomew the Englishman, who provides a false etymology, citing Isidore of Seville, that the name *Germania* (Germany) arose from the ease with which its inhabitants conceive (*germinando*).[13]

Just as Albertus rejects the Galenic seven-chambered womb, he also decisively rejects the view that treats hermaphrodites as a third sex generated in the middle chamber between the male and female. Instead, he defends the Aristotelian view that recognizes only two sexes (male and female) and that treats hermaphrodites with redundant genitalia as a birth defect and flaw of nature. Albertus treats the presence of male and female genitalia on a single individual much the same way as he does extra digits on a hand: the sperm divides superfluous material into extra body parts. Like many of his contemporaries, Albertus feels compelled to provide an explanation for hermaphroditism because it implied an unwelcome ambiguity in nature that threatened binary sexual differentiation. His explanation may reflect his own observation. He remarks,

In a certain man born in our time the testicles were
contained higher up within the skin in such a way that
their outward bulge gave the suggestion of the two lips
of a woman's vulva. There also seemed to be a split in
the middle which was closed over by skin. Since the
parents thought he was a girl, and that the split should
be opened to ready her for intercourse, an incision
was made and out leapt his testicles and his penis. He
afterward took a wife and bore many children from her.

Just as Albertus introduces either his own observations or
those of credible witnesses to his discussions of twins, conjoined
twins and hermaphroditism, he also frequently provides personal
observations of childcare. He claims that he has seen many
women employ the trick of rubbing nettles on their breasts to

Albertus Magnus pointing to the hermaphroditic Androgyne holding
the Y symbol of immortality. Note the fully formed male and female
genitalia. Illustration from Michael Maier, *Symbola aureae mensae
duodecim nationum* (1617).

stimulate the production of milk and states that 'some were widows and some virgins and yet milk flowed abundantly from the breasts of them all.' His Latin – *ego vidi hoc facere multas mulieres* – leaves little doubt that he was a first-hand observer of this action that may be associated with wet-nurses. At the same time, he adds another ethnographic observation that goes far beyond Aristotle's text on which it is based, that 'the milk of dark, dusky women is better and has more nourishment than that of white women.' This comment seems to echo Avicenna's remark that Black women have healthier milk (*Abbrevatio de animalibus*) but relies more on Michael Scot's remark that the milk of a Black or brown woman is always better than that of a white woman. The choice of a wet-nurse would have been of great interest to their readers since, as Michael Scot affirms, the quality of her breast milk not only contributes to the infant's physical development but affects its moral development and character.

He speaks too of holy women who, through excessive fasting and vigils, suffered irregular menstruation. Elsewhere, he says that he had seen a certain old woman who had a white vaginal discharge. In another passage, he describes a woman he saw in Cologne who often fasted for twenty or thirty days at a time and a man who fasted for seven weeks, only taking one cupful of water a day or every other day. This incident is notable because Albertus says he diligently checked the seals locking him in and found them unbroken. He thus might have been present as an official Church witness.[14]

Albertus regards no topic related to sexual function as too delicate. If 'hindered by some flaw', the male sperm's heat will produce a female or it may not result in conception at all. For this reason, he remarks too on the length of the penis, both in humans and in other animals. On the one hand, 'in those that have long penises, the sperm evaporates as it flows and becomes cold by being a great distance from its principle.' The longer distance it must travel cools the sperm, and pregnancy will occur very infrequently. On the other hand, 'those animals, however, with a penis that is too short do not propel the sperm to a place from which the womb can absorb it.' The solution seems to lie in the Aristotelian mean: 'those which have average sized penises do generate for the most part.' 'Average', Albertus concludes, is best.[15]

Albertus, like Michael Scot, offers a method to predict the size of the genitalia. Such a method might be useful for physicians who must determine why a couple cannot conceive. Michael Scot identified the nose as a visible physiognomic predictor of the size and appearance of the male genitalia, including the penis, or *hasta baiardi*.[16] For example, a long and thick nose signifies a large prepuce, thick and broad nostrils signify thick and broad testicles, but thin and narrow nostrils indicate thin and small testicles.[17] Similarly, from the appearance of the tip of the nose (*pirula*), one can determine whether virginity has been lost: if the cartilage is undivided, it is a sign of virginity; if the cartilage is divided, however, it indicates virginity has been lost. For Michael Scot, the size and shape of a woman's foot bears a similar predictive relationship to her genitals:

> If her foot is long and narrow and thin it indicates a long and narrow and thin vulva. And contrariwise. Likewise, the measure of the middle of the bare foot is the measure of the length of the whole of the vulva for each one. Therefore, a certain one said: 'by the form of the foot you will know the woman's vessel.'[18]

Unlike Michael, however, Albertus (*QDA²*, p. 63) affirms a physiognomic correlation between the hand and male and female genitalia:

> a large-sized hand is a good sign in the male because
> it indicates a large-sized penis, but it is a bad sign
> in a woman because it is an indicator of a large-sized
> womb in which the sperm is not well concentrated
> and, as a result, the sperm does not become fertile.

Just as a large penis may produce 'cooled' sperm that poorly correlates with conception, so too an exceedingly capacious womb is poorly disposed to conception.

Albertus, like Michael Scot, offers various tests for virginity. He does not rely on a physiognomic indicator but, in one instance, echoes the lapidary section of *On the Flowers of Natural Things* by the early thirteenth-century encyclopedist Arnold of Saxony to suggest instead that a woman drink water that contains some scrapings of jet, a lignite coal.[19] If she can retain the water, she is a virgin, but if she urinates immediately, she is not. 'And this', Albertus pronounces, 'is the way virginity should be tested.' In *On Animals*, however, Albertus proposes a physical examination to determine whether the fine membranes at the vaginal opening are intact: 'When seen, they are taken as proof of virginity. They are destroyed through intercourse or else by the insertion of fingers, and when this occurs the little bit of blood that is in them flows out.' The examination must be conducted by those with experience in these matters, however, in order to avoid deception, since

> there are, moreover, certain women who, through
> the use of medicaments designed for this purpose,
> cause the womb to appear wrinkled at the neck
> of the vulva even after a great deal of intercourse.
> This wrinkled condition creates the appearance
> of pannicular-membranes, and these women then
> appear as virgins to the inexperienced.[20]

While the size of the genitalia plays a role in conception, Albertus also provides advice on the best coital positions to achieve pregnancy. One will not be surprised that this church-man recommends the 'missionary' position. The woman, he remarks,

> will be naturally positioned if she is on her back with
> her legs spread well apart and quite elevated so that
> the opening of the vulva is raised toward the thighs.
> For this is where the hollow of the womb is and the
> sperm is then projected directly into the womb.

Should she lie on her side, the sperm typically fails to hit its mark. Moreover,

> When the woman mounts the man the womb is twisted
> around and that which is in it is therefore poured forth.
> When the woman stands up, however, the womb is
> stretched out and this contracts its opening so that it
> does not receive the sperm and if it does, pours it forth
> on account of its being stretched. A woman that has
> relations from the rear only takes in the semen
> between the lips of her vulva because the thickness
> of her buttocks hinders the penis from reaching to
> the mouth of the womb.

Finally, Albertus adds, 'Whenever the pleasure of the male and the female occur at the same time during intercourse impregnation is easier.'[21]

Since Christian marriage had procreation as its primary purpose, obstacles to conception necessarily concerned not only physicians but medieval ecclesiastics who commented, like Albertus, on the best coital positions as well as on various procedures to identify sterility and infertility. After rejecting several folk practices intended to detect sterility or infertility, Albertus addresses 'blockage of the womb' in human females and approves the claim of those who assert that

> if a fumigant is made for the woman out of aromatic herbs and . . . if the fumes are directed toward her womb with a funnel, and if the woman senses the odor of the aromatic herbs in her mouth and nose, it is a reasonably certain sign that she is not blocked up by bad humours.

Similarly, 'if garlic is peeled and placed in a woman's vulva and if she sleeps this way and if, after her sleep, she finds the odor of garlic in her mouth and nose, it will signify that there is no blockage in her womb.' Albertus' Dominican confrère Vincent of Beauvais recommends a test to determine whether the woman or the man is responsible for a failure to conceive: have the woman sit upon a bench covered with a cloth and let her be fumigated, he advises. If the fumes reach her nose and mouth, then it is not she but rather the man who is the cause of the difficulty.[22]

Although coition is necessary for reproduction, and reproduction is a mark of perfection, it remains for Albertus nonetheless a source of both shame and delight. Unlike other animals who, when they copulate, make a great deal of noise,

> the human animal is discreet and prudent, thanks to reason, and has discretion, and therefore can abstain on account of shame from those acts toward which coition is ordered, and this is why he does not make a lot of noise. To the contrary, if he can, he lies down hiddenly, and the more hiddenly the more sweet it is.

For Albertus, humans' seeking privacy for sexual intercourse is not a psychological indicator of repression but instead points to an innate and natural moral repugnance that is only overcome by the pleasure sex accords. That pleasure can be so intense, Albertus remarks, that 'I have seen a certain man who did not feel a wound made with a knife on his penis when he was in the heat of passion.' He remarks that the capacity for shame is distinctly human and indicates our capacity for moral judgement, but he also recognizes something akin to shame in other animals. Albertus records Aristotle's anecdotal reports of nature's repugnance for incest, for example. According to the philosopher, 'A certain camel had coitus with its mother, and after she knew that she was his mother,' she killed the man who had covered her head to conceal her partner's filial identity. Aristotle also 'tells of a certain noble horse in the northern region that had coitus with his mother and after he discovered it he fled and cast himself off into a ditch and died'. The explanation offered is that 'the act of coitus induces shame, and the horse and the camel strive to observe the order of nature by a natural instinct. And this is why the son naturally hates to have coitus with his mother.'[23]

Is Nature White? Albertus Magnus on Race and Complexion

Earlier, we asked whether one might describe nature as 'male' for Albertus because it seeks to produce only males. Here we might ask a related question: is nature 'white', and is whiteness nature's default condition? Already we have recorded a few of Albertus' ethnographic remarks concerning Black women: they have sexual intercourse more frequently than white women, and intercourse with them is 'sweeter'. Their breast milk is also more nourishing than that of white women. Do these comments reflect the erroneous modern conviction, which had come to prominence by the twentieth century, that humanity is divided into biologically different races and that these races are indicated by different skin colours?

The presence of race and racism in medieval texts remains hotly contested. A principal reason is that medieval authors did not perceive race – or skin colour, for that matter – as a set of permanent, biologically determined characteristics. Instead, the physical and psychological attributes associated with modern racial categories are better explained by medieval authors as a theory of humoral complexion. Complexional theory is simple in its basic principles, but complex in its application. According to Avicenna's influential *Canon of Medicine*, 'Complexion is that quality which results from the mutual interaction . . . of the four primary qualities residing within the elements,' namely fire, earth, air and water. These elements are associated with four primary qualities – the moist, the hot, the dry and the cold – and combine to form material bodies. Complexion, then, results from the interaction of these qualities to produce composite bodies that are hot and dry (choleric), hot and moist (sanguineous), cold and moist (phlegmatic), or cold and dry (melancholic). In a perfect state, the body's four qualities are equal, temperate or balanced. But since Adam's Fall and expulsion from paradise, bodies are always more or less imbalanced: when the imbalance is acute, it presents as illness and, untreated, leads ultimately to death. The challenge for physicians is to restore the body most nearly to a harmonious balance. Although 'complexion', Albertus remarks, 'is an accidental quality arising from the composition of opposite qualities', a balanced complexion withdraws as far as possible from destructive contrariety. Conversely, when the ratio of the humours (viz., the moist, dry, hot and cold) departs from a balanced mixture, it creates a 'distempered' complexion that is a source of illness, corruption and decay.[24]

Among all animals, 'the human especially comes near to balance in complexion' and possesses the most noble complexion, which produces a concomitant nobility or excellence in intellectual operations. This is because a link exists, says Albertus, between the body's complexion and the intellect since, as Plato taught, forms are bestowed upon matter according to merit, and a balanced complexion merits the noblest soul (viz., the human soul), which is one capable of intellection. Were our complexion in perfect balance, then we would appear to be earthly gods capable of understanding all things. Because life depends on the heat and moisture found in blood, a sanguineous complexion (hot and moist) is best suited for a long life. Therefore, 'those animals with a more balanced and temperate complexion live longer,' Albertus claims, whereas 'those that stray from this balance have a shorter life span.' Contrariwise, 'a melancholic complexion [cold and dry] in particular results in a brief life span, according to the opinion of the physicians.' In old age, moreover, a body typically possesses a cold and dry complexion, since the heat and moisture necessary to sustain life have been nearly exhausted. In our prime, however, humans provide the most perfect example of a balanced sanguineous complexion, since 'among all the animals the balance of his [the human's] complexion belongs more to the nature and balance of heaven', where no contrariety exists. 'This is not to say', Albertus adds, 'that the human consists of balanced amounts of all the elements, for this is impossible, but rather that the human's complexion is furthest from the excesses of the contraries.'[25]

Although humans withdrew from a perfectly balanced humoral complexion after the Fall, one should not be surprised that for Albertus and other medieval theologians, 'the most noble soul demands, with respect to nature, the most noble complexion. But Christ had the most noble soul with respect to nature; therefore, he had the most noble complexion.' Christ presents, then, not only a model of moral and intellectual perfection, but of humoral perfection. Consequently, an unedited text from the second half of the thirteenth century proposes that Jesus necessarily possessed a sanguineous complexion.[26] For us, such perfect balance remains an aspirational ideal that, Albertus claims, will only be recovered by our resurrected, impassible body.[27]

Individuals are born with an innate complexion (*complexio innata*) that is derived from material principles that combine to produce the foetus. We receive our complexion in the first instance, then, as an inheritance from our parents, although principally from the father.

But complexion can be influenced or altered by numerous causes. For example, illness or disease will distemper complexion. A body's complexion also can be influenced, according to medieval physicians, by the six 'non-naturals', which include the influence of diet, sleep, exercise, sexual intercourse, mental affections like fear or joy, and environmental factors like the quality of the surrounding air and water. Albertus opines that geography and the influence of the environment cause different human populations to have their own distinctive complexions. These vary according to their location among seven climes (*climata*), that is, the parallel bands that divide the earth into latitude and longitude. Each human group has a 'natural place' and shares its complexion, since 'place and what is placed in it enjoy a shared nature.' Conversely, 'men who move to a different climate on account of the unnaturalness of the place grow weaker and are destroyed; and when they return to their native places, they recover health.' Therefore, Albertus remarks,

> an Indian who possesses an entirely middle and balanced complexion that suits his habitation would not live well in England, Scotland, or Dacia. And a Dacian who nears

balance of complexion for his habitation would quickly
die in India or Ethiopia, and it is the same for other
differences in *clima*.[28]

Leaving one's 'natural place' produces an adverse humoral
opposition, but Albertus introduces the possibility that migrat-
ing populations could *gradually* adapt to a new clime:

> Indians have their own complexion and live according to
> it, and the Germans and French have their own as well,
> according to which they live in the seventh *clima*. One
> would not live well in the *clima* of the other even though
> *we have often seen certain Moors living very well in the seventh*
> clima *once they grew used to the diet of the northern regions.*
> (our italics)

The seventh clime includes northern European lands and is the
northernmost clime, furthest from the equator. Albertus remarks,
for example, that the city of Cologne is found in the seventh clime.
Beyond the seventh clime, the earth is uninhabitable, owing to
extreme cold. A migrant can become 'acclimated' to this new
environment, however, and this will be facilitated by the adop-
tion of the local diet. Because behaviour or 'character [*mores*]
follows complexion', Albertus proposes that the complexions of
diverse geographical regions or climes will produce different moral
behaviours, cultural customs and even skin colouring. In contrast
to those in the equatorial first clime, those who live in northern
climes like Albertus' own Germany have a colder and moister
complexion that produces a white or very fair skin colouration,
as well as a distinct mental 'temperament', like a natural boldness
and talent for war. Those who live in the northernmost seventh
clime, which is most distant from the equator,

are all cold, and their places are quickly cooled,
and this is why the wombs of the women are cold
and moist, and for this reason an intense whiteness
and fairness [*subalbedo*] occurs in them, as occurs
among the Slavs and the Parthians and those of
Dacia and the Teutons and Angles and such nations
of this sort, which dwell around the shore of the
northern ocean.

The surrounding cold of their environment also makes them
phlegmatic (cold and moist) and causes them, generally, to be
more dull-witted and less inclined to intellectual pursuits and
the discipline required for study. Albertus remarks:

But when they are moved to study they persevere longer
and they are much better by far after mental exercise.
The proof of this is that southern people in general always
study law, liberal studies, and the arts, about which the
Dacians and the Slavs care little.

Indians, who live in the hotter second clime, thrive in their
environment and

excel more in ingenuity on account of the moving heat
and the keenness of their spirits. Of which this is the sign
(proof): there have been distinguished philosophers in
India especially in mathematics and the magic arts, on
account of the power of the stars over those climates.

The inhabitants of the more temperate sixth and seventh climes
(which Albertus identifies as approximately 40 degrees north latitude) may not equal those in India, for example, in mathematics
and the magic arts, but owing to the surrounding environment,

'they are very handsome of body, are of noble and fair stature, and they are beautiful in colour, while the men of the fourth clime are small and dark.'[29]

On the other hand, those who live in the exceedingly hot and dry region of the first clime, which is nearest the equator, 'are exceedingly wrinkled from dryness . . . and very black on account of their heat, as are the Ethiopians'. 'Ethiopian' does not designate those living in the modern nation-state of Ethiopia, but rather identifies a population spread across a large area of East Africa. Because the extreme heat causes the moisture to evaporate more quickly from their bodies, those living in this clime will have a choleric (hot and dry) complexion. The body responds by opening the pores to 'vent' the heat to the outside, and, as a result, 'their hearts are made timid and cold' and they will be 'frivolous in mind' and unsuited for war. Because of the sun's extreme heat in the first and second climes, 'the bodies of those born all participate in an intense blackness, and they have curly hair.' From the sun's heat, too, 'those who are from India, those from the city of Iamen and the Zyndi and all Ethiopians are black and curly-haired and dry.' We have noted above the effect a hotter climate has on female sexual mores, for example that Black Ethiopian women more easily give birth, although they do not easily conceive. Just as Moors can become acclimated to a more northern climate once they grow used to the local diet, so too Albertus imagines that even Black Ethiopians can become gradually acclimated to other regions. Over time, complexion may so thoroughly adapt to a change of place that although 'black Ethiopians . . . are sometimes born in other climes as in the fourth and the fifth, [and] nevertheless, they take their blackness from their first ancestors who are complexioned in the first and second climes', gradually, they adapt, 'and a little at a time, they are altered to whiteness when they are transferred to other climes'.[30]

Such transformations are dependent upon successful adaptation, are by no means assured and may require several generations to achieve completion. Albertus construes these transformations as natural processes, however, grounded in scientific principles. These principles are true for animals as well. Just as one finds that people in cold, moist, northern climes are white, so too are the animals: there one finds white bears (polar bears) and white hares, whereas these same animals in more southern climes are black or brown. If one moves a black bear to the most northern clime, Albertus opines, over time the black bear will become white in response to this change in environment. Unlike his confreres Vincent of Beauvais and Thomas of Cantimpré, however, Albertus does not appear to treat whiteness as nature's default and present in humans *naturaliter*, whereas he does regard 'specific' nature as male and striving to produce other males.[31]

Precisely because Albertus imagined skin colour and other group characteristics to arise largely in response to environment, he concludes too that a change in environment would produce a gradual change even in colour. Although Albertus may seem less forceful in his assertion that a Black Ethiopian will turn white once his habitation is moved to a northern clime, he never repudiates this notion. For this reason, many medieval historians challenge the notion that medieval authors share our modern conception of race. Instead their ethno-anthropology stems from an 'environmentalism'. They may have been guilty of 'racialism' – that is, the association of negative qualities or attributes with Blackness – but in Albertus' natural philosophy, his 'racialism' is rooted in climate-based humoral theory.

TEN

Monsters

No discussion of Albertus Magnus' understanding of nature is complete without reference to monsters. The word 'monster' may bring to mind the frightening creature created by Frankenstein encountered on cinema screens at Saturday-afternoon matinees. Indeed, Albertus Magnus appears in Mary Shelley's classic *Frankenstein*: when a teenaged Victor Frankenstein discovers the writings of Albertus Magnus and the sixteenth-century Paracelsus, his interest in science and alchemy is 'sparked', leading him to construct his artificial human.

There exists a further link between Albertus and the Frankenstein tradition that is not Shelley's invention but can be traced back to a work published within a century of Albertus' death: the *Rosaio della vita*, often attributed to Matteo Corsini (d. 1402). This text promotes a legend that Albertus fabricated a metal automaton endowed with the power of speech. One day, a monk visited Albertus' cell. He called out to Albertus, but Albertus was not there, and instead the automaton replied. The monk, who regarded it as an evil invention, destroyed it. When Albertus discovered that his creation had been destroyed, he was incensed and lamented that it could not be replaced for 30,000 years, until the planets were once again in a proper alignment. By the fifteenth century, the legend had evolved to identify the monk who had destroyed it as Albertus' student

Thomas Aquinas.[1] Some of Albertus' later defenders, like his biographer Peter of Prussia, seek to discredit the legend that Albertus fashioned an artificial man with a capacity for human speech in order to promote his canonization.[2]

One could be forgiven, then, for the inference that when Albertus refers to monsters, he is speaking of horrifying creatures like Frankenstein's. In truth, however, Albertus' 'monsters' are far more mundane, and we encounter them frequently. Following a discussion of appropriate terminology, Albertus makes clear that a monster is not a miracle, a portent or a prodigy. A monster is something that merely exceeds or surpasses the primary

Albertus seated before his talking automaton, detail from the ceiling mural of the library vault at the Cistercian monastery of Aldersbach, painted by Matthäus Günther, 1760.

intent and measure of nature. Among the 'monsters' in Albertus' natural world are females, twins, hermaphrodites and individuals with ordinary birth defects, abnormalities or disabilities. All these signify nature's failure to hit its mark. Thus Albertus views females as 'monsters' in the rather ordinary sense that, as demonstrated above, a female is a flawed male. Females remain necessary for the perpetuation of the species, but if nature's aim were unimpeded, it would produce only males. And

> this is why every woman desires to exist under [the category of] manhood [*virilitas*]. For there is no woman who would not wish to put off the basis of her femininity [*femineitas*] and naturally to put on manhood. And in this same way matter desires to put on form.

Thus, although females are flawed products of nature, they remain natural all the same, and as a result, 'the female does not exist outside the natural course of universal nature.'

Hermaphrodites also depart from the primary intention of nature. Therefore, Albertus remarks that 'there are accidental monstrous traits which occur in certain generated ones which people call hermaphrodites because during the first generation they take on both the male and the female members.' Therefore, 'for various reasons, male and female can occur in the same one owing to a flaw in nature, as is evident among hermaphrodites, who have each member. But this is a monster in nature.'[3]

Monstrous traits arise generally from one or more of four causes during generation: from an inadequate quantity of material, from a superabundance of material, from a disproportion of material qualities (that is, the qualities of the four humours: heat, cold, dryness and moistness), or from a defect in the foetus's material 'container' (*secundina*). The nature of the 'container' will vary among animals. Among oviparous animals, Albertus notes that once he saw a hen's egg with two shells, one inside the other, which he then identified as 'one of nature's failings and monstrosities'. He also remarks on hens that produce double-yolked eggs, from which twin chicks emerge. Of the twin chicks, however, 'it occurs quite often that the small one is deformed [*monstrosus*] or both may be.' This monstrous birth results from some corruption to the container. Among viviparous animals, the 'container' typically designates the placenta or amniotic sac. Albertus imagines that when there is superabundant material in the womb at conception, the male sperm may form more than one foetus, resulting in multiple births. When the male sperm acts to create twins, the two foetuses are separated into two 'containers' in the womb. Should the containers rupture, the foetal material of one may adhere to the other to create conjoined twins. When superabundant material is present, but perhaps not enough to create separated twins, and when complexional heat and coldness are simultaneously present, a hermaphrodite will be generated.[4]

Above we discuss the factors affecting whether progeny display any resemblance to their parents and ancestors, but Albertus takes this line of thinking one step further: 'Sometimes, moreover, it does not even retain the resemblance of the species and will be a monster,' and

> sometimes [progeny] . . . do not even retain a human shape or that of those that generated them, but take on instead a monstrous and wondrous form. An offspring which is in no way like its parent, either in the nature of the species or individual shape, is monstrous and is called a wonder of nature.

Albertus remarks that although those of closely related species may produce 'hybrid' animals, just as a horse and an ass produce a mule, or a dog and wolf produce a wolf hybrid, or a goat and a stag produce the *tragelafus*, this will never occur in species more remote from one another, such as a human with a cow or pig. Albertus attributes the description of the ancient minotaur, which is said to have a human body but the head of a ram or bull, to 'the tales of the poets'. 'Such flaws', Albertus remarks, 'occur more often in other animals than in humans.' He rejects, moreover, the opinion of 'certain physicians' that such monstrous creatures arise when animals of different species copulate and their sperms mix. Instead, Albertus treats monstrous births principally in terms of a flaw (*peccata naturae*) in the material available for generation.[5]

Albertus turns, then, to a consideration of 'monstrous births', which appear when the progeny not only fails to resemble its parents or their species, but retains merely a resemblance to their *genus*. A resemblance to the *genus* is always preserved, however, 'for no animal is found which has ever given birth to a plant or a stone, but at a minimum the *genus* is preserved in all things which are generated.' As a result, Albertus insists, a 'monster' is not entirely beyond nature, but rather exists within the natural order. Although in its production nature fails to achieve its primary goal or aim, which is to produce one like the father, and this failure represents an evil, 'nevertheless the monster itself, insofar as it possesses the definition of being [*ens*], is good.'[6]

What causes such monstrous births? The cause may be astrological influence – that is, a power of the planets and stars – or a flaw related to the material. 'There are some stars in the sign of Aries', Albertus acknowledges, 'that bring about monstrous births . . . and such monsters have occurred among us and have come to our attention.' Albertus provides another reference in his commentary to Peter Lombard's *Sentences*, a twelfth-century textbook for theological education:

Ptolemy says in the *Quadripartitus*,[7] that when the sun
exists in a certain part and minute of Aries,[8] human
generation does not occur; and if the semen falls into the
womb then, a monster will be born. And so that this may
be believed, I have proved it by experience in two modest
and good matrons, from whom I learned that they gave
birth to monsters, and inquiring of them the season and
comparing the stars, I found that they had conceived when
the sun was at the same degree and minute, according to
their estimates.

But 'the primary source of monstrosity', Albertus notes, 'is
rooted in matter.' If the active formative power in the sperm is
supplied with an appropriate material, it will produce an appropriate progeny. Yet if there is too much or too little material, it
will be reflected in the progeny. As a result, Albertus remarks:

A monster is something that surpasses the measure of
nature. And this happens in many ways resulting, to be
sure, from a defect, like a hand for an upper arm (*humerus*),
or from abundance. It occurs from abundance in three
ways, namely from an abundance of power toward the
form of one member, such as [will produce] several mouths
or noses or ears on one [body]. Or it occurs from an
abundance of material in one member, like six or more
fingers. Or it occurs with respect only to quantity, just as
the sons of the Anakim are said to be monsters because
others when compared to them seemed like locusts.[9]

Although we might be inclined to call polydactylism a simple
birth defect, for Albertus, as indicated in the passage above, it
is 'monstrous'. He remarks, 'When the formative power has
completed the five fingers for the hand, if there is still sufficient

matter for one more finger and nature is not idle, it will produce a sixth finger.' He adds, 'I have thus seen a person who has six digits each on his hands and feet. His brother, born after him, likewise has six digits on his hands and feet.' Nature, then, adds additional fingers because there is more material available to the formative power than is necessary. In the same way, he views conjoined twins and hermaphrodites as 'monsters' because there is a lack of proportion between the matter and the agent's power: either there is too much matter or too little, resulting in superfluous members, like the superfluous genitalia in herm-aphrodites or superfluous horns on a ram: 'I have seen a ram which bore four large horns on its head.'[10]

Conversely, monstrousness may result from a shortage of material: 'I have also seen a goat which had only front feet and which walked about on them, carrying the rear portion of its body on them in the air and not dragging it along the ground.' Since there was an insufficient amount of material available at conception, the goat was born with only front feet. 'Monstrous' defects appear among the internal organs as well, which may be too large or too small, improperly positioned in the body, or absent entirely. While Albertus has seen an animal with only one kidney, 'an animal has never been found which lacks a heart . . . [or] which lacked a liver.' Monstrousness also arises in relation to 'quantity' or size. This is because nature establishes a boundary or limit to size in a species that it should not exceed. If it does, a monster results. In this sense, as seen above, the Anakim are monsters because they surpass the upper boundary and seem like giants. The same sense may be observed in references to sea monsters, whose size surpasses all reasonable boundaries. Alter-natively, a monster may arise when it fails to achieve the lower boundary. Albertus provides an example: 'I once saw a girl nine years of age who did not even have the requisite size of a one-year-old infant.'[11]

It is clear, then, that Albertus' 'monsters' are not quite the stuff of Hollywood movies. They may be infrequent, but they reveal or point to (*monstrare*) nature's failure. This is especially true for those that do not share the parents' species. Monsters are not unnatural, however; rather, they have natural, physical causes. They occur outside nature's primary intention as 'errors' or defects of nature. In Albertus' commentary on Aristotle's *Physics*, such individual 'errors' present the surest proof that nature is directed to a final cause or end, just as an error in grammar attests that grammatical rules exist or as an artist's failed work attests to the goal the artist had hoped to achieve. And art, Albertus reminds us, imitates nature. Surprisingly, then, monsters offer proof of the purposiveness of nature. Similarly, Albertus describes certain behaviours and 'great crimes' that transgress the moral order as 'monstrous'. For this reason, Albertus rejects entirely that monsters arise by 'chance' or without an identifiable cause. Although he acknowledges that there exist 'in the tales of the poets' monstrous beings like the minotaur, he does not give them much credence. Monsters such as these are rare and, he remarks, 'occur more often in other animals than in humans'. If monsters such as these appeared with more regularity, then we should expect to see the same sort of 'monstrousness' among plants: for example, a plant that presents a grapevine on one side and an olive tree on the other. But this is not established by experience.[12]

Nonetheless, in the bestiary portion of *On Animals*, Albertus lists monstrous beasts from antiquity, such as a pegasus, possessing an eagle's wings but the body of a horse, and the *pilosus*, or 'hairy man', a faun-like creature who is human above and goat below. Despite – or indeed because of – its anthropoid face, Albertus assigns the latter to the monkey genus. Owing to its composite nature, he adds that 'it is quite monstrous and sometimes walks erect and is tamed.' Albertus' source, Thomas of

Jan van Schayck, oak panel with a wild man supporting an
escutcheon, from an organ case in the church of St Vitus
in Naarden, c. 1510–20.

Cantimpré, provides a much lengthier description of the *pilosus* and remarks that in his own day one of these creatures, having the head of a dog but appearing human in other respects except for the hair on its back, was brought to the king of France. At court, it drank wine and ate its food so delicately that no one doubted that it seemed human in this respect. It stood erect like a human and 'united' with (*jungebatur*) women and girls. It also had a large genital member, Thomas adds, completely out of proportion to its body.[13]

Even though Albertus includes a description of the *pilosus* – could he have seen the one brought to the French king? – he expresses reservations concerning many mythical monstrous animals. Although Albertus identifies a creature called a unicorn, his description seems clearly to be that of a rhinoceros. In fact, he glosses the Latin *unicornis* with the Greek *rynnoceros*. And although Albertus identifies the harpy, 'a bird of prey

Griffin in a miniature from the Northumberland Bestiary (*c.* 1250–60).

having hooked talons and a human face', he also attributes its description 'to a certain man of no great authority and whose statements are not proven by experience'. He includes in his description the claim that if this bird kills a human, when it sees its own humanoid face reflected on the surface of water, it grieves forever for killing one that it resembles: 'but these things are not borne out by experience and seem to be fabulous, especially the things a certain Adelinus relates, as well as Solinus and Jorach'.[14] Albertus frequently criticizes Solinus and Jorach, and complains that 'these philosophers tell many lies'. In the same way, although Albertus provides a description of the mythical griffin – a bird with the head of an eagle but with the hindquarters of a lion – he casts doubt upon its existence, adding, 'that griffins are birds is more a statement made by the histories than something asserted by the expert findings of philosophers or by proofs based on natural philosophy [rationes physicae]'.[15]

Likewise, although he includes an account of the basilisk, 'a serpent like a cock in all respects except for having a long serpent's tail', he also expresses his doubts: 'now I do not think this is true, but it was said by Hermes and has been accepted by many on the authority of the one saying it.' Similarly, he attributes the description of the Sirens to 'poets' tales' and notes that 'the poets likewise say that Scilla is a sea monster . . . [with] the shape of a young woman . . . a huge mouth opening and very sharp teeth.'[16]

This is not to say that Albertus dismisses all accounts of mythical, monstrous beasts. He records Pliny's account of nereids – mermaid-like creatures – without objection (DA, 24.45, no. 86; SZ, vol. II, p. 1693). He also includes a description that came to him from 'natural philosophers who write about the monsters of the world'. He identifies a certain 'Persian named Astyages' who, 'if we are to believe his stories', reports on an Indian animal resembling a bear but belonging to the wolf genus, with feet

Siren and centaur in a miniature from a Franco-Flemish Bestiary
(*c.* 1270).

Basilisk in a miniature from the Northumberland Bestiary (*c.* 1250–60).

H mdia nafat teftia que manucoza dz mpltci tcuum ordine to
cunto inctho: altitus facte hominus folautif oculus fanoumteo tolo

Manticore (creature with the body of a lion, the head of a man and
the tail of a scorpion) in a miniature from the Northumberland Bestiary
(c. 1250–60).

like a lion, a scorpion-like tail and a human face (but with an
'imperfect' human voice). This is the *maricon morion* that,
Albertus claims incorrectly, means 'insane man' (*vir insanus*)
in Latin and is similar to the manticore. Despite the fantastic
elements in this description, Albertus finds it credible based on
a report that he may have heard from hunters, perhaps, in
Germany:

> For a little before our time in the forests of Saxony near
> Dacia, in a certain deserted heath, two monsters were
> captured which were hairy and had a shape in all respects
> like that of a human. The female was dead from the bites
> of the dogs and the wounds of the hunters, but the male
> was captured and tamed. It learned to get around erect on
> two feet and it learned to talk quite imperfectly and using
> only a few words. It had a thin voice like a roebuck and
> had no power of reason at all and was thus not in the least
> ashamed about the privy, excretion, or other such matters.

It had a great appetite for intercourse with women and
tried to overcome such women as were around whenever
it was in rut.[17]

Despite a willingness to accept this account of 'monsters'
captured in the forests of Saxony, more often than not Albertus
expresses his doubts and sometimes counters accounts of mythical or fabulous creatures with his own observations. This is
apparent in his treatment of the 'ant-lion' (*formicaleon* or *mur-
mycaleon*), a mythical man-eating creature whose body is like a
lion in the front and to the rear like an ant. Albertus provides
a thoroughly naturalistic and accurate account, insisting that
the ant-lion is a type of insect and that

> this animal does not start out as an ant, as some say.
> For I have seen myself and have pointed out to my
> companions that this animal has the approximate
> shape of an *engulas* [tick] and that it hides in the
> sand by digging a hemispherical hole.

This is an excellent description of the ant-lion, most likely
Euroleon nostras, which is found throughout Europe. Albertus
also records his doubts concerning the so-called monstrous races
that were thought to reside at the furthest reaches of the world.
For example, he notes that nature has established that every
animal will have feet in pairs. In an apparent reference to the
fabled Sciopods, or 'umbrella-foot' people – who, since antiquity,
were said to have hopped about on one foot – Albertus remarks,
'Therefore, what is said about the monopeds is proven to be false
and what people say about their getting around by hopping about
is nothing.' The Sciopods were also said to protect themselves
from the sun and rain with their enormous umbrella-foot while
lying on their backs. But, says Albertus, 'what is said about the

Monstrous races: Antipode, Scinopode, Coastal Ethiopian and
Psalmlarus, miniature from a Franco-Flemish Bestiary (c. 1270).

large-footed people is an absurd falsehood.' Albertus also denies
that the 'dog-people' (canini homines) found in the Mappa mundi
are hybrid monsters. Instead, they are a type of monkey that
'seems to have the head of a dog and which is called the dog-
monkey [canina simia, baboon]'. He then provides a reasonably
accurate description of a baboon.[18]

Unlike most of his contemporaries, Albertus had a naturalist's interest in monsters. He was fascinated more than horrified
by them and wanted to find causal explanations for their

occurrence. As we have seen, most often he will assign the cause to the matter available at conception: either there is too little or too much, and the informative power of the male sperm then produces a monstrous progeny with a birth abnormality. A monster is not only a physical anomaly, however. Albertus also identifies monstrousness (*monstruositas*) in behaviour and character, which seems to follow from the body's deformity. Just as earlier Albertus explains that 'character [*mores*] follows complexion', he also remarks,

> Plato's statement was wise when he said that 'monsters of character [*monstra morum*] occur just like monsters of nature.' For a monstrosity of nature, because it is evidence of corruption to the organs in which the moving spirits exist, often causes monstrosity of character [*monstruositatem morum*]; and this is why Moses the Egyptian said that 'a monster in body is also a monster in soul and in character.'[19]

It is the 'monster in soul and in character' who introduces disorder to the moral universe that causes Albertus to retreat in horror. This is the Frankenstein that disturbed *his* dreams.[20]

ELEVEN

Albertus' Legend and Influence

On 15 November 1280 Albertus Magnus breathed his last at the Dominican Cloister in Cologne. Three days later he was interred, undoubtedly with the words 'Rest in Peace' spoken over his body at his funeral Mass. Yet, as we will see, just as in life, Albertus was not allowed to rest in peace. Before addressing this fact, however, it would be useful to survey the sources we possess for Albertus' reputation. The most contemporary are laudatory statements concerning Albertus that came from his students such as Thomas of Cantimpré (1201–1272) or Ulrich of Strasbourg (d. 1277). Certain other mentions of Albertus occur in works such as the chronicle of Henry of Herford (d. 1370), but the greatest amount of material concerning Albertus' life and influence comes from biographies of Albertus commissioned by the Dominicans of the fifteenth century as they sought to have Albertus canonized as a saint. Luis de Valladolid was a Spanish Dominican who, in 1414, produced an index of Albertus' works and appended to it a short life of Albertus, whose cult was rising in the fifteenth century. Peter of Prussia produced a life around 1485, as did Rudolph of Nijmegen circa 1488. David J. Collins argues convincingly that these lives were created to provide evidence to have Albertus canonized.[1] While there may be a certain amount of exaggeration in this hagiography, its stories inform what we know of the legend of Albertus.

Albertus was laid to rest in the church of the Cologne Cloister, which lay not far from the present church of St Andrew (shown in Chapter One). The site today bears a bronze marker at the intersection of An den Dominikanern and Stolkgasse. Some fifty years later, Albertus' name was submitted to Pope John XXII (r. 1316–34), along with those of Thomas Aquinas and Raymond of Peñafort, as a candidate for canonization. Of the three names submitted, only Aquinas, Albertus' student, was canonized at the time. Raymond of Peñafort, a fellow Dominican and contemporary of Albertus known for his saintliness and expertise in canon law, was eventually canonized in 1601, more than three hundred years before Albertus. The pope, Luis tells us, did grant permission to erect a chapel in Lauingen, Albertus' birthplace and almost surely one of the places where devotion to Albertus began.

In 1483, as the Dominicans prepared once more to submit Albertus for canonization, his sepulchre was opened in the presence of many Dominican dignitaries. Rudolph of Nijmegen actually provides evidence that it might have been opened earlier. After describing Albertus' death, Rudolph immediately states that 'after the passage of a bit of time', the tomb was opened 'for the sake of [a] devotion'; the body was found to be entirely incorrupt (a traditional sign of sainthood) and a sweet odour filled the room.[2] The implication is that this event took place shortly after Albertus' death. Peter of Prussia describes the event in minute detail.[3] The stone sarcophagus was covered with dirt since its wooden coverings had rotted away. The body, however, had fared much better, and Albertus was still accompanied by the objects that had been put in his coffin. These included his bishop's staff, which he held in his hand; his episcopal mitre; a copper ring on his finger; and sandals on his feet. Around his neck he still bore several relics that he had carried while alive, a coin pierced with a nail from the Crucifixion, and pieces of the cross. He also bore an Agnus Dei made of wax and wrapped in silk. An Agnus Dei is a small disc made annually from the remnants of the Paschal candles in Rome and blessed by the pope.[4] These were distributed as papal favours throughout the year, and it is fitting that Albertus owned one. Peter, as if speaking for the committee that would review the evidence for Albertus' canonization, goes through a description of the partially decomposed body from head to toe. The bodily parts remained connected, the eyes still possessed a certain light, and his chin had bristles of beard. Flesh adhered to one humerus and to parts of his legs. The body and relics were enclosed behind glass after the exhumation to facilitate viewing by the faithful, the one exception being Albertus' right arm, which was removed and sent to Pope Sixtus IV. Later, on 2 June 1693, Albertus' tomb was reopened, and another relic was detached from the body for the bishop of Regensburg.

Miracles are a sign of sainthood, but in Albertus' case, witnesses to possible miracles were long dead. Nevertheless, the biographers did their best to present credible instances of miraculous intervention. Shortly after the exhumation, for example, a young man was cured of blindness and a woman of her chronic illness. Another man who had lost his sense of smell had it restored when he immediately smelled the sweet odour Albertus' body gave off. Many other cures have also been claimed for ailments ranging from dysentery to violent headaches, but three reports of apparitions of Albertus are even more impressive. The Dominican Godfrey of Duisburg was deeply saddened by Albertus' death and prayed continuously with fasting and tears for his soul. As he was praying, Albertus appeared to him dressed in episcopal garb that was covered with precious gems radiating light. He explained to Godfrey a mortal's eyes could not endure viewing his heavenly presence and that his appearance was symbolic, with each jewel representing one of his books, spreading light and knowledge throughout the world. At Trier, a recently deceased noblewoman known for her piety appeared to her confessor. After inquiring how she fared in the afterlife, he asked, 'Do you know Albertus Magnus, a brother of our Order of Preachers, who recently died in Cologne?' The woman replied that she did and added that he was enjoying ineffable joy far beyond her own. A certain Theutoca, a Cistercian abbess, saw Albertus one morning in church shortly after his death, standing in front of the altar as if to preach to the congregation, but doing so floating in mid-air.

This evidence did not prevail, however, and once more Albertus was denied canonization. Pope Innocent VIII did allow altars to be set up in Dominican cloisters in Cologne and Regensburg, and said that Dominicans could celebrate 15 November as his feast day. This status remained until 1670, when Pope Clement X officially beatified Albertus, making the cult worldwide. Yet canonization was not granted, and one might well ask why such a staunch theologian, biblical commentator and high cleric who had preached a crusade should have met this sort of opposition. The answer lies not in Albertus' deeds but in the fact that his investigations into natural philosophy left him open to criticism. Rudolph of Nijmegen explains that some of Albertus' later detractors complained that Albertus was *too* interested in the things of nature (rather than in the articles of faith) and too devoted to the works of the pagan philosophers. His excessive curiosity led them to incriminate him and even accuse him of practising magic.[5]

More problematic for Albertus were charges of his being a practising alchemist and magician, charges that began in his own lifetime and grew after his death. His own pupil Ulrich of Strasbourg (also known as Ulrich von Engelbrecht) is even quoted as having said Albertus was an expert or had experience in magic (*in magicis expertus*).[6] Various legends about suspect behaviour also arose around Albertus, as we have seen above in the tale of the talking automaton Albertus supposedly created. Another story that emphasizes his apparent skill as a magician is that in the winter of 1249, when Duke William II of Holland visited, Albertus caused a garden to bloom amid the snow.[7] Another tale from the troubadours concerns an evil princess who lured young men into her abode only to seduce them and then cast them into the river. Such tactics failed to work on Albertus, who added that he knew of the previous victims. The princess ordered Albertus tied up and thrown into the river, only to see the ropes burst asunder and Albertus skilfully navigate the waves. Arrows were shot to finish the job, but they turned into birds and flew about his head. Albertus, it is said, then tied messages revealing the princess's evil deeds to each of the birds and set them free across the land. Other stories include magical cups, travels with Alexander the Great, riding to Rome on the back of the Devil, and the story that Albertus whisked away the daughter of the king of France from her home to Cologne through the air.

In fact, Albertus studied fields that some considered contrary to religious beliefs, such as astronomy, astrology and alchemy.[8] For Albertus, the movements of the heavens were an integral part of an ordered cosmos, and their study was as justified as that of animals, plants or minerals. Aristotle, after all, discussed astronomy in his works and was a believer in the ability of the movements of the heavens to influence aspects of human life. Albertus took up Aristotle's beliefs and comments on them in such works as On Generation and Corruption (De generatione et corruptione) and On the Heavens (De caelo), and it is clear that he shared the overall belief that the movement of the celestial bodies can influence life below. In general, however, Albertus is more interested in describing these effects as part of the science of astronomy than he is in astrology, that is, using these phenomena to achieve certain results in the lower world. The dividing lines are thin. Astrologers create horoscopes and make prognostications, like those for the outcome of a new business venture or the result of a pregnancy, and astronomy also has practical goals such as weather forecasting or the effects climate can have on agriculture and animal husbandry. Albertus' case was not helped by the fact that the medieval Latin word *astronomia* can be used to mean either astronomy or astrology.

It is an easy thing to believe that one who is engaged in astrology is dabbling in magic. Collins recently studied this in an excellent article that explains how Albertus Magnus came to be perceived by some as Albertus the magician (*magus*).[9] Bias against Albertus was worsened by *The Mirror of Astronomy/Astrology* (*Speculum astronomiae*), a work attributed to Albertus as early as the fourteenth century. It treats both the astronomical and astrological aspects of *astronomia* and, when discussing the practical ones, categorizes some practices as legitimate and others as not.

Parts of Albertus' *On Minerals* surely contributed to the beliefs that he favoured illicit practices. At the very beginning of the third tractate of *On Minerals*, he states:

Now we must speak of the images and sigils in stones; for although this [subject] belongs to that part of necromancy which is dependent on astrology . . . yet, because it is good doctrine, and because the members of our Order have desired to learn this from us, we shall say something here . . . about whatever has been written of these things by many people. Few really understand the writings of the wise men of antiquity about the sigils of stones, nor is it possible to understand them without at the same time understanding the sciences of astrology, magic, and necromancy. (*DM*, p. 127)

Despite this careful attempt to distance himself from the illicit uses of natural science, it is easy to see how statements by Albertus on the efficacy of a given stone could be taken in the wrong light. This is especially true for his discussions of the powers of amulets in DM, pp. 146ff. Albertus relates beliefs that amulets can cure any number of diseases and can even possess odd powers, such as the ability to extinguish fires, and speaks of magnets that attract gold, silver, tin, lead and even bones, hair, human flesh, water and fish. On occasion, he denounces the use of a substance, such as the fact 'white naphtha' attracts fire and that the 'keepers of temples' in Chaldea deceive the common folk by using it to claim that they can bring fire down from heaven. Yet Albertus insists that claims like this are borne out by experience and proven by great men.

Albertus also shows more than a passing interest in alchemy in his *On Minerals*. Further, Albertus expressly says that 'I have inquired into the transmutations of metals in alchemy, so as to learn from this, too, something of [metals'] nature and accidental properties.' Later in the same passage, he goes even further:

> As to the transmutation of these bodies and the change of one into another, this is to be determined not by natural science but by the art called alchemy. Likewise, in what places and mountains [metals] may be discovered, and by what indications, are matters partly for natural science and partly for the science of magic called treasure-finding. Therefore the signs by which these places that produce metals may be recognized we shall mention below; and as to the other method of discovery, we shall [omit] it, because that science depends not upon [scientific] demonstrations but upon experience in the occult and the supernatural.[10]

It must have been easy for those seeking evidence that Albertus dabbled in alchemy to overlook his caution here. Later, when describing the possibility of turning lead into gold, he is cautious once more, saying, 'Besides, we have rarely or never found an alchemist . . . who could perform the whole process'; that the best he had seen was the ability to impart a golden colour to the lead and not its actual transmutation. When describing the natural creation of gold, he allows for the possibility of creating it artificially through alchemical means if the alchemists 'work with nature'. But in another place, he clearly says that those who claim to turn metal into gold are deceivers and that he had tests performed on some alchemical gold and silver. These products endured six or seven firings but after that were reduced to dross. J. R. Partington sums up the sometimes-confusing evidence well:

> There is no doubt . . . that Albert firmly believed in the possibility of the transmutation of metals, which, however, he considered very difficult, and that he also knew from personal experience that many alchemists were impostors and their products mere imitations.[11]

It is no surprise, then, that Albertus' somewhat-wavering cautions and caveats could be overlooked and that, as a result, the titles of over fifty books of alchemy were attributed to Albertus after his death.[12] The most famous of these attributed works is *The Right Path* (*Semita recta*), a veritable handbook for alchemists, written to correct the many failures 'Albertus' had observed. In fact, Jammy's 1651 edition of Albertus' complete works includes five alchemical works that were likely attributed to Albertus to give them greater authority and legitimacy.[13]

Albertus' reputation as an alchemist was so enduring that his image appeared on a 1929 French trading card for 'Real Liebig Meat Extract', which identified Albertus as a thirteenth-century

Trade card for Extrait de viande de la Cie Liebig (Liebig Meat Extract Company) depicting Albertus Magnus, 1903.

alchemist. Such alchemical works bearing Albertus' name undoubtedly had an adverse effect on his progress towards canonization. Pope John XXII, for example, to whom the first request had been presented, was an assiduous critic of alchemists. Albertus' canonization process would only be completed in 1931 when Pope Pius XI used the vehicle of equipollent canonization to name Albertus a saint and bestow on him the name *Doctor universalis*, setting 15 November, the day of Albertus' death, as his feast day. This 'equivalent' canonization is somewhat rare and is used especially for people long dead whose miracles could not be verified by witnesses appearing before a committee of inquiry. In 1941, in the decree *Ad Deum*, Pope Pius XII declared Albertus the patron saint of students of the natural sciences.

Albertus' body was to be disturbed on three more occasions. In 1802, due to the invasion of Napoleon and the subsequent dissolution of the monasteries, his remains were moved to the church of St Andrew, which lay close to the cloister, and in 1859 they were moved to the Gothic Shrine in the church.

St Andrew's was damaged by bombing during the Second World War, and in the process of restoration, a crypt decorated with murals was discovered under the altar that had been destroyed in the fifteenth century. In 1954 Albertus' remains were moved for a final time to where they can be visited today, reposing in a third-century Roman sarcophagus repurposed for the task. St Andrew's lies just a few blocks' walk from the much more famous Cologne Cathedral and is well worth the visit. In fact, in 1980, on the seven hundredth anniversary of Albertus' birth, Pope John Paul II did just that.

In the end, Albertus' influence is on par with the astonishing number of his written works. No less a figure than G.W.F. Hegel (1770–1831), one of the greatest philosophers of the modern age, described Albertus Magnus as 'the most celebrated German schoolman'.[4] Many high schools in the United States bear his name, as does Albertus Magnus College of New Haven, Connecticut, and his statues can be found in such diverse places as the universities of Houston and Cologne. In 1931, the same

Albertus' sarcophagus in the crypt of St Andrew's Church, Cologne.

year as Albertus' canonization, the prestigious Albertus-Magnus-Institut was founded, with one of its main goals being the publication of the *Cologne Edition*, which will be composed of critical editions of the entire corpus of Albertus' works. Until that monumental task is accomplished, almost all the previously complete works of Albertus published in 21 volumes by Jammy in 1651 and in 38 by Auguste and Émile Borgnet from 1890 to 1899 are available through the 'Alberti Magni e-corpus', sponsored by the University of Waterloo (Canada). The future, then, is bright for a continuation of the substantial work on Albertus, his writings and his thought.

In conclusion, no better testimony to the influence of Albertus' works on the study of the natural world exists than these words of Pope Benedict XVI, taken from a general audience he granted on 24 March 2010 in St Peter's Square:

> He still has a lot to teach us. Above all, St Albert shows that there is no opposition between faith and science, despite certain episodes of misunderstanding that have been recorded in history . . . With a classical similitude in the Middle Ages and in the Renaissance one can compare the natural world to a book written by God that we read according to the different approaches of the sciences.

APPENDIX

Boots the Bishop

Most lives of Albertus Magnus mention his nickname, 'Boots the Bishop', a delightful translation by James A. Weisheipl of the medieval Latin *Episcopus cum bottis* (the bishop with boots) or *Episcopus cum magnis sotularibus* (the bishop with big sandals). The nickname is rightly invoked as an indication of how far Albertus – who, as a Dominican, was forbidden to use luxurious means of transportation such as horses or wagons – walked during the course of his life. In fact, in *On Animals*, Albertus often refers to various hides that are good for making sandals, recommendations certainly based on experience. But how far did Boots the Bishop actually walk? What follows is an attempt to approximate an answer to this question. In constructing it, we have relied heavily on the work of Paul von Loë, supplemented with that of Wyckoff.[1]

It must be said at the start that absolute accuracy is impossible in this matter for a number of reasons. Modern civil engineering, for example, has been able to level roads for automobiles that were once arduous climbs for travellers on foot. Modern bridges and tunnels defeat obstacles that often caused travellers to divert their paths to find a longer 'way around'. As a result, there is no adequate way to find out the amount of effort Albertus had to expend in his various travels. Nonetheless, through the wonders of the Global Positioning System, one can rather easily calculate the current length and time of a given journey on foot. Yet difficulties also arise from gaps in our records and conflicting accounts of Albertus' travels. For example, Albertus' earliest journey seems to be his round-trip travel to Padua and Venice, and the means of his travel depends on the thorny issue of when he became a Dominican, since before taking vows he could travel by horseback or in a conveyance. For our calculations here, we follow the tradition that Albertus joined the order in Padua, although without arriving at a final decision on the matter.

Let us consider one period that exhibits these problems. According to our sources, when Albertus was a lector, he visited four priories during a period in the 1230s or 1240s in the following order: Hildesheim, Freiburg, Regensburg and Strasbourg. Albertus also tells us that 'at one time I had become a wanderer [*exul enim aliquando factus fui*], travelling to metal-rich places so that I might experience the natures of metals' (DM, p. 53). Albertus' own words, along with Wyckoff's knowledge of the metallurgy of the area, pinpoint some of the mines and smelting places he visited on this 'mining tour': Hildesheim, Goslar, Eisleben and Freiberg.[2] Wyckoff believes this 'tour' took place before Albertus joined the Dominicans, but some of these places overlap with or lie along the route of his travels as lector, a period when he may well have felt like an *exul*, one without a home. On the other hand, Goslar is only a ten-hour trip from Hildesheim and may only represent a side trip when he was in residence there. Nor is there any guarantee he did not visit it more than once. Considering all this uncertainty, we have chosen not to include the mining tour in our calculations, even though it certainly would add significant miles to the total. Similar questions arise concerning the travels of Albertus as preacher of the Crusade during 1263–4. We are fortunate to have records of his activities during this period (consecrating altars and churches, settling disputes and so on), and the work done by Stehkamper in turning these data into plausible routes is of great help.[3] We have chosen to use only the documented routes Stehkamper proposes. Certainly, Albertus visited many more places than these, however.

There are also notable gaps in our records. When Albertus was prior provincial of the German Dominicans, he became responsible for visiting as many Dominican houses under his guidance as he could. These included approximately forty priories and convents within his province, which encompassed Alsace, Lorraine, Luxembourg and the Low Countries, Germany, Austria, Switzerland, Bohemia, parts of Poland, Lithuania and even Riga in Latvia. Yet our knowledge of the actual number and order of the visits is incomplete. If the names of some destinations can refer to more than one place, tentative choices must necessarily be made. The reader is directed to the biographical section of this book, where details surrounding such choices are given.

An additional problem arises from the fact that, when Albertus was named bishop of Regensburg in 1260, he was likely granted a dispensation from the rules of his order. Furthermore, he was probably between 55 and 60 years old, and it may be that on some occasions, especially later in his life, he allowed himself the luxury of a wagon. Wyckoff reports that this was the case in 1270 when, only ten years before his death, Albertus visited Mecklenburg.[4] On certain occasions, such as the time Albertus spent at the Curia as it moved about Italy, it is difficult to imagine that as the pope rode, the Dominican bishop tried to keep up on foot. Nevertheless, the very existence of the nickname 'Boots the *Bishop*' is telling, and later biographies insist that he travelled throughout his diocese on foot, supported by a walking stick and leading a donkey bearing his episcopal vestments and books. Even if some of the journeys Albertus undertook, especially later in life, were by conveyance, they nonetheless help demonstrate the extent of his travels. And if they are listed below as journeys on foot, they are certainly offset by the innumerable journeys about which we know but for which itineraries cannot be reproduced.

In an attempt to be cautious, we have omitted the reports of some journeys, such as Albertus' supposed visit to Riga in modern Latvia or the story that, as quite an elderly man, Albertus travelled to Paris in 1277 to speak in defence of Thomas Aquinas. In an instance where all we know is that Albertus was in a particular place, we omit the travel since we lack a starting place. When GPS offered alternate routes, we consistently chose the longest one, presuming that it better reflects thirteenth-century conditions. In order to estimate how many days a journey took, it was necessary to attempt the impossible task of establishing a miles per day average for a medieval monk on foot at various stages of his life. After consulting various charts online, it was determined that the average walking pace is 5 kilometres (3 mi.) per hour. A generous estimate of actual time spent walking would be eight hours, yielding 40 kilometres (24 mi.) per day. No adjustment was made for age, terrain or weather and numbers are rounded up. Actual walking times were undoubtedly greater, especially later in Albertus' life.

In the end, what do these numbers indicate? We can say with reasonable certainty that Albertus probably walked more than 30,000 kilometres (19,000 mi.) in his lifetime and that he spent over a full year of his life walking. To give this some perspective, Albertus' total mileage is approximately the equivalent of four roundtrips from Cologne to Jerusalem.

Date	Trip (* = round trip)	Mileage	Kilometres	# of days	Notes
1221	Lauingen to Padua	330	531	14	With uncle, for education
1224/5?	Padua to Venice	30	48	1	Observes earthquake
1224/5?	Venice to Padua	30	48	1	
1228	Padua to Cologne	573	922	24	
1233	Cologne to Hildesheim	178	286	7	As lector
1238	Hildesheim to Bologne*	1,290	2,076	54	General chapter
1230s–40s	Hildesheim–Freiburg–Regensburg–Strasbourg	762	1,226	32	As lector
1240s	Strasbourg to Paris	277	446	12	University of Paris
1248	Paris to Cologne	283	455	12	Opens studium generale
1254	Cologne to Worms*	256	412	11	Provincial chapter; declared prior provincial
1254	Cologne to Ottenheim*	436	702	18	Hosted by Count of Ottenheim
1255	Cologne to Brandenburg*	640	1,030	27	Visits Dominican house
February 1255	Cologne to Soest*	152	245	6	Professes the first nuns
June 1255	Cologne to Milan*	1,004	1,616	42	General chapter
after June 1255	Cologne to Regensburg*	616	991	26	Presides over provincial chapter
June 1256	Cologne to Paris*	566	911	24	General chapter
after June 1256	Cologne to Erfurt*	408	657	17	Presides over provincial chapter
end of September 1256	Cologne to Anagni	893	1,437	37	Papal visit
December 1256	Anagni to Rome	42	68	2	
May 1257	Rome to Viterbo	57	97	2	

May 1257	Viterbo to Florence	136	219	6	General chapter
Summer 1257	Florence–Bologna–Cologne	692	1,114	29	
June 1257	Cologne to Augsburg*	582	937	24	Provincial chapter
June 1259	Cologne to Valenciennes*	346	557	14	General chapter
Mid-March–29 March 1260	Cologne to Regensburg	308	496	13	To take position of bishop
August 1260	Regensburg to Lerchenfeld*	106	171	4	Consecrated altar
September 1260	Regensburg to Landau*	406	653	17	Conference of bishops
1260	Regensburg to Strasbourg*	472	760	20	General chapter
1261	Regensburg to Donaustauf*	16	26	1	For study and contemplation
End of May 1261	Regensburg to Viterbo*	1,162	1,870	48	Seeks release from episcopacy
1263	Regensburg to Polling	68	109	3	Preaching Crusade
May 1263	Polling to Würzburg	183	295	8	Preaching Crusade
June 1263	Würzburg to Frankfurt am Main*	144	232	6	Preaching Crusade
July 1263	Würzburg to Cologne	181	291	8	Return
October 1263	Cologne to Brandenburg	320	515	13	Resolves local issues
December 1263	Brandenburg to Freiburg	232	373	10	Preaching Crusade
February 1264	Freiburg to Speyer	356	573	15	Preaching Crusad By March 1264
By March 1264	Speyer to Regensburg	189	304	8	Preaching Crusade
By August 1264	Regensburg to Mainz	210	338	9	Preaching Crusade
By December 1264	Mainz to Würzburg	88	142	4	Mediates dispute
July 1267	Würzburg to Burtscheid	215	346	9	Consecrates chapel and altar

4 August–September 1267	Burtscheid to Cologne	45	72	2	Consecrates church
Autumn 1267	Cologne to Strasbourg	197	317	8	DM, p. xxii
29 April 1268	Strasbourg to Esslingen*	186	299	8	Consecrates church
1268	Strasbourg to Adelhausen*	156	251	7	Consecrates church for leprosarium
Summer 1268	Strasbourg to Mecklenburg*	914	1,471	38	Settles dispute
1269	Strasbourg to Basel*	156	251	7	Consecrates church
1269	Strasbourg to Unterlinden*	92	148	4	Consecrates choir
1270 (?)	Strasbourg to Cologne	200	322	8	Mediates dispute, remains until death
13 May 1274	Cologne to Lyon*	822	1,323	34	2nd Council of Lyon
After August 1274	Cologne to Fulda*	286	460	12	Papal commission
1274	Cologne to Vochem*	16	26	1	Consecrates altar
1274	Cologne to Brauweiler*	16	26	1	Consecrates altar
30 January 1275	Cologne to Werden*	74	119	3	Consecrates church
9 September 1276	Cologne to Antwerp	125	201	5	Consecrates church and altars
13 September 1276	Antwerp to Leuven	30	48	1	Consecrates church and altars
1276	Leuven to Cologne	109	175	5	Return
20 October 1278	Cologne to Colmar*	472	760	20	Present at erection of convent of Colmar
Totals		19,131	30,789	464	

CHRONOLOGY

c. 1200	Born in Lauingen on the Danube
c. 1221	Sent to Padua to study
1223 or c. 1229	Enters the Dominican Order at Padua in 1223 or at Cologne c. 1229
c. 1229	Provides theological instruction at the Dominican house in Cologne
1233–4	Begins teaching as a lector at Dominican houses in the German Province (in Hildesheim, in either Freiburg-im-Breisgau or Freiberg in Saxony, in Regensburg, and then in Strasbourg)
c. 1240	Arrives in Paris to continue his studies at the University of Paris
1245	Master of theology and then regent master at the University of Paris
1248	15 May: Albertus' name appears as a signatory to the Parisian condemnation of the Talmud
	Returns to Cologne in the summer (accompanied by Thomas Aquinas) to establish and direct a *studium generale* at the Dominican priory of the Holy Cross
1254	Elected Dominican Prior Provincial for the German province
1256–7	Present at the papal court at Anagni for the condemnation of On *the Dangers of the Last Times* and to provide a refutation of the Averroist doctrine of the unity of the intellect
1257	Resigns as Prior Provincial and returns to Cologne, by spring 1258, to lecture
1258	Participates in the Great Arbitration to negotiate a settlement between Cologne's burghers and Cologne's Archbishop Conrad von Hochstaden
1260	Named bishop of Regensburg by Pope Alexander IV and consecrated in March 1260
1262	Travels to the papal court to receive permission to resign his Regensburg bishopric; this was granted by Alexander IV's successor, Pope Urban IV

1263–4	Pope Urban IV commissions Albertus to preach the Crusade in German lands
1264–70	Albertus resides in Würzburg and travels widely across Germany in service to the Dominican Order and the Church (see Appendix)
1270	Returns to the Dominican the priory of the Holy Cross in Cologne to teach and to write
1271	Negotiates peace between the townspeople of Cologne and Archbishop Engelbert II
1274	Likely attended the Second Council of Lyon in May
1280	15 November: Albertus dies in Cologne
1670	Albertus is beatified by Pope Clement X
1931	Albertus is canonized as a saint by Pope Pius XI
1941	Pope Pius XII declares Albertus the patron saint of students of the natural sciences

REFERENCES

1 The Life and Works of Albertus Magnus

1 Feet ablaze: *Inferno*, canto XIX.45ff.; far from: *Paradiso*, 10.98.
2 Roger Bacon, *Opus tertium*, cap. 2, in *Opera quaedam hactenus inedita*, ed. J. S. Brewer (London, 1859), vol. I, p. 13.
3 Ulrich of Strasbourg, *De summo bono*, 4.3.9.
4 Henry of Herford, *Liber de rebus memorabilioribus sive Chronicon Henrici de Hervordia*, cap. 94, ed. A. Potthast (Göttingen, 1859), p. 196.
5 Rudolph of Nijmegen, *Legenda Beati Alberti Magni*, ed. Heribert C. Scheeben (Cologne, 1928), p. 94.
6 Simon Tugwell, *Albert and Thomas: Selected Writings* (New York, 1988), pp. 3–129.
7 James A. Weisheipl, 'Albertus Magnus', in *Dictionary of the Middle Ages*, ed. Joseph R. Strayer (New York, 1982), vol. I, p. 127.
8 Volcano: *CPE*, p. 114; cobblers: *sz*, vol. I, p. 710; Swabian fowlers: *sz*, vol. I, p. 716; upper Germany: *sz*, vol. II, p. 1247; mouse: *sz*, vol. I, p. 768.
9 *ThDA*, 2.57.
10 Nursery: *Taming of the Shrew*, act 1, scene 1, l. 2; in Venice: *DM*, p. 128; earthquake: *Meteora*, 3.2.9.
11 *Epistula* 20, in *Beati Iordani de Saxonia Epistulae*, ed. Angelus Walz, Monumenta Ordinis Fratrum Praedicatorum Historica 23 (Rome, 1951), p. 24.
12 James A. Weisheipl, 'The Life and Works of St Albert the Great', in *Albertus Magnus and the Sciences: Commemorative Essays 1980*, ed. James A. Weisheipl (Toronto, 1980), pp. 13–51, at p. 19.
13 Tugwell, *Albert and Thomas*, p. 4.
14 Ibid., p. 7.
15 John B. Freed, 'St Albert's Brother Henry of Lauingen OP', *Archivum fratrum praedicatorum*, XLVIII (1973), pp. 63–70, at p. 70.
16 Desire of the flesh: *vfOP*, 3.14, pp. 110–11; no other son: *vfOP*, 3.14, p. 111.
17 Gwyn A. Williams, *Medieval London: From Commune to Capital* (London, 1963), p. 315.
18 Caesarius of Heisterbach, *Dial.*, 2.30, vol. I, p. 102.

19 For this text, see *The Jews in the Legal Sources of the Early Middle Ages*, ed. and trans. Amnon Linder (Detroit, MI, 1997), pp. 353–8.

2 From Cologne to Paris

1 *DM*, p. 153.

2 Weisheipl also seems uncomfortable with 1243 or 1244 for Alb.'s arrival in Paris. In his entry 'Albert the Great' in *The New Catholic Encyclopedia* (New York, 1967), vol. I, pp. 254–8, at p. 254, he suggests 1241 as the year in which Alb. was sent to Paris to study theology.

3 Simon Tugwell, *Albert and Thomas: Selected Writings* (New York, 1988), p. 8.

4 Comet: *Meteora*, 1.3.5; wanderer: *DM*, p. 151.

5 Caesarius of Heisterbach, *Dial.*, 5.22, vol. I, p. 304.

6 City of philosophers: *DNL*, p. 121; demon: *ThDA*, 2.57.

7 Did this in Paris: *DM*, p. 123; the rocks of Paris: *CPE*, p. 117, cf. *DM*, pp. 55ff.; someone in Germany: *DM*, p. 129.

8 *Conciliorum oecumenicorum decreta*, canon 1, ed. J. Alberigo, J. A. Dossetti, P. P. Joannou, C. Leonardi, P. Prodi and H. Jedin (Bologna, 1973), pp. 230–71, at p. 230.

9 See *Chartularium Universitatis Parisiensis*, ed. Heinrich Denifle and Émile Chatelain (Paris, 1889), vol. I, no. 128, p. 170. For a discussion of the various theologians caught up in the Parisian controversy, and Albertus' role, see esp. Jeffrey P. Hergan, *St Albert the Great's Theory of the Beatific Vision* (New York, 2002).

10 Michael Scot's translation of Aristotle's *De animalibus* is based on the Arabic translation of Pseudo-Ibn al-Biṭrīq. Scot's translation remained enormously popular into the sixteenth century, even after William of Moerbeke completed a Greco-Latin translation beginning in 1260. See Aafke M. I. Van Oppenraay, 'Avicenna's *Liber de animalibus* ("*Abbreviatio Avicennae*"). Preliminaries and State of Affairs', *Documenti e studi sulla tradizione filosofica medievale*, XXVIII (2017), pp. 401–16.

11 Lynn Thorndike, *Michael Scot* (London, 1965), p. 1.

12 *Meteora*, 3.4.26.

13 *Chartularium Universitatis Parisiensis*, vol. I, no. 59, p. 116.

14 *Summa*, II.1.4.3, vol. XXXII, 108b–111a.

15 For Albertus' text, see 'Compilatio de novo spiritu', no. 76, in *Documenta ecclesiastica Christianae Perfectionis, Studium Spectantia*, ed. Joseph de Guibert (Rome, 1931), pp. 114–25, at p. 123.

16 For the text of this letter, as well as the Latin and Hebrew accounts of the 1240 Paris disputation, see *The Trial of the Talmud: Paris, 1240*, trans. John Friedman and Jean Connell Hoff, Mediaeval Sources in Translation 53 (Toronto, 2012), esp. pp. 93–5.

17 Ibid., p. 96.

18 Ibid., pp. 100–101.

19 All *The Trial of the Talmud*. For inspection, p. 100; testimony of the Jews: p. 102.

20 *Extractiones de Talmud per ordinem sequentialem*, ed. Ulisse Cecini and Óscar de la Cruz Palma, CC CM 291 (Turnhout, 2018).

21 Alexander Fidora, *Albertus Magnus und der Talmud*, Lectio Albertina 20 (Münster, 2020), p. 43.

22 *Super IV libros Sententiarum*, 4.43.1, ed. Borgnet, pp. 501–2.

23 For further discussion, see Irven M. Resnick, 'Talmud, *Talmudisti*, and Albert the Great', *Viator*, XXXIII (2002), pp. 69–86, and esp. pp. 74–7.

24 *De res.*, p. 129.

25 Manuela Niesner, 'Wer mit juden well disputiren'. Deutschsprachige Adversus-Judaeos-Literatur des 14. Jahrhunderts (Tübingen, 2005), p. 485. For the roughly contemporary accusation that the Jews regard the Talmud as if it were law, see also Alex. Hales, *Summa theol.*, 2.2, vol. III, p. 729.

26 *Der Passauer Anonymus. Ein Sammelwerk über Ketzer, Juden, Antichrist aus der Mitte des 13. Jahrhunderts*, ed. Alexander Patschovsky, Schriften der Monumenta Germaniae Historica 22 (Stuttgart, 1968).

27 Fidora, *Albertus Magnus und der Talmud*, p. 38.

28 As we have indicated in a note to this passage (*SZ*, vol. I, p. 594, n. 33), Albertus has apparently jumbled a passage in which Aristotle refutes the belief that the octopus eats its own flesh or body, insisting instead that they are nibbled at by conger eels. This is because Albertus' text transmitted 'eats itself' as *intra se*, which Albertus glosses as 'in its own species'. The identity of the *galahe* is uncertain.

29 See *SZ*, vol. II, pp. 761–2 and n. 127; split marble at will: *SZ*, vol. II, p. 1762; *vermis Solomonis*: Vincent of Beauvais, *Speculum doctrinale*, 15.124.

30 *De homine*, p. 562, ll. 51–5.

31 *Extractiones de Talmud*, p. 206, ll. 18–19.

32 *The Trial of the Talmud*, p. 165.

33 Thomas Aquinas, *Super Ad Timotheum I reportatio*, 1.2.9, p. 214.

34 *Summa*, pars II, tr. 11, q. 64, vol. XXXII, p. 613a.

35 *De mul. forti*, 15.1, p. 111b.

36 G. K. Hasselhoff, *Dicit Rabbi Moyses. Studien zum Bild von Moses Maimonides im lateinischen Westen vom 13. bis zum 15. Jahrhundert* (Würzburg, 2004), pp. 123–4.

37 For a summary account, see Henryk Anzulewicz, 'Die Perspektive auf jüdische Exegese und Philosophie bei Albertus Magnus. Versuch einer ersten Bestandsaufnahme', *Archa Verbi, Subsidia*, XIV (2016), pp. 197–222.

38 William of Tocco, *Ystoria sancti Thomae de Aquino*, cap. 13, ed. Claire le Brun-Gouvanic (Toronto, 1996), p. 116.

3 From Paris to Cologne

1 Peter Abelard, *Theologia Christiana*, 3.45, ed. E. M. Buytaert, CC CM 12 (Turnhout, 1969).

2 Paul von Loë, '[*Legenda Coloniensis*] Vita B. Alberti Magni Circa an. 1483 conscripta', *Analecta Bollandiana*, XIX (1900), pp. 272–84, at p. 279.

3 William of Saint-Amour, *De periculis novissimorum temporum*, ed. and trans. G. Geltner, Dallas Medieval Texts and Translations 8 (Paris, 2008), p. 124.

4 *Phys.*, 1.1.1, pp. 1, 13–14.

5 Pieter De Leemans, *Aristoteles Latinus* XVII 1.iii, *De motu animalium. Fragmenta Translationis Anonymae* (Turnhout, 2011).

6 *Albert the Great's Questions concerning [Aristotle's] 'On Animals'*, trans. Irven M. Resnick and Kenneth F. Kitchell Jr, Fathers of the Church, Medieval Continuation 9 (Washington, DC, 2008).

7 *Albertus Magnus 'On Animals': A Medieval Summa Zoologica*, trans. Kenneth F. Kitchell Jr and Irven M. Resnick, 2 vols (Baltimore, MD, 1999); and *Albertus Magnus 'On Animals': A Medieval Summa Zoologica*, trans. Kenneth F. Kitchell Jr and Irven M. Resnick, revd edn (Columbus, OH, 2018).

8 See Giocchino Curiello, '"Alia translatio melior est": Albert the Great and the Latin Translations of the *Corpus Dionysiacum*', *Documenti e studi sulla tradizione filosofica medievale*, XXIV (2013), pp. 121–51.

9 The *'Opus Maius' of Roger Bacon*, pars 3, cap. 1, ed. John Henry Bridges, 3 vols (London, 1900), vol. III, p. 82.

10 Isabelle Draelants, *Le Liber de virtutibus herbarum, lapidum et animalium (Liber aggregationis): un texte à succès attribué à Albert le Grand*, Micologus Library, 25 (Florence, 2007).

11 These letters date from 1236–7. *The Letters of Robert Grosseteste, Bishop of Lincoln*, 40 and 41, trans. with introduction and annotation by F.A.C. Mantello and Joseph Goering (Toronto, 2010), pp. 160–61.

4 From Cologne to Regensburg and Back Again

1 The name itself suggests these foundations were for *Scotti* or Scots.
2 Benjamin Laqua, 'Nähe und Distanz. Nachbarrechtliche Regelungen zwischen Christen und Juden (12.–14. Jahrhundert)', in *Pro multis beneficiis. Festschrift für Friedhelm Burgard. Forschungen zur Geschichte der Juden und des Trierer Raumes*, ed. Sigrid Hirbodian, Christian Jörg, Sabine Klapp and Jörg R. Müller (Trier, 2012), pp. 73–92, at p. 82, citing *Regensburger Urkundenbuch*, vol. I: *Urkundender Stadt bis zum Jahre 1350*, ed. Josef Widemann, Monumenta Boica 53 (Munich, 1912), p. 74, n. 143.
3 Henry of Herford, *Chronicon*, p. 201.
4 Hannes Möhle, *Albertus Magnus*, Zugänge zum Denken des Mittelalters, 7 (Münster, 2015), pp. 200–209.

5 Those Who Came Before

1 Many authors, of course, appear in multiple categories. The following topics seem only tangentially related to what we would call 'natural sciences': architecture, doxography, harmonics, mathematics, mechanics, metrology, optics, psychology.
2 *Historia* is a transliteration of the Greek ἱστορία, meaning 'inquiry' or 'investigation'. Although the works are written in Greek, they are generally referred to by their Latin, equivalent names.
3 On the weasel: *sz*, vol. II, pp. 1523–4; Isidore: *Etym.*, 12.3.1; version of Pliny: *HN*, 8.226.
4 Brocotoz: *sz*, vol. II, p. 1183; Eradytis: *sz*, vol. II, p. 889; the philosopher Heraclitus: *PA*, 645a18f.; Aradotus the poet: *sz*, vol. I, p. 432; the original Aristotle: *PA*, 645a18f.; aware of the problems: *sz*, vol. II, p. 926.
5 'Less than it should be': *diminitus*, which seems to imply physical gaps or omissions in the text and a poor state of preservation.

6 Albertus and the Encyclopedists

1 The *Speculum naturale* alone consists of 3,718 chapters in 32 books; the *Speculum doctrinale* 2,374 chapters in seventeen books; the

Speculum historiale 3,793 chapters in 31 books; whereas the *Speculum morale* (not by Vincent himself, but produced by anonymous authors a generation later) consists of only three books.

2 Much useful information about Vincent and his work can be found at www.vincentiusbelvacensis.eu.

7 Albertus and the Experts

1 All *sz*. Vultures at Worms: vol. II, pp. 1653–4; nightingales: vol. II, p. 1647; fox pelt: vol. II, p. 1552.

2 'Finest of philosophers': *De gen. et corr.*, p. 206, l. 32; hares: *sz*, vol. II, p. 1256; Aristotle can err: *Phys.*, 8.1.14, p. 578, ll. 26–7; mole eyes: *sz*, vol. I, pp. 98–9.

3 All from *sz*. Magpies: vol. I, p. 650; cuckoo: vol. I, p. 548; ostriches: vol. I, p. 533; cranes: *sz*, vol. I, p. 615; wolves: vol. II, p. 1518; wasps: vol. I, p. 749.

4 All *sz*. Scorpion: vol. II, p. 1761; cricket: vol. II, p. 1748; salamander: vol. II, p. 1731, cf. Barth., *De prop.* 18.20; spider: vol. II, p. 1732.

5 All *sz*. Sea water: vol. I, p. 592; woodpecker: vol. I, p. 694; ostriches: vol. II, p. 1648; honey: vol. I, p. 640.

6 All from *sz*. Kingfishers: vol. II, p. 1633; eat other birds: vol. I, p. 674; swallows: vol. I, p. 689; monogamous: vol. I, p. 690; cranes: vol. I, pp. 537–8.

7 Robin S. Oggins, 'Albertus Magnus on Falcons and Hawks', in *Albertus Magnus and the Sciences*, ed. James A. Weisheipl (Toronto, 1980), pp. 441–62, offers an excellent review of Albertus on falcons and hawks, including his sources.

8 *sz*, vol. II, pp. 1377–1400, 1453–93.

9 All from *sz*. Sparrowhawk: vol. II, p. 1639; catch a falcon: vol. II, pp. 1581–2.

10 All from *sz*. Latvia: vol. I, p. 599; falconer called: vol. II, p. 1756; territories: vol. I, pp. 546–7; gorged itself: vol. II, pp. 1653–4.

11 Wolfhounds: *sz*, vol. I, pp. 668–9; hunting deer: *sz*, vol. I, p. 684. Cf. Hermann Stadler, 'Geschichtlich-zoologische Studien über des Albertus Magnus Schrift *De animalibus*', *Mitteilungen zur Geschichte der Medizin und der Naturwissenschaften*, VI/3 (1907), pp. 249–54.

12 Frederic W. Farrar, *An Essay on the Origin of Language* (London, 1860), p. 10.

13 Text from C. A. Willemsen, ed., *Frederici Romanorum Imperatoris Secundi de arte venandi cum avibus* (Leipzig, 1942), translation ours. Cf. Friedrich Solmsen, 'The Emperor Frederic the Second on the

Limits of Aristotle's Autopsy and Empirical Knowledge', *Hermes*,
CVII (1979), p. 381.

14 What follows is based on Charles Homer Haskins, *Studies in the
History of Mediaeval Science* (Cambridge, MA, 1927), pp. 254–6;
and Ernst Kantorowicz, *Frederick the Second, 1194–1250*, trans.
E. O. Lorimer (New York, 1957).

15 Kantorowicz, *Frederick*, pp. 310–11.

16 *Camelopardulus*: sz, vol. II, p. 1465; *anabula*: sz, vol. II, pp. 1449–50;
seraph/nabun: Pliny, HN, 8.69; *oraflus*: sz, vol. II, pp. 1527–8, ThDNR,
4.84.

17 Avic. DA, 8r.

18 Trident: sz, vol. I, p. 483; flies: vol. I, p. 471; weir: vol. I, p. 633.

19 John B. Friedman, 'Albert the Great's Topoi of Direct Observation
and His Debt to Thomas of Cantimpré', in *Pre-Modern Encyclopaedic
Texts: Proceedings of the Second COMERS Congress, Groningen, 1–4
July 1996*, Brill's Studies in Intellectual History, vol. LXXIX,
ed. P. Binkley and F. Trombley (Leiden, 1997), pp. 390–92.

20 Whales: sz, vol. II, pp. 1666–71; those with experience: sz, vol. II,
p. 1668.

21 Markets: sz, vol. II, p. 1671; among the experts: sz, vol. II, p. 1671.

22 All *sz*. *Illibezzus* and *ankatynos*: vol. I, p. 688; vol. I, *krebs*: vol. I,
p. 83; *orhun*: vol. I, p. 617; *warchengel*: vol. I, pp. 702–3; *wisent,
gemeze, equicervus*: vol. I, pp. 294–301 and vol. II, pp. 1504–5.

23 Friedman, 'Albert the Great's Topoi', pp. 379–92.

24 All *sz*. Other quadrupeds: vol. I, p. 301; points: vol. I, p. 301;
water: vol. II, p. 1471.

25 Edward Heron-Allen, *Barnacles in Nature and in Myth* (London,
1928), pp. 100–108. Some of his conclusions may be suspect, as
they seem to be at odds with the birds' observed migration patterns.

26 Heron-Allen, *Barnacles in Nature*; Maaike van der Lugt, 'Animal
légendaire et discours savant médiéval: la barnacle dans tous ses
états', *Micrologus*, VIII (2000), pp. 351–94.

27 Wisdom teeth: sz, vol. I, p. 310 and vol. II, p. 979; bald man: vol. I,
p. 388 and vol. II, p. 1345; two passages: vol. I, p. 305.

8 Albertus and Everyday Life

1 The reader should know that each instance cited in what follows
was checked against the Stadler text to ensure that it is Albertus'
addition and was not in the text of Aristotle he received from
Michael Scot.

2 See our Appendix.

3 The text is uncertain at this spot; see our discussion on the passage at *sz*, vol. I, pp. 311–12.

4 All *sz*. Ass hide: vol. II, p. 1451; hippopotamus: vol. I, p. 312; walrus: vol. II, p. 1671.

5 All *sz*. *Perna*: vol. II, pp. 1694–6, with notes; *bombex*: vol. II, pp. 1746, 1749; *varius*: vol. II, p. 1542; otter: vol. II, p. 1520.

6 Stitch cloth together: QDA², p. 103; ape makes a tunic: QDA², p. 272; imitates what it sees: *sz*, vol. II, p. 1419; most easily taught animal: *sz*, vol. II, p. 1460.

7 All *sz*. Fishmongers: vol. I, p. 269; sturgeon and cod: vol. I, p. 385; footstools: vol. I, p. 300; brushes: vol. I, p. 295. 'Footstool' seems the best translation of *scabella*, although it can also denote a kneeler in a church or crutch and hand supports for disabled individuals who used them to make their way along the ground.

8 Wyckoff's (DM, p. xxxvii) arguments that Albertus undertook this journey before he became a Dominican are convincing.

9 Dorothy Wyckoff, 'Albertus Magnus on Ore Deposits', *Isis*, XLIX (1958), pp. 109–22, at p. 112.

10 Hyena: *sz*, vol. II, p. 1512 and DM, pp. 96–7; handles: *sz*, vol. I, p. 451; engraved teeth: *sz*, vol. I, p. 380; threads: *sz*, vol. II, p. 86; the nature of metal: DM, p. 153; miners/smelters: DM, pp. 153, 200; renovation: DM, p. 181, n. 6; Montmartre: DM, p. 120; jet: DM, p. 93.

11 All DM. Gold leaf: p. 189; bells: p. 216; ten pearls: p. 105; brass: pp. 221ff.; jasper: p. 100; steel tool; p. 133; *falcones*: p. 92.

12 Gulp: QDA², p. 101; thin/fat: QDA², p. 183; nationalities: QDA², p. 257.

13 Thrush: *sz*, vol. II, p. 1651; snipe: *sz*, vol. II, p. 1640; dormice: *sz*, vol. II, p. 1510; chestnuts and eggs: *sz*, vol. II, pp. 1368–9; broths: *sz*, vol. I, p. 411; hares: *sz*, vol. II, p. 1515; cheese: *sz*, vol. I, pp. 429–30; food and drink: QDA², p. 234; formic wine: *sz*, vol. I, p. 727; laxatives: *Meteora*, 2.3.17.

14 All *sz*. Eyesight: vol. II, p. 1645; rook: vol. II, p. 1631; tough: vol. II, p. 1564 (swan), p. 1626 (crane); jackdaw: vol. II, p. 1639.

15 *Murena* often refers to a moray eel, but the lamprey is commonly called the 'nine-eye' (*Neunauge* in German). The number nine refers to the two eyes and the seven round gill slits behind each eye. Heston Blumenthal, a noted British chef, has created a video in which he follows just this recipe. Search using the terms 'Blumenthal lamprey medieval' to find it on the Internet.

16 All *sz*. Dolphins: vol. II, p. 1678; mullet: vol. II, p. 1691; anemone: vol. II, p. 1686; *huso*: vol. II, pp. 1682–3, 1698.

17 All *sz*. Castration: vol. II, pp. 761–3; capons: vol. II, p. 1629; sexing chicks: *sz*, vol. I, p. 528, cf. *HA*, 559a27f.; tow: vol. I, p. 529.

18 All *sz*. Capons: vol. I, p. 761 and vol. II, p. 1629; *putorius*/fox: vol. I, p. 688, vol. II, pp. 1523–4, 1532–3, 1542.

19 Umberto Albarella and Richard Thomas, 'They Dined on Crane: Bird Consumption, Wild Fowling, and Status in Medieval England', *Acta zoologica Cracoviensia*, XXXXV (2002), pp. 23–38.

20 All *sz*. Partridge: vol. I, p. 496; ducks and geese: vol. II, pp. 1556–9; cranes: vol. I, pp. 537–8; swan: vol. II, pp. 1564–5.

21 For a readable and scholarly history of medieval equine medicine see Klaus-Dietrich Fischer, 'A Horse! A Horse! My Kingdom for a Horse', *Medizinhistorisches Journal*, XXXIV (1999), pp. 123–38, and on Albertus see p. 128, n. 15.

22 Every bird: *sz*, vol. II, p. 1607; Frederick's falconer: *sz*, vol. II, p. 1603.

23 All *sz*. Rent: vol. II, p. 1565; lion's skin: vol. II, p. 1514; elephant dung: vol. II, p. 1477; horse hair: vol. II, p. 1504; mosquitoes: vol. II, pp. 1746–7.

24 All *sz*. Olive oil: vol. II, p. 1463; cuckoo's earth: vol. II, p. 1568; substances: vol. II, p. 1753; hedgehog fat: vol. II, pp. 1507, 1753; mercury and lead: vol. II, p. 1754; centipedes: vol. I, p. 436 and vol. II, p. 1747; frogs: vol. II, p. 1754.

25 Fleabane: *sz*, vol. I, p. 475; ass's lung: *HN*, 28.73.155 and *sz*, vol. II, p. 1452; poisons: *sz*, vol. II, p. 1525.

9 Human Sexuality, Gender and Race

1 All *sz*. Woman and mare: vol. I, pp. 581, 792 and vol. II, p. 1316; prevents conception: vol. II, p. 1516; adore him: vol. II, p. 1475; walking with him: vol. II, p. 1520.

2 All *sz*. Wolf's penis: vol. II, p. 1520; whore: vol. II, p. 1520; antaphrodisiac: vol. II, p. 1520; conception: vol. II, p. 1475; spider: vol. II, p. 1752; urinate: vol. I, p. 845, cf. *QDA²*, p. 411; hare rennet: vol. II, p. 1516; *algazel*: vol. II, p. 1520.

3 Baldness: *sz*, vol. I, pp. 389, 391; eunuchs: *sz*, vol. I, p. 762 and vol. II, p. 1348; too frequently: *QDA²*, p. 556; sunken: *sz*, vol. II, p. 1235.

4 Katharine Park, 'The Life of the Corpse: Division and Dissection in Late Medieval Europe', *Journal of the History of Medicine*, L (1995), pp. 111–32, at p. 111.

5 Near it: *sz*, vol. II, p. 1444; no longer deliver: *sz*, vol. II, p. 1235, 1444; with experience: *De nutr.* 6; damages eyesight: *Spec. nat.*, 31.2;

Lib. phis., 2; bled often: *sz*, vol. II, p. 1135; *QDA²*, p. 335, cf. *Lib. phis.*, cap. 3.

6 *QDA²*, pp. 468–9.

7 Confused beginning: *sz*, vol. I, p. 420; than to form one: *sz*, vol. II, p. 1132.

8 The opinion: *sz*, vol. II, p. 1135; to generate sperm: *QDA²*, p. 468.

9 Stimulated: *QDA²*, p. 196; lechers: *QDA²*, p. 468; easily conceive: *DNL*, p. 102; nocturnal emission: *sz*, vol. II, p. 1441; changes the body: *sz*, vol. I, p. 778; black: *sz*, vol. II, pp. 1443–4; for the others: *QDA²*, p. 230; every part: *QDA²*, p. 536; generations ago: *sz*, vol. II, pp. 1112–13; of the child: *ThDNR*, 4.1, p. 107.

10 Lombard, flawed male: *Sent.*, IV, 35.1; crooked tibia: *Phys.*, 2.1.5; produce a female: *Phys.*, 2.1.5; for this generation: *QDA²*, p. 441; being the humour: *sz*, vol. II, p. 1195; ugly the beautiful: *sz*, vol. II, p. 1195.

11 Female on the right: *QDA²*, p. 531; *anatomia*: *sz*, vol. II, p. 1286.

12 One hermaphrodite: *Lib. phis.*, 7.2; turned itself: *sz*, vol. II, p. 1305; abundant material: *sz*, vol. II, p. 1313; middle of the body: *Phys.*, 2.3.3.

13 Egypt: *sz*, vol. I, pp. 791–2; sixty children: *sz*, vol. I, p. 792; with difficulty: *DNL*, p. 102; *germinando*: *De prop.*, 15.13; children from her: *sz*, vol. II, p. 1314; breasts of them all: *sz*, vol. I, p. 428; Aristotle's text: *HA*, 523a9; that of white women: *sz*, vol. I, p. 432; of a white woman: *Lib. phis.*, 13.

14 All *sz*. Irregular menstruation: vol. I, p. 781; vaginal discharge: vol. I, p. 777; church witness: vol. I, p. 660.

15 From its principle: *sz*, vol. II, p. 1094; can absorb it/average is best: *sz*, vol. II, p. 1094, cf. *sz*, vol. II, pp. 1207, 1235; what is at this location: *QDA²*, p. 329.

16 Charles DuCange cites Michael Scot's text to define *hasta baiardi* as 'the part of the body by which men are men' (*pars corporis, qua viri sumus*). See *Glossarium mediae et infimae Latinitatis* (Paris, 1843), vol. III, p. 632. The term (literally 'wheelbarrow pole' or 'wheelbarrow handle') seems to be slang for the penis. Indeed, Nicola F. McDonald has drawn attention to an image of a woman pushing a phallus-filled wheelbarrow. See McDonald, ed., *Medieval Obscenities* (Woodbridge, 2006), p. 3, image 1.3.

17 *Lib. phis.*, 22–3: 'in viso vasus [sic] longus et grossus significat praeputium magnum & econverso' (Venice, 1486). Joseph Ziegler correctly reads *nasus* for *vasus*. See his 'The Beginning of Medieval Physiognomy: The Case of Michael Scotus', in *Kulturtransfer und*

Hofgesellschaft im Mittelalter: Wissenskultur am sizilianischen und kastilischen Hof im 13. Jahrhundert, ed. Gundula Grebner and Johannes Fried (Berlin, 2008), pp. 299–319, at p. 316; small testicles: *Lib. phis.*, pp. 23, 65.

18 Virginity has been lost: *Lib. phis.*, 23; woman's vessel: *Lib. phis.*, pp. 22–3.

19 Arnoldus Saxo, *De gemmarum virtutibus* 37a, in *Die Encyklopädie des Arnoldus Saxo, zum ersten Mal nach einem Erfurter Codex*, ed. Emil Stange, Beilage zum Jahresbericht (Erfurt, 1906), p. 72.

20 Be tested: DM, p. 93; flows out and inexperienced: *sz*, vol. I, p. 221.

21 Into the womb/mouth of the womb: *sz*, vol. I, p. 844; impregnation is easier: *sz*, vol. II, p. 1208.

22 Bad humours: *sz*, vol. I, p. 845; no blockage: *sz*, vol. I, p. 845; cause of the difficulty: *Spec. nat.*, 31, 29, p. 2315.

23 More sweet: QDA^2, p. 37; heat of passion: *sz*, vol. I, p. 814; in other animals: *sz*, vol. I, pp. 64–5 and vol. II, p. 1446; his mother: *sz*, vol. I, p. 758, cf. Ar. *HA*, 630b31f.; into a ditch: *sz*, vol. I, p. 759, cf. Ar. *HA*, 631a1; with his mother: QDA^2, p. 298.

24 Fire, earth and water: *Can.*, 1.1.3.1; opposite qualities: *sz*, vol. II, p. 895.

25 Balance in complexion: *De homine*, p. 255, l. 23; capable of intellection/all things: *De anima*, 2.3.2; long life: QDA^2, p. 139; shorter life span: QDA^2, p. 281; the physicians: QDA^2, p. 279; balance of heaven: *sz*, vol. II, p. 1413; no contrariety: *De anima*, 2.3.23; contraries: *sz*, vol. II, p. 914.

26 Noble complexion: *Sent.*, III, 3, dist. 16, art. 2; unedited text: *Legitur in annalibus hebraeorum*, found in the British Library's MS Egerton 843. See Joseph Ziegler, 'Text and Context: On the Rise of Physiognomic Thought', in *De Sion exibit lex et verbum domini de Hierusalem: Essays on Medieval Law, Liturgy, and Literature in Honour of Amnon Linder*, ed. Yitzhak Hen (Turnhout, 2001), pp. 159–82, at p. 171, n. 32.

27 Impassable body: *De res.*, p. 286.

28 Shared nature: CPE, p. 33; recover health: DNL, p. 33; differences in *clima*: *sz*, vol. II, p. 915.

29 The northern regions: *sz*, vol. II, pp. 901–2; seventh clime: *Meteora*, 3.4.11; character follows complexion: QDA^2, p. 272; northern ocean: CPE, p. 35; care little: *De nat. loc.*, p. 27; over those climates: DNL, p. 102; small and dark: DNL, p. 77.

30 The Ethiopians: DNL, p. 101, cf. *Meteora*, 3.1.11; frivolous in mind: DNL, p. 102; unsuited for war: QDA^2, p. 278; curly hair: CPE, p. 34;

curly-haired and dry: *CPE*, p. 35; Iamen: may indicate Yemen, while
the Zyndi seem to be an East African people; easily conceive: *DNL*,
p. 102; transferred to other climes: *DNL*, p. 102.

31 Black or brown: *DNL*, p. 108. See Peter Biller, 'The Black
in Medieval Science', in *La Pelle Umana/The Human Skin*,
ed. Agostino Paravicini Bagliani, *Micrologus*, XIII (Florence, 2005),
pp. 477–92.

10 Monsters

1 For the legend, see Minsoo Kang and Ben Halliburton, 'The Android
of Albertus Magnus: A Legend of Artificial Being', in *AI Narratives:
A History of Imaginative Thinking about Intelligent Machines*,
ed. Stephen Cave, Kanta Dihal and Sarah Dillon (Oxford, 2020),
pp. 72–94.

2 Peter of Prussia, *Vita B. Alberti* (Antwerp, 1621), pp. 140–41.

3 Measure of nature: *Sent.*, II, 18.5; manhood: *QDA²*, p. 191; universal
nature: *Phys.*, 2.1.5; female members: *SZ*, vol. II, p. 1312; monster in
nature: *QDA²*, pp. 445–6.

4 Material 'container': *Sent.*, II, 18.5; failings and monstrosities: *SZ*,
vol. I, p. 75; both may be: *SZ*, vol. I, p. 542.

5 Will be a monster: *SZ*, vol. II, p. 1303; a wonder of nature: *SZ*,
vol. II, p. 1295; *tragelafus*: *SZ*, vol. II, p. 1538; cow or pig: *CPE*, p. 91,
cf. *SZ*, vol. II, p. 1304; tales of the poets: *SZ*, vol. II, p. 1304; than
in humans: *SZ*, vol. II, p. 1304; available for generation: *De anima*,
2.2.1.

6 Generated: *SZ*, vol. II, p. 1303; being is good: *QDA²*, p. 539.

7 A reference to Ptolemy's *Tetrabiblos* or *Quadripartitus*, viz., a text in
four books on the philosophy and practice of astrology, composed
about the middle of the second century. Albertus repeats this claim
at *Phys.*, 2.3.3.

8 Albertus refers here to Aries, the first astrological sign, spanning
the first 30 degrees of celestial longitude. The sun begins to transit
or cross Aries at the vernal equinox (21 March). When the sun is at
Aries 0°, the initial point in the sign of Aries, this marks the vernal
equinox. A 'minute' is a unit of measurement, $\frac{1}{60}$ of a degree.
Medieval astronomers sought correspondences between various
astronomical phenomena and events here below. This produced
genethialogy, or the art of predictions based on horoscopes cast at
birth. Ptolemy tries to systematize these various elements in his
Tetrabiblos. *Tetrabiblos*, 3, chap. 8 bears the title 'Of Monsters'.

9 Cf. Deuteronomy 9:2. The Anakim are giants and therefore they are 'monsters' because of their size or 'quantity'.

10 Our attention: *CPE*, p. 91; their estimates: *Sent.*, II, 7.9; rooted in matter: *QDA²*, p. 539; in the progeny: *De anima* 3.4.3; seemed like locusts: *Sent.*, II, 18.5; sixth finger: *QDA²*, p. 540; hands and feet: *sz*, vol. I, p. 1306; horns on its head: *sz*, vol. I, p. 1307.

11 All *sz*. Along the ground: vol. II, p. 1307; lacked a liver: vol. II, p. 1307; one-year-old infant: vol. II, p. 1309.

12 Parents' species: *sz*, vol. II, p. 1295; order as 'monstrous': *sz*, vol. I, p. 241; than in humans: *sz*, vol. II, p. 1304; established by experience: *Phys.*, 2.3.3.

13 Pegasus: *sz*, vol. II, p. 1531; *pilosus*: *sz*, vol. II, p. 1531; and is tamed: *sz*, vol. II, p. 1531; proportion to its body: *ThDNR*, 4.90.

14 'Adelinus', the name introduced by Thomas of Cantimpré at *ThDNR*, 9.22 for the author of a *Liber monstrorum*, appears to be Aldhelm, Abbot of Malmesbury, author of a late seventh-century *Enigmata ex diversis rerum creaturis composita*. See John Block Friedman, *The Monstrous Races in Medieval Art and Thought* (Syracuse, NY, 2000), p. 248, n. 43. At *sz*, vol. II, p. 1450, Albertus identifies Jorach as the author of a work *On Animals*. Little is known of this author, who is cited numerous times by Arnold of Saxony in his *De floribus rerum naturalium* and later by Thomas of Cantimpré, Bartholomew the Englishman and Vincent of Beauvais. Recent scholarship has suggested that Jorach may be identified with King Juba II of Mauritania. See Isabelle Draelants, 'Le dossier des livres *sur les animaux et les plantes* de Iorach: traditions occidentale et orientale', in *Occident et Proche-Orient: contacts scientifiques au temps des Croisades: Actes du colloque de Louvain-la-Neuve, 24 et 25 mars 1997* (Turnhout, 2000), pp. 191–276. Again, at *sz*, vol. II, p. 1549, Albertus remarks that Adelinus and Jorach make certain claims regarding the eagle that are not proven by experience. Solinus summarized Pliny's work on natural history circa 200 CE.

15 All *sz*. *Rynnoceros*: vol. II, p. 982; proven by experience: vol. II, p. 1555; tell many lies: vol. II, p. 1565; *rationes physicae*: vol. II, p. 1565.

16 All *sz*. One saying it: vol. II, p. 1628; 'poets' tales': vol. II, p. 1701; *Scilla*: vol. II, p. 1701.

17 All *sz*. Monsters of the world: vol. I, p. 308; Astyages: vol. I, p. 308; similar to the manticore: vol. II, pp. 1521–2; was in rut: vol. I, pp. 308–9.

18 All *sz*. Hemispherical hole: vol. II, p. 1749; hopping about: vol. I,
   p. 78; absurd falsehood: vol. I, p. 78; dog-monkey: vol. I, p. 312.
19 That is, Rabbi Moses ben Maimon or Maimonides, whose work
   Albertus frequently cites.
20 Character follows complexion: *QDA²*, p. 272; in soul and in
   character: *De mot. an.*, 2.2.5.

11 Albertus' Legend and Influence

1 David J. Collins, 'Albertus, Magnus or Magus? Magic, Natural
   Philosophy, and Religious Reform in the Late Middle Ages',
   Renaissance Quarterly, LXIII (2010), pp. 1–44.
2 Rudolph of Nijmegen, *Legenda Beati Alberti Magni*, 3.1
   (Cologne, 1928), p. 73.
3 Peter of Prussia, *Vita Alberti Magni* (Antwerp, 1621), pp. 333–5.
4 Aislinn Muller, 'The *Agnus Dei*, Catholic Devotion, and
   Confessional Politics in Early Modern England', *British Catholic
   History*, XXXIV (2018), pp. 1–28.
5 Rudolph of Nijmegen, *Legenda*, 3.8, pp. 84–9.
6 Peter of Prussia, *Vita Alberti Magni*, p. 126.
7 J. R. Partington, 'Albertus Magnus on Alchemy', *Ambix*, I (1937),
   pp. 3–20, at p. 7.
8 This area of study is treated in detail by H. Darrel Rutkin, *Sapientia
   Astrologica: Astrology, Magic, and Natural Knowledge, ca. 1250–1800*
   (Cham, 2019). See a shorter version, H. Darrel Rutkin, 'Albert the
   Great and the *Speculum Astronomiae*. The State of the Research at
   the Beginning of the 21st Century', in *A Companion to Albert the
   Great: Theology, Philosophy, and the Sciences*, ed. Irven M. Resnick
   (Leiden, 2013), pp. 451–505.
9 Collins, 'Magnus or Magus'.
10 Accidental properties: DM, p. 153; occult and the supernatural: DM,
   p. 154.
11 Creation of gold: DM, pp. 200–201; actual transmutation: DM,
   p. 176; reduced to dross: DM, p. 179; J. R. Partington, 'Alchemy',
   p. 13.
12 See Pearl Kibre in three articles spanning seventeen years:
   'Alchemical Writings Ascribed to Albertus Magnus', *Speculum*,
   XXVII (1942), pp. 499–518; 'An Alchemical Tract Attributed to
   Albertus Magnus', *Isis*, XXXV/4 (1944), pp. 303–16; and 'Further
   Manuscripts Containing Alchemical Tracts Attributed to Albertus
   Magnus', *Speculum*, XXXIV (1959), pp. 238–47.

13 The five are the *Libellus de alchemia, Concordantia philosophorum de lapide philosophico, De rebus metallicis, Compositum de compositis* and *Breve compendium de ortu metallorum.* See Jammy's vol. XXI.

14 G.W.F. Hegel, *Lectures on the History of Philosophy*, trans. E. S. Haldane and Frances H. Simson, 3 vols (London, 1892–6), vol. III, p. 75.

Appendix

1 Paul Von Loë, 'De Vita et Scriptis B. Alberti Magni', *Analecta Bollandiana*, XX (1901), pp. 272–84; Wyckoff, DM, pp. xiii–xxv.

2 DM, pp. xxxvii–viii.

3 Hugo Stehkamper, ed., *Albertus Magnus: Ausstellung zum 700. Todestag.* Historisches Archiv der Stadt Köln, XV (Cologne, 1980).

4 DM, p. xxii.

FURTHER READING

The literature on Albertus Magnus is vast. The entries below emphasize work available in English anthologies or compilations and are intended to provide a mere taste of the scholarly literature. For a more detailed investigation see especially Resnick and Kitchell Jr, eds, *Albert the Great: A Selectively Annotated Bibliography (1900–2000)*, and Bruno Tremblay, 'Modern Scholarship (1900–2000) on Albertus Magnus: A Complement', *Bochumer philosophisches Jahrbuch für Antike und Mittelalter*, XI (2006), pp. 159–94.

Bonin, Thérèse, *Creation as Emanation: The Origin of Diversity in Albert the Great's 'On the Causes and the Procession of the Universe'* (Notre Dame, IN, 2001)

Cunningham, Stanley B., *Reclaiming Moral Agency: The Moral Philosophy of Albert the Great* (Washington, DC, 2008)

Honnefelder, Ludger, et al., eds, *Albertus Magnus und die Anfänge der Aristoteles-Rezeption im lateinischen Mittelalter/Albertus Magnus and the Beginnings of the Medieval Reception of Aristotle in the Latin West* (Münster, 2005)

Kovach, Francis J., and Robert W. Shahan, eds, *Albert the Great: Commemorative Essays* (Norman, OK, 1980)

Meyer, Gerbert, and Albert Zimmermann, eds, *Albertus Magnus. Doctor universalis 1280/1980* (Mainz, 1980)

Möhle, Hannes, *Albertus Magnus* (Münster, 2015; in German)

Resnick, Irven M., ed., *A Companion to Albert the Great: Theology, Philosophy, and the Sciences* (Leiden, 2013)

—, and Kenneth F. Kitchell Jr, *Albert the Great: A Selectively Annotated Bibliography, 1900–2000* (Tempe, AZ, 2004)

Tugwell, Simon, ed., *Albert and Thomas: Selected Writings* (New York, 1988)

Weisheipl, James, ed., *Albertus Magnus and the Sciences: Commemorative Essays* (Toronto, 1980)

Zambelli, Paola, *The 'Speculum astronomiae' and Its Enigma: Astrology, Theology, and Science in Albert the Great and His Contemporaries* (Dordrecht, 1992)

PHOTO ACKNOWLEDGEMENTS

The author and publishers wish to express their thanks to the below sources of illustrative material and/or permission to reproduce it. Some locations of artworks are also given below, in the interest of brevity:

akg-images/Erich Lessing: p. 28; Bibliothèque municipale de Valenciennes: p. 125 (MS 320, fol. 192r); Bibliothèque nationale de France, Paris (MS Lat 16169): pp. 38 (fol. 151r), 60 (fol. 331v), 69 (fol. 272r), 138 (fol. 302v), 160 (fol. 280r), 172 (fol. 286r), 182 (fol. 145r), 186 (fol. 209v), 191 (fol. 243r), 196 (fol. 134r); British Library, London: pp. 10–11 (Yates Thompson MS 36, fol. 147r), 72 (Add MS 15254, fol. 13r), 153 (Harley MS 4751, fol. 36r); InsightPhotography/Pixabay: p. 29; iStock.com: pp. 32 (Wassiliy), 34 (Sergei Baldin); The J. Paul Getty Museum, Los Angeles: pp. 109 (MS 100, fol. 5v), 135 (MS Ludwig XV 3, fol. 95v), 149 (MS 100, fol. 47), 223 (MS 100, fol. 26v), 225 (top; MS Ludwig XV 3, fol. 78), 225 (bottom; MS 100, fol. 54v), 226 (MS 100, fol. 27v), 228 (MS Ludwig XV 4, fol. 118); from Albertus Magnus, *Philosophia naturalis* (Basel, 1506): p. 122; from Michael Maier, *Symbola aureae mensae duodecim nationum* (Frankfurt, 1617): p. 200; The Metropolitan Museum of Art, New York: p. 21 (The Cloisters Collection, 1964; 64.215); National Library of Sweden, Stockholm/World Digital Library: p. 30; photo Luisa Ricciarini/ Bridgeman Images: p. 27 (Kunsthistorisches Museum, Vienna); Rijksmuseum, Amsterdam: p. 222; courtesy Science History Institute, Philadelphia, PA: p. 238; Wallraf-Richartz-Museum, Cologne: pp. 24–5.

wfilm (a natural thing), the copyright holder of the image on p. 215, has published it online under conditions imposed by a Creative Commons Attribution-ShareAlike 2.0 Generic License. Rufus46, the copyright holder of the image on p. 14, has published it online under conditions imposed by a Creative Commons Attribution-ShareAlike 3.0 Unported License. Wellcome Collection, the copyright holder of the image on p. 63, has published it online under conditions imposed by a Creative Commons Attribution 4.0 International License. Laurentius, the copyright holder of the image on p. 170; Raimond Spekking, the

INDEX

Page numbers in *italics* indicate illustrations